CW00820857

"What does *theology* look like after the
might still think such a 'turn' is optional,
reading and theological reflection are situated in a dynamic in-between
space' that enables ongoing inquiry into and discernment about God's
agency in a fluid world through Jesus Christ by the Holy Spirit. This is not
about divine usefulness but about Christian leadership and discipleship being continually renewed and reformed by what God is doing."

—AMOS YONG

Fuller Theological Seminary

"*Leadership, God's Agency, and Disruptions* is a wonderfully brilliant book
by two world class thinkers on leadership. Read it and allow the leadership
you have known to be unraveled. Know that, by the time you're finished
reading, you'll be re-constructed as a Christian leader. Instead of techniques, you'll be given a new way of being that is found in the very center of
God's agency, not your own."

—DAVID FITCH

Northern Seminary

"In a noisy field of Christian leadership books touting the secrets to effective ministry, Branson and Roxburgh have raised a clarion call to reorient
leadership around God's agency rather than management techniques. Its
biblical depth and theological rigor may make you doubt you've ever read a
book that deserves to be called a 'theology of leadership' before. This mas-
terpiece of practical theology is now my go-to recommendation on leadership for teachers and practitioners."

—CHRISTOPHER B. JAMES

University of Dubuque Theological Seminary

"There are many books that offer descriptors of that which is wrong with
the church in the Western world. Few, however, offer a way forward that is
not merely a reflection of the current fixation of the West with methods,
techniques, and programmes. . . . Mark and Alan's offering brings together
a well-tuned intellectual and academic perception, practical engagement in
ministry, and a significant insight into what the journey ahead might be."

—MARTIN ROBINSON

ForMission College, Birmingham, United Kingdom

Leadership, God's Agency, and Disruptions

Leadership, God's Agency, and Disruptions

Confronting Modernity's Wager

MARK LAU BRANSON

and ALAN J. ROXBURGH

CASCADE *Books* · Eugene, Oregon

LEADERSHIP, GOD'S AGENCY, AND DISRUPTIONS
Confronting Modernity's Wager

Copyright © 2020 Mark Lau Branson and Alan J. Roxburgh. All rights reserved.
Except for brief quotations in critical publications or reviews, no part of this book
may be reproduced in any manner without prior written permission from the
publisher. Write: Permissions, Wipf and Stock Publishers, 199 W. 8th Ave., Suite 3,
Eugene, OR 97401.

Cascade Books
An Imprint of Wipf and Stock Publishers
199 W. 8th Ave., Suite 3
Eugene, OR 97401

www.wipfandstock.com

PAPERBACK ISBN: 978-1-7252-7174-6
HARDCOVER ISBN: 978-1-7252-7173-9
EBOOK ISBN: 978-1-7252-7175-3

Cataloguing-in-Publication data:

Names: Branson, Mark Lau, author. | Roxburgh, Alan J., author.

Title: Leadership, God's agency, and disruptions : confronting modernity's wager / Mark
Lau Branson and Alan J. Roxburgh.

Description: Eugene, OR: Cascade Books, 2020 | Includes bibliographical references.

Identifiers: ISBN 978-1-7252-7174-6 (paperback) | ISBN 978-1-7252-7173-9 (hardcover)
| ISBN 978-1-7252-7175-3 (ebook)

Subjects: LCSH: Christian leadership. | Change—Religious aspects—Christianity. | Mis-
sion of the church.

Classification: BV4509.5 .L435 2020 (paperback) | BV4509.5 (ebook)

12/10/20

Mark dedicates this book to the four "Dons" who connected
scripture, context, and attention to God in ways that formed his
imagination and practices for church and leadership:
Dr. Don Williams
Dr. Donald Buteyn†
Bishop Donald Green
Dr. Donald Gelpi, SJ†

Alan dedicates this book to four people who over the years were
huge influences on his imagination in leadership:
John McLaverty, whose love, humour, wisdom
and presence have carried me
Wally Mills, a tool and die maker who modelled love and leadership
Dr. Paul Gooch, one of my early teachers
who nurtured a love of philosophy
Dr. Martin Robinson, a wise friend who shows me
gracious ways of leading

Contents

Permissions | xi

Introduction | 1

PART I: FRAMING

CHAPTER 1: **God's Agency and Biblical Narratives** | 9
    Introduction | 9
    Jeremiah | 12
    Matthew | 17
    Luke's Account in Acts | 22
    Ephesians | 28
    Inhabiting Worlds | 31

CHAPTER 2: **The Inhabited Leadership Context** | 33
    Introduction | 33
    Modernity's Wager | 35
    Force and Power | 36
    God as Useful | 40
        Method and Control as Central Characteristics of the Wager | 41
        Leadership in a Euro-Tribal Imagination | 41
        Willie Jennings on a Diseased Theological Imagination | 44
        The Problematic Particularity of the Christian Narrative | 49
    An Architecture of Leadership | 51

CHAPTER 3: **Theological Themes** | 53
    Introduction | 53
    God's Agency, Trinity, and Incarnation | 53
        Trinity: Relationality, Intimacy, and Risk | 54
        God's Agency and the Incarnation | 55
    God's Agency and a Christian Anthropology | 60
        Anthropology: Theocentric and Modern | 60

An Anthropology Rooted in the Revelation of God in Christ | 60

The Modern Anthropological *modus vivendi* | 61

    The Project of Order, Mastery, and Its Rationality | 62

    Modernity as a Wager | 63

    The Modern Person—Autonomous, Cut Off | 64

An Anthropology of Hope in a Context of Fear and Disillusionment | 65

Eschatology, God's Agency, and Being the Church | 66

    Not Private or Projects or Postponed | 67

    Creation and the Eschatological Shape of Leadership | 69

INTERMEZZO 1: **Practical Theology and Discernment** | 71

Introduction | 71

Overview and Movements | 73

Engaging the Process | 74

    1. Name and Describe Current Praxis | 74

    2. Analyze Praxis and Context Using Cultural Resources | 75

    3. Study and Reflect on Christian Texts and Practices | 76

    4. Recall and Discuss Stories from Our Own Lives, Church, and Community | 78

    5. Discern and Shape New Praxis through Prayer, Imagination, and Experiments | 79

Summary | 79

PART II: BIBLE & LEADERSHIP

CHAPTER 4: **Jeremiah as Interpretive Leader** | 83

Introduction | 83

    The Context of Jeremiah's Leadership | 84

    Jeremiah 22—Memories of Josiah | 85

Contemporary Frameworks | 86

    Jeremiah and Interpretive Leadership | 87

    Interpretive Leadership, Discontinuous Change, and Holding Environments | 88

    Taylor and Social Imaginaries | 90

How Jeremiah Shapes an Interpretive Community | 91

    Jeremiah 36—Texts, Options, and Avoidance | 91

    Jeremiah 29—Texts and New Practices | 94

Jeremiah and Our Social Dislocation | 99

CHAPTER 5: **Matthew and Learning Communities** | 101

Introduction | 101

    The Context of Matthew's Learning Communities | 102

    Matthew 1:1—4:25: Genealogical Framing | 104

Contemporary Frameworks for Learning Communities | 106
    Learning Communities | 107
    Gergen and Social Construction | 109
    Freire's Action-Reflection Pedagogy | 110
The Gospel and Context: God's Disruptive Presence | 112
    Disruptive Tensions Requiring New Interpretive Perspectives | 112
    The Telos of Learning for Matthew | 114
Reading Matthew as Communities of Learning | 115
    Matthew 7: Hallowed be Your Name | 116
    Matthew 9:35—11:1: Calling and Sending the Twelve | 117
    Matthew 28:1–20: Disciples Suitable for Disruptions | 119
Summary and Conclusion | 121

CHAPTER 6: **Acts: Luke's Narrative on God's Disruptions** | 122
Introduction | 122
    Setting Up Luke's Narrative in Acts | 123
    Acts 2: Pentecost & Praxis | 124
Contemporary Frameworks | 128
    Improvisation | 128
    Diffusion | 131
    Alterity | 134
Reading Acts as Leaders | 136
    Acts 6–7: The Spirit Disrupts Leadership | 136
    Acts 16: Alterity & Improv in Philippi | 139
Leaders Amidst Disruptions of the Spirit | 142

CHAPTER 7: **Ephesians and New Social Arrangements** | 144
Introduction | 144
    The Context of Ephesians | 145
        Ephesus and Artemis | 145
        Ephesus and the Empire | 146
    Ephesians 1: Churches and Powers | 148
Theoretical Frames: Critical Theory and Changing Organizational Culture | 151
    Critical Theory | 151
    Organizational Theories and Change | 153
Reading Ephesians as Alternative Culture | 156
    Ephesians 2 and 3: New Social Arrangements Impact the Powers | 156
    Ephesians 4: Vocation and Equipping | 158
Getting Reoriented in Ephesus | 161

PART III: IMAGES & PRACTICES

INTERMEZZO 2: *Habitus* and Practices | 165

Introduction | 165
Why *Habitus* and Practices | 166
   Habitus | 168
   Practices | 170
   Virtues | 172

Chapter 8: **Metaphors: Leadership for the Space-Between** | 174
Introduction: Why Metaphors Matter | 174
Some Current Metaphors of Leadership | 177
   Inside/Outside | 177
   Public/Private | 179
The Clergy Industry | 181
Ferment of the Spirit | 185
   A Metaphor for the Context of Leadership | 185
   Metaphors for a Theology of Leadership: The Space-Between | 188
Metaphors Amidst the Unraveling | 190

CHAPTER 9: **Practicing Amidst God's Agency** | 192
Introduction | 192
Attending to God in Everyday Life | 194
Attention, Location, and Alterity | 197
Making the Road as We Walk | 199
Jeremiah: Dwell Where You Are | 201
   The Path Begins in the Local | 202
   Discernment Only Comes on the Path | 203
Matthew: Action-Reflection and Learning Communities | 204
   Interpreting Contexts in Terms of God's Disruptions | 205
   Antioch and Disruption | 206
Acts: Alterity and Improvisation | 207
   Locations and Associations | 207
   Imaginations and Improvisations | 208
   Relinquishing Power and Control | 209
Ephesians: Critical Reflection and Change | 210
   The Use of Critical Theory | 211
   Organizational Change | 213
Taking the Journey | 213
   Learning Together | 213
   Starting from Where People Are | 214

Bibliography | 217

Permissions

George Gower's Armada Portrait of Elizabeth I (1588?) at Woburn Abbey.

This work is in the public domain in its country of origin and other countries and areas where the copyright term is the author's life plus 100 years or fewer. https://commons.wikimedia.org/wiki/File:Elizabeth_I_(Armada_Portrait).jpg.

An excerpt of the poem "Proverbios y cantares," from *Campos de Castilla* (1912) by Antonio Machado, is from "Traveler, your footprints," *There is No Road*, trans. Dennis Maloney and Mary G. Berg (Buffalo, NY: White Wine Press, 2003).

Earlier versions of chapters 4 and 5 appeared under the authorship of Mark Lau Branson in the *Journal of Religious Leadership*: "Interpretive Leadership during Social Dislocation: Jeremiah and Social Imaginary," *Journal of Religious Leadership* 8, no. 1 (2009) 27–48; and "Matthew and Learning Communities," *Journal of Religious Leadership* 15, no. 2 (2016) 37–68.

The authors have used the Common English Bible (CEB) in citations throughout this work, and those uses are hereby acknowledged: © Copyright 2011 COMMON ENGLISH BIBLE. All rights reserved. Used by permission, (www.CommonEnglishBible.com).

In some instances, Bible verses are noted as NRSV. These quotations are from the New Revised Standard Version Bible, copyright © 1989 National Council of the Churches of Christ in the United States of America. Used by permission. All rights reserved worldwide.

Scripture taken from the New American Standard Bible, copyright ©1995 by the Lockman Foundation. Used by permission.

Introduction

THIS IS A BOOK about leadership. But it's not a generalized book about leadership for all kinds of leaders across all sectors within late modern societies. This is a book written for Christian leaders working within all kinds of systems—from congregations/parishes, to denominational systems, educational institutions, and not-for-profit organizations shaped by a Christian imagination. The emphasis on *Christian* leaders is important. We are proposing that a Christian imagination, dwelling inside the Christian story of God's engagement and involvement in the world in Jesus Christ, cannot be secondary to or background support for leadership that has been developed inside other stories. Our experiences indicate that leaders in these organizations, whether or not they reflect on their work, are inside other narratives, such as the social sciences or the latest models that emerge from the business world. This is not to denigrate the value and insight that can be found from within these models or proposals. Rather, we are arguing that the starting point for a consideration of the practice of leadership as Christians must come from a radically different source. Indeed, we will argue that a priority on theology will radically relativize understandings of leadership that have become normal defaults for a majority of Christian leaders across the late modern West.

Alan was recently in a small city located in a coastal mountain range in the Pacific Northwest. Fifteen leaders from church and not-for-profit organizations were gathering for their weekly morning of breakfast and conversation about being the church in our time. This group was intriguing because of their diversity and the degree of mutual respect. Many were evangelicals who would probably run the range from moderately right of center to just left of center in terms of politics and social values. Others would describe themselves as progressives, leaning much to the left on such matters. With all these differences, they demonstrated a care for each other and a readiness to listen with a sense of trust that must have developed slowly over time.

While noting the significant differences among these leaders, Alan became aware of striking similarities. They were all wrestling with questions about what it means to be faithful people of God in our current cultural milieu. This general question, inevitably, kept leading them back to their churches and congregations—these places where God's people gather to worship and figure out together what it means to be Christian today. The invitation to Alan was rooted in their interest in missiologist Lesslie Newbigin. They knew that Newbigin had addressed important matters concerning the modern world, living in plural societies, and rethinking theology in ways that shaped us to participate in God's mission.[1] As Alan continued this reflective work with these leaders he introduced the term "Euro-tribal churches."[2] This concept is a shorthand for noting the roots of these leaders and their organizations. Their denominations and theological traditions had been formed as Europe moved into the modern era. And that meant that their organizational and leadership habits had been shaped by numerous cultural forces that were more powerful than their espoused theology. Two themes, which we will engage in later chapters, can help explain what we mean. First, the concept of "Modernity's Wager" posits that the primary characteristic of modernity has not been the great ideologies of the nineteenth and twentieth centuries but what has undergirded these ideologies, a conviction that life can be lived well without God. This overarching belief has now settled deep into the bones, sinews, habits, and defaults of the Western imagination. This wager has overwhelmingly colonized the churches (no matter what the stripe—left or right, conservative or progressive) and it now shapes their understanding and practice of leadership.

The second (and related) characteristic of Euro-tribal churches is described by the French philosopher and somewhat Christian mystic Simone Weil. For her, it wasn't any one of the great "isms" of the these centuries but what she called technical rationality and, along with it, beginning in the early decades of the last century, the development of a whole culture of technocratic elites—professionals trained in the best methods of the social sciences to manage and control the systems and organizations for which they were trained to lead. This is the world in which almost all Christian leaders have been formed and for which they were professionalized (earning

---

1 See Roxburgh, *Structured for Mission*; *Joining God*; and *Practices for the Refounding* (with Martin Robinson).

2. We are indebted to the work of Jehu Hanciles for the introduction of the tribal nature of European Christianity, from which our term "Euro-tribal" arises; see his brilliant analysis of the Western Christian situation: *Beyond Christendom*, 88–92.

degrees and ordination). This has been the world in which Christian leaders have learned to operate and practice their calling.

As the morning continued among these leaders, Alan was aware of several important themes in their conversations. First, there was no disagreement with the proposition that almost all churches within the Euro-tribal denominations are wrestling with the issues of their own unraveling. This theme was woven into almost every issue that arose. Even those with successful churches (measured by some as growth and by others as stable and active organizations) recognized that they were largely disoriented and often anxious. Second, there was no argument that most of the activities of these leaders in such churches was continually directed toward finding ever new ways of "fixing" the churches and getting them back to some form of "health" (always an empty, ambiguous word waiting to be filled by someone's bright ideas about growth, evangelism, diversity, or social action). Third, it was helpful to give language to what is happening not just to these churches concerning their unraveling but also the wider culture of late modern states and societies. Those around the table could all express their dis-ease with what was happening across society—economic disparity, gender debates, differences over immigration, political dysfunction—and they noted the continual formation of ever more defensive sub-groups. Leaders were often at a loss concerning how to engage the proliferating camps that adopted variations of partisan names—left/right, conservative /liberal/progressive—often with variations regarding victim culture and political correctness.

What was interesting about elements of this conversation was that the ways of explaining what was happening were not, to use a word, theological—but socio-cultural and political. They were based on one form or another of models, experiences, and frameworks borrowed from every field except that of a theological reflection on the nature of God's engagement with the world in and through Jesus Christ. It was not that these leaders weren't deeply committed Christian men and women; it was that their basic frameworks were formed by the socio-cultural paradigms coming primarily from the social sciences, psychology, and the business world. God as agent was largely absent from the conversation. This is fully consistent with Modernity's Wager—we have all been formed, whether in church or seminary or other social structures—to be blind to God's agency. This wager has overwhelmingly colonized the churches (no matter what the stripe—left or right, conservative or progressive) and now shapes their understanding and practice of leadership. Indeed, this default is so powerful that the notion of Christian leadership being about forming communities where God is experienced as the primary agent represents a powerful idea but has little to no content.

Mark has had numerous parallel conversations in both church and academic settings. In a conversation among students and professors, regarding the purpose and methods of practical theology, those in the room voiced how much they appreciated how they were gaining the tools offered by other disciplines—cultural studies, organizational and leadership studies, migration studies, social theory, personality theories, Christian social ethics. Most frameworks for practical theology seek out correlations between these fields and the classic seminary studies in theology, church history, and biblical studies. Then Mark and a colleague asked a question, "What if practical theology is not about finding correlation—what if our core task is, as leaders, to engage groups so that together we discern what God is doing and we take steps toward faithful participation? What if this is what 'doing theology' means?" As Alan noted in the Pacific Northwest gathering, there was genuine and appreciative interest—while also a deep sense that our habits and skills did not move in this direction.

In both of these experiences, the conversations took a familiar turn. The questions immediately focused on "How?" Quickly, the conversations slipped into questions of how to go about engaging the ways Modernity's Wager has colonized the churches and their leadership. Several things emerged from that turn in the conversation. We observed both the encouragement that the challenges were being named and owned—while the questions about next steps were still deeply formed by the old narrative that was shaping the problem. Again, in both conversations, participants then observed and named this misstep. Numbers of them, in their questions and later conversations, intuitively grasped that confronting Modernity's Wager would not be about learning another technique or method that could be applied to a problem as a fix. One could detect in their conversation this resistance to technique that we are seeing among so many leaders. Something has happened over the past five to ten years that suggests that the Spirit is already disrupting the taken-for-granted presumptions that leadership is about finding techniques to fix the challenges faced by the churches. One could see in the faces of these leaders the awareness that this well-worn road could no longer be taken.

Leaving that meeting with those wonderful leaders, Alan was aware again that the Spirit is in a process of not just unraveling the forms of church and social life that have shaped Modernity' Wager, but the Spirit is already ahead of us fermenting a radically different kind of church that can call forth forms of society that are more directed toward kingdom life. What this calls for are leaders whose imagination and practices are shaped far less by the existent models of human agency and far more about discerning the ways in which God is present as agent in the process of calling into being the kingdom. This book is about the kinds of journeys this will require from leaders today.

To some extent this disruptive context in which we now operate as leaders is about location. Overall, the Euro-tribal churches and their leaders have operated in a space of expertise and the correlative assumptions so that we have been positioned to not only know what is needed but also have the technical skills to manage desired outcomes. The unraveling world that is now before us invites leaders into a radically different theological imagination about our location as leaders and churches. In this book we introduce a metaphor we will use to provide theological perspective on the location of leadership. That metaphor is space-between. As we will contend in the following chapters, God, who is the primary agent in the world, comes to us in a particular kind of way—without the pretense of power and control. God meets us in this space-between where there can be neither power nor control. This theological imagination, we argue, must now form the basis of Christian leadership and must become the means of assessing all other leadership models we choose to take up.

This book presents a theology of leadership. This does not mean that it presents a supportive theological rationale for some model of leadership nor for the leadership theories drawn from the social sciences or other modern frameworks. It is written from the assumption that the basis of leadership within the Christian narrative begins with the question of God and what God is doing in the world. In this book we offer ways of asking this critical question drawn from both Scripture and from theological convictions concerning God's agency in contexts of massive unraveling.

We will approach our work in three parts, plus two bridges. In part I we will introduce how we will engage Scriptures, explore the complexities of cultural forces in late modernity, and name some key theological matters. In part II we expand our biblical work with chapters on Jeremiah, Matthew, Acts, and Ephesians. In part III we name the role of metaphors and then explore key practices for leadership that are shaped by God's agency. The two intermezzos provide bridges between the parts. Intermezzo 1 names practical theology as a practice; intermezzo 2 frames the final chapters as matters of *habitus* and practices.

We are very aware that we write as participants in various overlapping circles of friends and colleagues. We have learned together as we taught classes, led consulting projects, hosted webinars, and spent countless hours with hundreds of church leaders—doing *lectio*, praying, conversing, imagining, hoping. Complete lists are impossible. When Mark wrote a chapter for

Craig Van Gelder,[3] and then asked for his feedback on another article, Craig said Mark needed to author a book focused on engagements with Scripture; Mark said "maybe in ten years"—but it took a bit longer, and collaborations with Alan in other labors led to partnership here. As we complete the manuscript, Mark acknowledges that colleagues and students at Fuller Theological Seminary have fostered and fed his research, creativity, teaching, and leadership for over two decades. The Academy of Religious Leadership has been a learning community of professors, researchers, and leaders who have listened to, read, critiqued, and encouraged the development of materials that ended up on these pages. The Ekklesia Project has provided an annual gathering of friends who invest their lives in the kind of theological praxis and faithful practices that we encourage here. Alan has many of the same people who have influenced and shaped his thinking around leadership and theology, both in terms of mentors and important co-learners over a long journey. In the early days, the Gospel and Our Culture Network, with friends like Pat Keifert and Craig Van Gelder, was a source of learning and partnership in starting to work on these ideas of leadership (and these meetings were where we, the two coauthors of this book, met). Alan and Martin Robinson founded the *Journal of Missional Practice*, and over the last decade it has been a generative conversation space for both of us as we work with colleagues in the UK like Paul Weston, Sally Mann, and Harvey Kwiyani. Our thanks also go to colleagues like Juan Martinez, Chris James, Ian Douglas, and many others who show up in our footnotes.

3. Branson, "Ecclesiology and Leadership."

PART I: FRAMING

CHAPTER 1

God's Agency and Biblical Narratives

INTRODUCTION

WE ARE WRITING THIS book in a context of significant confusion for many North American churches and their leaders around questions of identity and practice.[1] Euro-tribal churches are characterized by declining participation, continued transience across religious communities, and waning of respect from the neighborhoods and communities within which they are located. Parallelling these challenges is a flurry of what gets described as late modern expressions of church that attract participants who tend to drop out or move on to the next new version of "contemporary" church. These churches market niche churches, such as multi-site mega-gatherings focused on worship bands and preaching, that bring a strong preacher into neighborhoods (sometimes with local music and an assistant pastor) via social media in efforts to market some ethos like inclusive, authentic, non-traditional, or diverse.[2] Some interpret these newer forms of church as responses to generational shifts; others critique them as being little more than adjustments to taste and preference. Some observers have concluded that

---

1. We are focused on North American churches from Euro-tribal traditions. As researchers and practitioners we have limited experience alongside other groups in North America and elsewhere. While we are grateful when colleagues from other cultures commend what we are advancing, we are still aware of important distinctives. For an introduction to these challenges, see Branson and Martínez, *Churches, Cultures and Leadership*.

2. Our desire is not to disparage the appropriate local expressions, but to note that they have been turned into marketing lures.

9

these are signs of the end of Protestantism.[3] None of these experiments and innovations have halted the drift of Protestant churches as the new language of the "dones," "nones," and "gones" indicates.[4]

Frequently we hear from those who know they are manufacturing temporary fixes to these challenges. They say that they are overwhelmed by the constant demands for vision, innovation, staffing, and more committed participation (often described in terms of the need for programs that ramp up substantive discipleship in congregations). We agree with people's suspicions concerning these efforts to address the unraveling of Christian life in North America. Nor do we believe the proposals that dodge challenges by putting the responsibilities on magic available from millennials.[5] This book is being written from a very different starting place. It is formed out of the conviction that right in these contexts that overwhelm and discourage, God is up to something far bigger and more important than fixing Euro-tribal churches or making them more attractive and relevant. We see God out ahead of us, fully engaged in the places where believers live and among the neighborhoods where they dwell. This turning requires the formation of a new social imaginary of leadership. Along with pastor friends who are already seeing and practicing this new imaginary, we want to dig into the contextual challenges and theological resources for its formation. God is revealing the way of Jesus out ahead of us in the form of risk-forming relationships with the people in our communities. This book is about the shape and practices of leadership that center on joining God in local contexts. These directions are not, in any way, intended to deny the work of ecclesiology,[6] but we are convinced that in the crisis of Christian life now confronting Euro-tribal churches, ecclesiology must be formed in retrospect. Ecclesiology must be the reflective response to a missiology that is shaped around joining God in the local.[7] With that theological core, this book is focused on the question of leadership—what kind of leadership promotes a way of life that pays attention to God's initiatives?

This chapter begins our inquiry in Scripture. With multiple parallels to our situation, the varied biblical authors of this chapter address believers who are, in diverse ways, just as confused, traumatized, questioning, discouraged, and clueless as we ourselves. Jeremiah, Matthew, Luke, and Paul

3. Leithart, *End of Protestantism*.

4. The "nones" designation has been used by Pew Research Center to refer to those who are unaffiliated with any religion, then the terms "gones" and "dones" have gained attention in less technical observations. See Pew Research Center, "'Nones' on the Rise."

5. See Seel, *The New Copernicans*.

6. See Micheal Goheen's fine book on this subject, *Church and Its Vocation*.

7. See Weston, "Leslie Newbigin."

make a singular claim: God is active. And there is a corollary: we are invited to participate, to join with God. Jeremiah, who countered the official palace version of God's priorities in the midst of the Babylonian invasion, dared claim that Israel needed to be converted to different interpretive perspectives and accompanying practices. Matthew, aware of disruptive events that challenged the church of Antioch, wrote a narrative about Jesus that sought to arouse this community to how God's initiatives were continuing after Jesus' resurrection and ascension and for them to join in what God was doing. In writing Acts, Luke knew that his readers, perhaps like the apostles in Jerusalem, had trouble interpreting how the jarring actions of Holy Spirit should be understood, so he repeats the stories told by Peter and Cornelius multiple times in the hope that repetition would increase awareness of God's initiatives. Paul's letter to the churches of Asia Minor, present in our New Testament as the Epistle to the Ephesians, does not dismiss the fierce challenges those churches faced in the form of Rome and the economies of the pagan gods—rather, he proclaims that God's on-the-ground activities were inviting them to practices of risky discernment and participation.[8]

These authors, attending to different places and diverse times, are neither dispassionate nor disengaged. They are deeply implicated in their own narratives. Their accounts about God and the options available to their readers frequently push against what those readers were assuming. And, more relevant to our writing from the context of late modern Christian communities, they offer narratives and perspectives that push into our own models, frameworks, and habits of learning and leadership. This opening chapter begins a process of what we believe to be critical work: paying attention. Our argument is that, overall, the Euro-tribal churches have not paid attention to the agency of God in a disruptive world but have subsumed God's agency to models and frameworks borrowed from the narratives of late modernity (see chapter 2). Therefore, one of the critical practices to be cultivated is that of how we pay attention to what God is already doing ahead of us. Discernment is more critical than innovation.

We write as practical theologians. By that term we do not mean that this is a book of functionalist, pragmatic steps. We are doing theology—which means the book is at the overlap of conversations regarding Scripture, theology, social history, contemporary experiences of churches in North America, leadership theories and habits, and opportunities for discerning and joining with God's initiatives.[9] But by *doing theology* we do

8. In part II, these four biblical books will each receive chapter-length attention. We are using traditional references regarding authorship. In part II we will reference commentaries and scholarly materials that engage those debates.

9. In intermezzo 1 we will provide more details on our approach to "practical

not mean we are just working with ideas—rather God's agency is assumed and doing theology is about discerning and embodying God's apocalypse or revelation. This "doing theology" is also about where we prioritize our "paying attention." We are arguing that it is the conviction of God as agent that should determine our engagement with models and practices of leadership rather than that our understanding of God be fitted into and subsumed beneath the models and frameworks we adopt. We believe that by attending to these biblical texts, we are awakened to the radical priority God's agency and, thereby, will be more available to a shift in leadership assumptions and practices. What we see in Scripture is this continual work of the Spirit wrestling with communities of God's people in order for them to grasp this always radically new place from which we are to engage our situation. It is to be the primacy of God's agency that determines our leadership frames, not, as is currently the case, the offering of theological rationales as support for the claims of various models of leadership drawn from other sources. In what follows we examine this dynamic of God's agency at work in a series of biblical texts drawn from both testaments.

JEREMIAH

Six hundred years before Jesus, Judah was facing the turmoil of internal anomie while being challenged from the outside by the Babylonian Empire. In that context, the prophet Jeremiah was countering the theopolitical praxis of official Judaism. We propose that Jeremiah's leadership at the cusp of the Babylonian exile gives us access to the challenges Christians today face in North America. Jeremiah provides insights into the work of leadership that faces the unraveling of its established world. As the book shows, plans and power are not foremost in Jeremiah's leadership approach. He contested those with plans, those who assumed they had power. So our reference to Jeremiah's leadership prompts the question, "In what manner is Jeremiah a leader?" It is not uncommon for Jeremiah's ministry to be interpreted as a failure because he did not convince Judah's officials to change course.[10] The narrative is set up in Jeremiah 1 with references regarding relational connections to religious persons (". . . son of Hilkiah, of the priests who were in Anathoth" 1:1 NRSV) and Jeremiah works with scribes (Baruch and Seraiah). Also, the influential family of Shaphan appears in this beginning chapter to provide some political access and protection for the prophet (Jer 26, 39, 40). Finally, various texts indicate that Jeremiah apparently has some

theology and discernment."

10. Schreiber, "Rethinking Jeremiah."

level of access to King Zedekiah (Jer 21, 37, 38, 39). These and other nota-
tions give us clues to the existence of a small group among whom Jeremiah
at least had limited access and influence. As Walter Brueggemann writes,
"These elements of personal history . . . altogether suggest that Jeremiah
is located in a subversive body of opinion in Jerusalem that was opposed
to royal policy and that supported Jeremiah as the point person for more
widely but dangerously held views."[11]

The text also gives witness to God's perspective: "Do not say, 'I am
only a boy'; for you shall go to all to whom I send you, and you shall speak
whatever I command you. Do not be afraid of them, for I am with you to
deliver you, says the LORD" (1:7–8 NRSV). The task given to Jeremiah is
described in very large terms: "I'm putting my words in your mouth. This
very day I appoint you over nations and empires, to dig up and pull down, to
destroy and demolish, to build and plant" (1:9–10). For those who wonder if
God is involved in Israel and in the wider world, these opening verses make
substantive claims about God's initiatives, and, because God is involved,
about Jeremiah's collaborative agency. These verses are proposing that in
all the unraveling there is already the radically new that, paralleling Lesslie
Newbigin's proposals, calls into question all previous assumptions and all
inherited tradition. God's activity is in fact the primal truth by which all else
has to be confronted and questioned.[12]

Because leadership can only be understood in light of context, we need
to survey some important aspects of Jeremiah's time and place. The kings of
Israel and Judah lived and ruled on a strip of land between continents, in
the midst of regional tribes and between superpowers. They were constantly
weighing political, economic, and military options. Frequently they were
in conversations with prophets who claimed to speak for God, and the differences between Jeremiah and those contemporary voices clarify much of
what is happening in this book.

Israel (before it was divided) chose this royal form of national life
when they asked God to give them a human king (something God opposed;
see 1 Sam 8). They envied other nations and the apparent power and honor
that accompanied kings and palaces. In this way they were hedging their
bets, concluding something like: "We want God's provision and protection,
but, based on what we see in the world around us, there are benefits to having a human king." God warned them that this would increase taxes, lead to
a standing army, and bring on accompanying temptations, but they wanted
both God and royalty. God makes clear that this preference was more about

11. Brueggemann, *To Build, To Plant*, 32.
12. Newbigin, *Light*, 2.

theology than management—Israel was rejecting him (1 Sam 8:7–8). There are parallels here to what we described in the introduction as Modernity's Wager in the modern West, and to the choices churches are making. Life without dependence on God looks like a viable plan, this wager claims. We can engage God for personal or social emergencies, or as a basis of support for prior methods and models, but confidence in God's continual presence and activity wanes into forms of a secondary presence in support of human agency.

Jeremiah's contemporaries cited traditions (and, we would note, some scriptural texts) that interpreted this history to mean that God would perpetually sustain them in that organizational form as a royal national institution. One possible historical referent had occurred a century before these Jeremiah texts. In 701 BCE, following decades in which Israel and Samaria had fallen to Assyrian forces, Yahweh countered an Assyrian siege and saved Jerusalem, as prophesied by Isaiah. This may have reinforced a theological perspective concerning God's unwavering support of the Jerusalem-centered monarchy. Royalty and clerics functioned inside this story that predetermined how they would both read and engage their situation. But the subsequent waywardness, as noted by Jeremiah, made that experience irrelevant.[13] This is Jeremiah's environment, a context of discontinuous change in which the usual approaches to anticipation, prediction, and royal management do not work. Change factors included not only the neo-Babylonian defeat of Assyria and the inflamed animosity between the Babylonian empire and Egypt, but also the internal disruption in Judah due to the loss of traditions, the seeming minimal presence of texts (except for the partial renewal under Josiah, see 2 Kgs 22), and the multivalent voices of prophets. The prophets that claimed God's preference for Jerusalem prevailed with court officials—insisting that God would not let Judah fall, or (perhaps) any defeat would be very temporary. So, as the Babylonian military power succeeded in a series of forays, captured citizens and the urban elites, and threatened further destruction, Judah's leaders at first said the threat would dissipate, then when survival appeared unlikely they sought the protection of Egypt. They were formed inside a narrative that privileged the means of power and control rather than the deeper story of God's agency in covenant.[14]

All of these elements are noted in the book of Jeremiah. He interprets the situation: leaders and people have deserted traditions, lived and worshiped wrongly, and ignored the warnings of prophets sent by God. God's

---

13. Robert Hubbard, email message to Mark Lau Branson, March 4, 2020.
14. See Oded, "Judah and the Exile."

words name the depth of the challenge: "Today I have made you [Jeremiah] an armed city, an iron pillar, and a bronze wall against the entire land—the kings of Judah, its princes, its priests, and all its people" (1:18). Then, as their anger becomes fixated on the truthful messenger, and Jeremiah is blamed and persecuted, he laments, "I was like a gentle lamb led to the slaughter" (11:19 NRSV).[15] Jeremiah is leading by disrupting the party line in Jerusalem; he is questioning the basis of their actions, the sources of their functional narratives. His voice, for some, gains credence because he bears the anger of waning officials. He has the ears of a few contacts, who diffuse his words in a dangerous situation. He is interpreting the current situation, their Jewish heritage, and God's present actions. Even though this interpretive leadership does not achieve the surrender or transformation of imagination he calls for, and efforts for a military alliance with Egypt proceed, Jeremiah's words create new opportunities in Babylon among the exiles, and his collected utterances shape a profound reorientation for Israel during and after the Babylonian exile.

Walter Brueggemann emphasizes the point that without proper utterance, Israel loses its identity, and its existence is threatened.[16] There are utterances from the palace, but they fail to adequately connect with historical texts and what God is doing on the ground. They fear being colonized by Babylon but in fact they already live as a colony that does not attend to God. This is the background to the kind of interpretive leadership Jeremiah is using to show the people what is actually going on. Their forgetfulness must be named. Another kind of utterance is required. They need leaders who stand in the space between the texts that rightly name their heritage, the threats of the world, their wayward rulers, and the on-the-ground provisions of an active and engaged God. If, in the midst of Israel's choices, any aspect of this utterance is lost, then identity and agency are endangered. Jeremiah's generation failed to give an accurate account of Yahweh's life with them, and that failure, as Brueggemann writes, "leads to a sense of autonomy, a life without Yahweh."[17] Without true utterances, with only the palace-sanctioned interpretations, God's saving words were neither recognized nor welcomed, so Israel attended to "things that do not profit" (2:8 NRSV). If an interpretive community[18] is to find a generative future, then, with its plural leaders, that

15. Ron Heifetz and Marty Linsky attend to this kind of blaming in *Leadership On the Line*, but we doubt if reading that book would have done much for Jeremiah. See page 41.

16. Brueggemann, *Texts That Linger*, 2.

17. Brueggemann, *Texts that Linger*, 3.

18. This concept of a community of interpreters comes from Royce, *Problem of Christianity*, 262. Concerning "communities of memory," see Bellah et al., *Habits of the*

community needs to recall and recite stories, meditate on and discern the presence and priorities of God in the narratives, and then test the discovered meanings in their current context. This iterative cycle of hearing and responding, of reflection and action (which we will address later), has the potential for showing the way out of the traps they have set for themselves.

Like Judah's rulers as they scramble to fix their chaos, Euro-tribal churches have developed habits and practices around institutional behaviors aimed at perpetuating organizational viability. Jeremiah utters a call to forget the structures and to reform around testimony and witness and practices regarding God's present activities. Jeremiah's work pushes us by naming our agnosticism. We value and quote elements of our traditions and texts as we write unending new texts to integrate our challenges and beliefs into mission statements and strategic plans. But, like the royal efforts seeking alliance with Egypt, Euro-tribal churches tend to over-invest in an imagination that had already excluded God's agency.

What we see here is Jeremiah practicing what we call interpretive leadership. It is about waking up and taking the risk of listening. Interpretive leaders do not begin by proclaiming—they attend to God's voice and the voices of those around them. Anyone around Jeremiah could have said "We're in trouble; this isn't working well." But since God said he would provide words and new life, the obvious destruction was not self-interpreting. There are parallels here with the late modern disequilibrium among North American churches. While numerous efforts for fixing the church are the topic of training, reading, planning, and management, our own observations indicate that God is at work outside of these efforts. So interpretive leaders help communities of believers to ask: What is God doing? How is the Spirit at work in this place, among these people? What observations, traditions, voices, and texts might increase our capacities for discerning God's initiatives? What habits block this engagement?

This is interpretive leadership, and Jeremiah is about this difficult task, made especially challenging because office holders not only counter his claims but also have capacities for coercion and retribution. However, as the longer story unfolds, Jeremiah's interpretive work eventually gains traction.[19]

Heart, 153–54. This framework is parallel to that of a "learning community," which gets more attention in our work on Matthew.

19. We will attend further to Jeremiah regarding interpretive leadership and discontinuous change in chapter 4.

MATTHEW

We will assume that Matthew wrote in the late seventies or early eighties. While some recent commentators propose that he lived and worked in Galilean cities like Sepphoris or Tiberius, we agree with a substantial number of Bible scholars that Matthew was resident in Antioch, Syria and he was writing with an awareness of the Christian community in that city.[20] Antioch was the third largest city of the Roman Empire, likely with over 200,000 residents, and shaped by the presence of Roman government, systems, trade, and military forces. Also, Antioch had long been a residence for the Jewish diaspora. This diverse population was formed by both local and larger factors. Over the centuries, Jews had lived there, sometimes in favored, wealthy circumstances, but often at the same time some Jews were impoverished—and on occasion persecuted. And, as in other locations, synagogues had been incorporating Gentiles—and that had increased in the decades of the Jesus movement. By the time of Matthew's writing, Christians had, for several decades, been living into and shaping their own core narratives, practices, and beliefs in this city. The ongoing connections between Christ-followers and Jews was occurring in both synagogues and in church gatherings.[21]

The more immediate circumstances, probably the topic of frequent conversations, concerned Rome's recent military conquest of Jerusalem. Regional Roman leaders had been frustrated by Jewish uprisings, and in the late sixties, after Roman troops centered in Antioch had failed to quell those rebellions, Titus led additional Roman troops in the sacking of Jerusalem and the Temple. This was not only a matter of human trauma, with a significant loss of life and thousands fleeing, but it was also a theological crisis—what was God's role in this event?

Matthew knows that earlier Jewish immigrants had received a certain favor through citizenship,[22] while more recent arrivals were marginalized by

20. This focus on Antioch does not discount that Matthew had a wider audience in view but it does help us connect his writing with a real on-the-ground context, including the belief that God was continuing to be an active agent of the gospel.

21. "The Jewish character of the Jesus movement remained strong. As late as the 380s CE, figures like Chrysostom were berating Christians in Antioch for going to synagogues on Saturdays and churches on Sundays and generally refusing to choose one form of association over the other. This indicates that a large number of people, in the third largest city of the empire, understood following Jesus as not only compatible with Jewish/synagogue life but inseparable from it." Tommy Givens, personal correspondence, April 16, 2020.

22. Adams et al., *Social and Economic Life*, 161.

imperial Rome and urban stratification.[23] Rome's hegemonic power is visible in the trade route that connects Antioch with the eastern regions of the empire and in the presence of military might (especially with Titus's legions in the area). Many refugees mourn as they flee Rome's victory in Jerusalem. Fear and anxiety would be present in Antioch's synagogues as they absorb the losses in Judea.

This is an environment in which the church is experiencing disorientation. Many Jewish Christ followers had experienced decades of rejection and even violence from their families and synagogues. Also, there were ongoing tensions regarding how Gentiles fit into the life of churches and the wider Jewish community. The Christian faith had been defined as a Jewish faith—and now the historic geographic center of that faith had been destroyed. In addition to the local challenges at the intersection of religious, economic, and political forces in an urban center under Roman rule, the Antioch church always suffered the overflow of suffering in Palestine—whether famine or persecution or war. If Jesus had proclaimed the presence of God's kingdom, and that his power would be revealed in God's apocalypse and the fall of the temple (Matt 24–25), how were they to interpret these events? How was God engaged with the empire? With Israel? Churches in North America are also in a complex time of immigration, ethnic and cultural disequilibrium, confusion about how to relate to an empire, ongoing (and new) wars, and the loss of narratives that previously provided (for some) assurances about identity and expectations. These disruptions are often met with management strategies and delimited modes of engagement. Our proposal, that God is active and creative in our contexts, requires *learning communities* that engage new ways of attending and improvising.

Matthew is shaping a community that needs to have a new awareness along with alternative practices and priorities, so he addresses their questions by directing their attention to a carefully crafted narrative. In this narrative he recalls words and actions of Jesus, and places those stories into the context of Rome's occupation of Palestine. In doing this he is inviting them to see what may otherwise be invisible. For example, after several opening chapters with a genealogy and stories about Jesus birth, baptism, temptation, and early ministry, Matthew invites his readers to hear Jesus' Sermon on the Mount as co-listeners with the original audience. In that earlier context of Rome's military occupation, marginal economics, and what could be called mixed reviews of Jerusalem's leaders, some hearers were simply, humbly waiting with hope for God's future. And there were

23. The social and economic strata are also noted by others: Brown and Meier, *Antioch and Rome*, 30–32; Carter, *Matthew and Empire*, 47; Carter, *Matthew and the Margins*, 17–19.

others (including those who came to be identified as Zealots) who were provoking rulers in hopes of an uprising. Jesus disrupts the experiences of those who gather to hear him and he names God's initiative: those who are poor in spirit, who mourn, and who are meek, are explicitly blessed because God is involved (Matt 5:3–5). That word—*blessed*—is not a matter of sappy internal attitudes but a powerful description about God's invasive actions. The kingdom from heaven transforms material conditions and social relationships, including the distribution of power. But for hearers, these sentences seem counterintuitive. Those who are marginalized and without options are favored by God's current initiative. If Jesus' disciples and Matthew's readers are going to gain capacities to understand what Jesus is up to, this reframing of how to interpret what is happening is critical. They need to be awakened to God's agency which, Jesus teaches, empowers their own agency. If we miss this reframing of what God is doing in Jesus then we are bound to misunderstand all that Matthew writes. Part of Matthew's purpose in writing is to invite these anxious Christians in Antioch to learn new perspectives on what is happening through an engagement with their own central Christian story.

To Jesus' audience, Rome said, "Enter into Roman life as it is presented by the collaborating Sanhedrin (official Jewish leadership) and Herod's dynasty (representing Rome). In this manner you will receive mercy, you can stay on the land, and you can be comforted and filled. Your reward can be now; you can avoid persecution; you can enter the kingdom of Rome." This is the *pax Romana*—the peace made available by a generous and benevolent empire and managed by Jewish elites. These words would shape a people in particular ways. The language indicated coherence between current arrangements and what some claimed that God was offering. This interpretive work of the Jewish elites (and how they used their power) was often the center of conflict between Jesus and those authorities as he contested their interpretation of the law. Not everyone lived at ease in this construction. Matthew's church in Antioch received the same message—compliance with Rome was the only obvious option. Rome is the only power, the only agent, the only provider of peace. This web—empire, religion, elites, sanctioned interpretations—is not dissimilar to North American societies and struggles regarding power and resources and who defines the good life.

Matthew's readers could consider Jesus' audience as they reflected on their own situation. In other words, Matthew's intention was to assist these Antiochian Christians to become more alert and faithful as they listen in on how Jesus addressed his own contemporaries. They hear how Jesus was forming them, especially his disciples, into a community that was learning to see God's story from a radically different place than that of established elites. Jesus' hearers were not quite sold on the Rome-Jerusalem arrangements. Economics had been unpredictable because of globalization: Rome had worked toward commodification in the Galilee fishing industry, and family farms were being merged into larger operations—necessary steps for supporting Rome's economy and its troops. And, though they couldn't say it too publicly, these listeners did not have confidence in many of the Jewish priests who were under Rome authority and generally compliant.[24] They knew the economic dislocations of that day; they knew that many were losing out to the Roman style of globalization. Many struggled with the temple compromises. They knew that some had spoken out and that some had even taken up arms in rebellion. Many prayed for a messiah. They meditated on the Psalms and Isaiah and Jeremiah, and sometimes on the Maccabean narrative. Now, in Antioch, Matthew's church knows that Rome's power seemed ubiquitous and those Jerusalem leaders, who had recently revolted, had suffered and died in the midst of Titus's violent overthrow. In what was a homeland for many of them, Israel was reduced to rubble. Matthew wanted the Antioch church to learn of God's purposes through all of this. So he invited them to read Jesus' words: "Blessed are the poor in spirit, for theirs is the kingdom of heaven. Blessed are those who mourn, for they will be comforted. Blessed are the meek, for they will inherit the earth" (Matt 5:3–5 NRSV).

Now, upon hearing these words from Jesus, what can the Palestinian villagers see? What does the Antioch church see? What access to reality do they now have that they did not have until Jesus' words are uttered? To these who are mourning, who feel powerless, who know they can't go up against Rome, Jesus announces another reality: those in mourning will receive comfort from God. This mourning is appropriate, and lamentations are appropriate, because the situation calls for personal and corporate sadness. But it doesn't end there, because God is involved: Jesus proclaims, "You will be comforted." Something more is going on.

Those villagers in Palestine and now the urban dwellers in Antioch were expecting a new kingdom with Jesus, though there were differing ideas concerning what that was. But now they experienced only loss. Then they hear Jesus say, "The meek will inherit the earth." Whether those original hearers were subsistence farmers or Jerusalem insiders, the Beatitudes were earthshaking because they spoke a world that could not otherwise be imagined. And now the Antioch readers hear of a reality that meets them in their dislocation and pain. Matthew is forwarding Jesus' message: God is present and active, so learn to be awakened to what has been beyond your vision.

24. Fletcher-Louis, "Priest, Priesthood," 700.

Commentators and preachers have often mistaken the Beatitudes for commands, or written them off as idealistic and naive, or relegated them to matters of internal disposition.[25] But they are actually something quite different—a lesson in communal sense-making. With this proclamation, which was foreshadowed in the law and the prophets, God's agency becomes clearer. As the crowd is hearing it, Jesus is providing renewed access, an access sharpened and empowered in the proclamation. In the language exchange, reality changes. In the proclamation, centered in the presence of Jesus, there is a reality that had not previously existed. A group of people—this circle of learners—is now different, and they become named players, agents of an incipient interpretive community.

Instead of "blessed are those who accommodate and acquire," Jesus says that God's blessing surrounds the poor and the meek, and that he incorporates them into something new. Rather than living as if Sanhedrin management and Roman globalization provide the truth, they now have an option. God's generative presence is available to those who mourn, who are meek, who are persecuted, and,

> Blessed are those who hunger and thirst for righteousness, for they will be filled.
>
> Blessed are the merciful, for they will receive mercy.
>
> Blessed are the pure in heart, for they will see God.
>
> Blessed are the peacemakers, for they will be called children of God. (5:6–9, NRSV)

Because of the coming of the reign of God in the presence of Jesus, there is a reality that is beyond the existing perceptions and interpretive capacities of the listeners. So Jesus begins by describing reality—a reality that the listeners and readers might too easily miss. In addressing the disciples (5:1–2), Jesus' discourse inaugurates this new learning community. The relationship between those shaped by Jesus and those shaped exclusively by other cultural forces is not merely a matter of values or doctrines. It is about life with God who knows reality and who engages that reality, shaping a community in which these blessings are announced and the community is transformed. This marks an invitation to be learning communities who engage what is being announced.

The churches of North America also exist in the complexities of diverse contexts. They inhabit cultural imaginations that limit sight and misalign practices. Even with theological confessions about God, Euro-tribal

25. For a helpful overview of interpretation, see Luz, *Matthew 1–7*, 229–31.

churches may speak of God's activities but frequently speak and plan and work quite independently of what Jesus announced in the Beatitudes. God may be addressed to bless or provide or resources, but activities proceed according to habits. Also, while previous decades and centuries gave preference to a European-framed religion regarding holy days, civic prayers, and faith claims of public officials, those social behaviors are less frequent or profoundly misshaped in our time, so that these experiences lead to reactive stances, blame, and a scramble for fixes. Some participants are negotiating matters of economics and social power with a level of satisfaction; some are wounded or even outraged by inequities and oppression. Continuing human migrations within North American and immigration across borders cause disorientation when newcomers in church neighborhoods fail to fit the cultural preferences of those churches. All of the cultural behaviors of seeking comfort or preferences or power or certainty or leverage are constantly at play. Matthew provides us with another perspective—learn to see what God sees, to discern what God is doing, to receive and engage God's initiatives. The Beatitudes are featured in the jarring beginning of Matthew's Gospel and they frame and interpret everything that follows.[26]

LUKE'S ACCOUNT IN ACTS

Why would Luke, writing in Acts about the numerous, amazing, noteworthy events in the early decades of the diffusion of the gospel, repeat one story multiple times? For example, Luke gives us details about a vision Peter had, noting that Peter had the vision three times. Then, later, he tells us that Peter referred to the vision for the benefit of others. Then he has Peter provide details of the vision, this time to other apostles. Luke is even more repetitious with a vision that Cornelius had. First, Luke narrates the details of Cornelius's vision, then the next day we read an account as Cornelius himself tells Peter about the vision. When Peter joins a group of Cornelius's associates at Cornelius's home, Cornelius recounts his vision. Finally, Peter gives an account of Cornelius's vision when he meets with other apostles in Jerusalem. In a book that seeks to provide the church with an account of numerous events, these two visions get an inordinate word count. Does this just indicate sloppy editing on the part of the publisher?

Writing around 80 CE, Luke is aware of the mood present among the churches of the Mediterranean world. Because of his travels, and the communications available among churches and traveling teams, Luke knew of

---

26. Our work regarding the Gospel of Matthew, with attention to theories about learning communities and social construction, will be the focus of chapter 5.

the local persecutions in various towns, the violent overthrow of Jerusalem by Titus and his father Vespasian (that also affected Palestinian Christians), and the traumas in Rome. Gaius Tacitus, a senator and historian wrote:

> Nero set up as culprits and punished with the utmost refinement of cruelty a class hated for their abominations, who are commonly called Christians. Nero's scapegoats [the Christians] were the perfect choice because it temporarily relieved pressure of the various rumors going around Rome. Christus, from whom their name is derived, was executed at the hands of the procurator Pontius Pilate in the reign of Tiberius. Checked for a moment, this pernicious superstition again broke out, not only in Judea, the source of the evil, but even in Rome . . .[27]

In discussing Gaius's writings, John Knox notes that, "members of the Early Christian movement often became political targets and scapegoats for the social ills and political tensions of specific rulers and turbulent periods during the first three centuries, CE; however, this persecution was sporadic and rarely Empire-wide, but it was devastating, nonetheless."[28]

This ongoing suffering did not seem to match Jesus' promise of a new reign of God. Jesus himself had promised his own personal return. He had made clear that the gospel was neither just some inward disposition nor a cult disconnected from on-the-ground realities. Salvation included matters of money, relationships, health, households, labor, and food. Decade after decade, participants and observers would question the vitality and power of a movement that seemed to consistently lack traction. Since Christians faced famine in Palestine, experienced treachery in the gladiator games in Rome, and were persecuted across the empire by their closest religious cousins the Jews, we might wonder if many were confused and discouraged. This is why Luke writes—to provide the stories, interpretive links, and hopes that centered on God's continuing initiatives. Our exploration of Acts will benefit from three lenses—diffusion (how something spreads among cultures and societies), alterity (experiences with those who are *other*), and improvisation (the process of receiving some experience, drawing on our own heritage and personal history, then responding so as to move the experience forward). Luke's narrative demonstrates how improvisation is always rooted in what has been received—especially the resources of Israel and experiences that Peter and others had in following Jesus.[29]

27. Gaius Tacitus, quoted in Knox, "Christianity," para. 15.

28. Knox, "Christianity," para. 12.

29. Joel Green notes that the main work of the disciples in Luke's first volume was to be "with" him—which was a prerequisite for apostolic witness in Acts (1:21) and,

Kavin Rowe writes about how the Lukan narrative in Acts "is a highly charged and theologically sophisticated political document that aims at nothing less than the construction of an alternative total way of life . . . that runs counter to the life-patterns of the Graeco-Roman world."[30] In reference to Luke 17:6, "the Christian mission is, in Luke's way of reading reality, a witness to a world that is upside down."[31] There is a play on perspectives—the accusers claim that Christians are turning the world upside down but actually the Christians are speaking and living in a way that reveals that the world is already upside down; in fact, God, with the participation of the church, is creating "instantiations of a world turned right side up."[32] Luke is aware that churches need these narratives in order to not succumb to the cultural powers and patterns. Rowe emphasizes that Luke is providing a full-on counter to Roman culture but not a prompt for a challenge to the military state. At the center of the project is the apocalypse—a continual revealing—of God.[33]

Volume one of Luke's writing is the longest Gospel narrative—a remarkably crafted account of Jesus' life and teachings, along with numerous insights into varied responses and consequences. Now, in volume two, Luke addresses the diffusion of the gospel across the Graeco-Roman world. But he is careful to not rush the geographic spread; he walks attentively through the initial critical turns of the story. Later we will engage several other episodes in Acts,[34] but this introduction focuses on chapters ten and eleven, where the above noted visions get an apparently inordinate amount of attention.

Luke's repetition of the testimonies of Cornelius and Peter makes clear that God is the initiator. Cornelius, an Italian, a centurion, a devout and generous God-fearer, saw an angel and was told that his prayers and alms (perpetual ways of being in a relationship with God) have made him available to something new that God is doing. He is instructed to send a team to Joppa to get Simon (Peter). Obviously, we are inside a narrative that disrupts its readers; if we believe even this initial setup, God is using a soldier who is part of Rome's military occupation and this soldier lives inside traditional

---

relevant to this study, the necessary preparation for faithful improvisation. We believe that the same practice of being with Jesus is the mode for our emphasis on being with God as God engages our contexts. See Green, *The Theology of the Gospel of Luke*, 108–9.

30. Rowe, *World Upside Down*, 4.

31. Rowe, *World Upside Down*, 6.

32. Rowe, *World Upside Down*, 6.

33. Rowe, *World Upside Down*, 5.

34. Our further work with Acts, including attention to matters of diffusion, alterity, and improvisation, comprises chapter 6.

practices of Jewish faith. Seemingly without any hesitation Cornelius does just what he is told, "Now send men to Joppa for a certain Simon who is called Peter" (10:5 NRSV). As the story unfolds, Luke recounts this vision three times.

Next, Luke describes a disruptive afternoon in Joppa where Peter's rooftop prayers draw him into a trance. In a vision he sees numerous animals and hears instructions to eat. When he argues, the voice, now credited to God, tells him, "What God has made clean, you must not call profane" (10:15 NRSV). Then, probably to limit Peter's avoidance, the vision is repeated two more times. Not only is God repetitious with Peter but Luke's narrative includes a reference back to this story plus a complete retelling.

Evidently Luke wants readers to be aware of some key matters: God is the initiator, prayer is a practice that places us in a listening posture, and those who are faithful in prayer will begin to improvise based on what they have heard. By *improvise* we mean that they take what has been given to them in a new experience, or situation, combine it with existing resources and competencies, and then take the next steps. The diffusion of the gospel was never a matter of strategic plans or expert tacticians. Cornelius, working with his own habits and resources, improvises when he hears instructions—he chooses a team to send and he gathers a group to receive a visit from Peter, a step that was not in the instructions. We will soon read that one act of his improvisation gets quickly corrected—when he prostrates himself to Peter he is told to stand.

In the world of the eighties, as churches experienced disorientation and numerous disruptions, we can imagine that they experienced increased anxieties, fears, and hopelessness. In this context, Luke insists that his readers attend to God's present and ongoing activities. While Jewish and Roman traditions are still at play, while numerous forces of Mediterranean cultures shape peoples and cities, God is a persistent initiator. Further, Luke notes, if God is the initiator then there are important, specific practices that make us more available to discern those activities, and we then have the work of improvising into God's creative engagements.

Given those basics, Luke names the jarring new orientation that God is promoting: God's particular enlistment of Israel has been expanded. Peter had already been stretched when he visited Samaria after Philip's expulsion from Jerusalem created new opportunities among that previously shunned people (8:4–25).[35] Through Acts 8 and 9, Luke is showing us a consistent

35. Johnson notes that Luke's narration of Peter's visit to Lydda and Joppa (Acts 9:31–43) and the miraculous healings creates a transition toward the explicit engagement with Cornelius and other Gentiles. Luke specifies that Peter responds to messengers, that the Holy Spirit is preparing and shaping these experiences, that Peter tells

progression as Peter is stretched. Biblical narratives indicate Peter as both faithful *and* hesitant (a hesitancy that does not get fully overcome even with this episode). Throughout this story, Peter argues with the angel, is "bewildered," "broods," and is "astonished." It will take the word of Cornelius, an outsider to pious Jews, for Peter to get enough sight to exclaim "Jesus is Lord of all" (10:36). God uses a thrice-repeated vision to tell him that exclusionary practices needed to be dropped, and then God instructs him to go with a group of men who are at his gate. That's it—Peter does not receive clarifying reasons or goals or methods or scripts. Peter does begin to ask questions of the men, and to listen to their answers. They implicate Cornelius, providing strong reference regarding his character and his service of Israel, and they claim that an angel prompted the journey to fetch Peter. Peter improvises by doing two things that are not specified by either vision—he provides a night's hospitality and then gathers a few believers to join him in this rather ambiguous adventure. Improvisation assumes disruptions and requires listening, in this case to God and to visitors, and it always includes elements and actions that are already at hand. It is our conviction that, similar to the disruption that Peter faced, North American churches today have opportunities to become aware of and participate in how God is active among our neighbors. Without the humility to listen, to God and to others, we cannot gain this awareness. Without improvisational steps toward neighbors (without scripts and answers) we will be without awareness or means of joining God. Luke writes in order to reform our expectations and options.

When this merged traveling group arrives in Caesarea, and after correcting Cornelius's posture, Peter discovers the assembly that has been gathered. He says only enough to address the awkwardness that everyone feels, emphasizing his own willingness to move beyond customary prejudicial behaviors: "You yourselves know that it is unlawful for a Jew to associate with or to visit a Gentile; but God has shown me that I should not call anyone profane or unclean" (10:28 NRSV). Then he says he wants to listen. Cornelius recounts his vision (this is Luke's third telling), commends Peter for his kindness, and requests whatever message God has sent via Peter. Peter begins with a key theological claim that arises because of the situation in which he finds himself: "I truly understand that God shows no partiality, but in every nation anyone who fears him and does what is right is acceptable to him" (10:34–5 NRSV). Acting on habits developed previously, he gives testimony regarding Jesus, invites them to believe, and is then interrupted by the Holy Spirit. Peter and the Jewish believers who are with him

---

the stricken to "get up" (using a term connected to Jesus' resurrection), and that Peter is in the home of a tanner (whose labors were seen as unclean). Johnson, *Acts*, 179–80.

hear the Spirit-prompted tongues and testimonies. Again, God is initiating and everyone else is improvising. For example, in response to what happened ("these people . . . have received the Holy Spirit just as we have" 10:47 NRSV) Peter improvises by calling for the new believers to be baptized.

As word of this event spread, Peter faced criticism; he was accused of being in an unclean house and receiving the hospitality of table fellowship among those who were uncircumcised.[36] In Jerusalem, facing critics, Peter blames God; the apostles receive a full telling of both visions, the steps that Cornelius and Peter took, and the Holy Spirit's baptism. As Luke Timothy Johnson writes,

> Luke shows through the narrative itself how the diverse experiences of God's action by individuals are slowly raised to the level of a communal narrative, which in turn must be tested by the entire community in a difficult and delicate process of disagreement, debate, and the discernment of the Scripture. By means of carefully constructed narrative, Luke communicates a vision of the Church as a community of moral discourse and of discernment of the Spirit.[37]

Possibly most disorienting here and in our later explorations in Acts 16 is the Spirit's engagement in households in a manner that displaces both Jerusalem and Rome. Luke's earlier narrative has seen the temple as a defining, sacred center. Now, in Peter's arguments with God on a Joppa rooftop, and then as he is schooled in a Caesarean house, there is a disruption. Green writes about the two axes of the temple, "The vertical axis marks the temple as the meeting place of God and humanity . . . (and the) horizontal axis, then, signals how the temple establishes the order of the world."[38] Both axes get reoriented in the Joppa and Caesarea houses—God's Spirit is present and active. Green concludes that "we should notice how the house(hold) has become the substitute for the temple as a place of prayer, a place of divine revelation, a place of instruction, and even as the locus of God's presence."[39]

For Luke's readers, who are experiencing rejection in many synagogues and sporadic violent persecution from Rome, these accounts bear witness to God's active involvement in their world and call them to practices of attentiveness, listening, and improvisation. Luke does not deny the traumas and

---

36. It is noticeable that the critique is not regarding a Gentile mission but about table fellowship. Maybe this can help us transgress in the ways that focus on God's agency.

37. Johnson, *Acts of the Apostles,* 16.

38. Green, *Luke as Narrative Theologian,* 174.

39. Green, *Luke as Narrative Theologian,* 176.

challenges, but he knows how disorientation and discouragement become overwhelming if believers lose sight of God's involvement and fail to engage their own agency. Basically, Luke is reminding them that they don't need prescribed strategies or experts of innovative programs. This is emphasized by Johnson, "by this repeated telling, Luke's reader is at least assured that the one guiding the community through this treacherous passage is God's Spirit."[40]

Churches in North America frequently work at managing strained commitments—professional clergy shaped by both priestly traditions and modern corporations, doctrines held with enlightenment certainty, missiology rooted in colonial hegemony and a continuing objectifying of the other. While it is important for leaders to be looking at both traditional texts and practices while also attending to contemporary cultures and resources, if God's agency is not primary then actions and habits will meander in an agnostic haze. Skills for reasoning, communication, innovation, and collaboration are important but usually they are operating with blinders. Throughout volume two of his writing, Luke provides numerous accounts of God's initiatives and the generative practices that have made alertness and responsiveness possible in regard to the churches' gospel vocation. We are also learning that without alterity—without the words of those we consider outsiders—we will not see and engage with God. Peter realizes and gives witness that "(Jesus) is Lord of all!"—not because some doctrines are rightly affirmed but because he listens to Cornelius and sees that God is active.[41] Now we are invited to connect the narratives of Scripture with our own lives. We believe that alertness to God's agency, risk, and humility in engaging others, practices of theological discernment, and a praxis of improvisation can help leaders find a space in which their work embodies a similar hope. We will explore these further in chapter 6 and in our proposals in Intermezzo 2 and the chapters that follow.

EPHESIANS

Paul made a brief visit to Ephesus around 52 CE, leaving Priscilla and Aquila behind to continue the work (Acts 18). Then in 54 CE he returned and spent three years there. Luke's narrative describes or alludes to the diverse forces that worked against the gospel in Ephesus, including Jews who made

---

40. Johnson, *Acts of the Apostles*, 201.

41. As Green notes, "For good reason, study of the Cornelius episode has, in recent years, shied away from a narrow focus on Cornelius's conversion in favor of an emphasis on Peter's." Green, *Luke as Narrative Theologian*, 175.

it impossible for Paul to teach in the synagogue, a Jewish exorcist who falsely claimed that he was working with Paul, and a silversmith who started a
riot among silver craftsmen who were losing money because of Paul's work
(which challenged their Artemis-centered idol-making). The church grew
in size and maturity in this environment of challenges that included religions, money, labor/business, and a town clerk's actions to maintain *Pax
Romana*. About five years later, while under arrest in Rome, Paul wrote a
letter that, in some early copies, has "to the Ephesians" in the heading; some
other copies lack any specified addressee. Sometimes this letter is evaluated
as too impersonal and too decontextual to be Paul's, but others note that the
time lag (since he last visited) and geographic distance could contribute to
those characteristics. There is still much that can be discerned in regard to
Paul's actions as a leader and what he commended going forward. While
actual authorship has been debated, we will refer to Paul because of both
tradition and the conceptual congruence with Paul's other New Testament
letters.[42]

Paul himself does not seem to be in a situation that demonstrates to
the Ephesians that all is well. Again, he is in prison in Rome, surrounded by
the empire's symbols, activities, and personnel. While there were mitigating
circumstances (living with a single guard and with some level of freedom),
this was likely during Nero's reign and the empire featured both instability
and violence. Many Christians saw Nero as the anti-Christ, and the great
fire of 64 CE (after Paul's acquittal and departure) was blamed on them.
Ephesus was a major Roman city, important for trade, philosophy, and worship of Artemis (with the impressive temple nearby, which was under Ephesus's stewardship). So Paul is writing from the empire's capital to a major
regional center.

In the letter's prologue Paul situates his readers vis-à-vis their world.
The citizens of Ephesus would have seen themselves under the fatherhood
of Caesar, proud recipients and guardians of Artemis's temple, benefactors
of great teachers, and recognized as a powerful outpost of the empire's economics and military. The Ephesians knew their role, and understood their
obligations to show their allegiance to Rome and Artemis, which are the
sources of identity, belonging, gifts, and purpose. Paul, in his earlier ministry and now in this letter, counters with an alternative narrative. In this
socio-cultural context, they need to be awake to what God has done and is
doing.

This first chapter of Ephesians orients us to the source and types of
blessings that Paul commends, and here we are faced with a conceptual

42. For an overview of authorship and audience, see Arnold, "Ephesians, Letter to."

challenge. The opening paragraphs have a word that has become increasingly unhelpful in late modernity—*spiritual*. It tends to refer to some unspeci-
fied postures or forces or activities that are disconnected from the earth.
Spirituality is an altered state of existence, non-physical, ethereal, without
substance. But for Paul, the word is actually more about the deeper, richer,
substantive, even earthy connections to God, rather than something intan-
gible and insubstantial.[43] Our modern imaginations are equally derailed by
the words *heavenly* and *heavens*. Creative literature and bad theology have
moved heaven away from physical presence and current chronology. In
Ephesians, Paul assumes that both words are landed, present, tangible—because he is challenging both Artemis and Rome in real time and in specified
geographies. Without this conceptual clarity, Christian faith is by definition
irrelevant and without substance. As we will explain in the next chapter,
modernity made that shift and God's agency was sidelined. In the most basic way, *spiritual* is, for Christ-followers, the real, daily, communal connections between God, the world, and the church. So, as becomes clearer below,
the work of spirituality is to discern and participate in what God is doing in
a locale and during this time. And, to take another quick dip into Ephesians
2, the "heavenly places" are the *current* location of the Ephesian believers
(2:6 NRSV), meaning these believers are situated in the midst of the lively
spiritual resources and traffic that come with participation in the Trinity on
the ground, in daily life, without leaving their current geographic location.
Without these conceptual shifts, Ephesians is flattened and agnostic.

So how does Paul work to orient them to this spiritual-heavenly-
grounded-blessed life? First, he reminds them that even though the mysteries of Artemis seemed permeating, powerful, and invasive, with secrets and
rituals and hidden knowledge, *God is not keeping secrets:* "With all wisdom
and insight God has made known to us the mystery of God's will, according
to God's good pleasure that God set forth in Christ, as a plan for the fullness of time, to gather up all things in him, things in heaven and things on
earth" (1:9–10 NRSV, adapted). In Christ, mysteries are not about things
hidden and proscribed, but about what God has already made, and continues to make, abundantly clear and tangible and consequential. What God
has revealed is not just a postponed goal that calls on believers to major in
delayed gratification, but blessings have already been distributed and, even
as Paul writes, continue to flow into their streets, homes, neighborhoods,
relationships, troubles, labors, learning, and imaginations. While only in
"the fullness of time" will God's full design become realized and visible,
Paul writes that God's telos for creation has invaded Ephesus. Second, God's

---

43. See Barth, *Ephesians 1–3*, 101–3.

glory—which is not ethereal and ceremonial but God's grounded and tangible self revelation—is the source of their vocation: "We are called to be an honor to God's glory" (1:12). That word *honor* is about how our lives and words, our thinking and acting, are an applause that arises from what God is doing around us (God's glory)—which requires that we pay attention, discern, so that we can live into our vocation. As we will see,[44] this is what leadership is about—making connections among the continually new movements of the Spirit and the women and men who are available and engaged in discernment and faithful participation.[45]

INHABITING WORLDS

We all see and think and feel and act inside cultural imaginaries. These maps or patterns are absorbed into our social ways of life as we continually learn ways of perceiving, imagining, acting, or evaluating. Just as Jeremiah and Matthew and Luke and Paul were shaped by their cultures, and enabled by the Holy Spirit to see something somewhat differently than their contemporaries, they provided those ways of interpreting and acting inside the frameworks of the very contexts in which they lived. Their books are not generic or timeless. As readers of Scripture, we also bring with us our societal habits—about spirituality and church and leadership and love and practice.

As leaders, continuing the metaphor of waking up, we are promoting a new alertness to how we read cultural forces, to how we embody societal habits of leadership, and to how we enter into biblical and theological texts. We believe that the apocalypse of God, throughout history and focused in Jesus Christ, and continuing in the ongoing presence and actions of the Trinity, must be the center of this exploration. These Bible books (and others) are crafted to help readers perceive and act in ways that are different from—even in direct counter to—the accepted ways of seeing and acting. Our vocation is to discern and be shaped by God's "breaking into" the grounded realities of our contexts. So we will name what we see in contemporary

44. In chapter 7 we will engage Ephesians with attention to modern leadership frameworks, including critical theory and various elements of organizational change.

45. This process makes obvious that interpretive leadership as utterance is essential but incomplete; rather, meanings arise from activities as words are enacted, and the experiences reshape the words. We create knowledge, we really learn, in this iterative process of personal and corporate praxis, which is the cumulative, mutually correcting, and reinforcing cycle of study/reflection and engagement/action. One place to begin such testing of utterance is the repeated list of basic practices connected to God and neighbor: hospitality, witness, love expressed in deeds, attention to orphans, foreigners, and the poor.

practices of leadership, then by engaging theology and Scripture we will begin describing alternatives. We are not promoting new techniques, and frequently we will commend some currently available frameworks that we believe are malleable, but our core affirmation is—to parallel Kavin Rowe's affirmation—that God engages a world that has been turned upside down and we need our own lenses to be flipped or we miss what God is doing and thereby we lose opportunities to participate in turning it right-side up. We are continually encouraged when we see leaders step into the practices that make discernment and participation more likely. We are also convinced that the biblical and theological resources we engage are profoundly generative for this task of seeing and practicing a different way.

CHAPTER 2

The Inhabited Leadership Context

Something terribly important happened in Europe sometime between the sixteenth and nineteenth centuries . . . From the European perspective these dizzying changes were proof of the superiority of the Western tradition. This is something new. It went beyond mere ethnocentrism, a bias to which nobody is immune . . . European supremacy in arms, science, economic productivity, and cultural accomplishment became the touchstone for all nations. Two points define a line, as soon as Europeans decided they lived in the most advanced of societies they endowed history with a course and direction. This set up a race from the past to the present in which Europe came first by definition. European history became universal history.

—Michael Steinberg, *The Fiction of a Thinkable World*[1]

INTRODUCTION

CHAPTER 1 PROPOSED THAT in Scripture we see God continually prodding and disrupting leaders as they faced upheavals that didn't fit their understanding of God's agency in their contexts. The changing of the on-the-ground realities that confronted these communities of God's people were neither expected nor imagined. As narrated in Acts, the Holy Spirit was the

1. Steinberg, *Fiction of a Thinkable World*, 149–52.

outpouring and continuation of all that God had begun in the Son through the incarnation, crucifixion, and resurrection. In the New Testament, the Spirit's work was both something new and the embedding of what had taken place in Jesus Christ. It was in these terms that the Spirit was continually prodding these new communities of Christians, and those who were their leaders. As the story of Acts continually announces, the Spirit was disrupting the assumptions of these first Christians, assumptions that were already limiting the scope of their expectations for what God had begun with Jesus and the pouring out of the Spirit. The texts in chapter 1 (these will be developed further in part II) are demonstrations of the ways that God was ahead of these young communities, reshaping their ways of life so that they might join with God in transforming their world.

We can hardly imagine it could be any different for us. At the same time, the specific forms of disrupting and learning going on in those early centuries aren't templates we simply copy into our own situations. The common denominator, or parallel, is that the Spirit is also disrupting us in our contexts today. Just as these first Christians had to figure out how to faithfully contextualize what they were learning through the Spirit's disruptions, so must we in our own time. The biblical texts propose a continuous contestation with dominant narratives that come and go, making their claims to be the true stories about the world, the true way of shaping it, and, therefore, demanding our allegiance. Even in the light of the resurrection wherein, for freedom, Christ has set us free, we must continually contest claims about both the purpose of life and the means of achieving that purpose. A profoundly destructive superstition frames the modern imagination, namely, the conviction that we are the primary agents in control of the forces at work in our contexts. This myth of agency lives at the heart of Modernity's Wager. It drives too many of the leadership models shaping the actions and attitudes of the churches.

What narratives, models, and methods will shape us in this time of our own unraveling as Euro-tribal churches? Are Christian communities to be shaped by the realpolitik all about us, the principalities and powers (the ways in which the powers become present in our forms of life such as politics, economics, and social movements) that ceaselessly work to bind us to their visions and practices, or are we to be shaped as communities whose ways of life are continually formed around the primacy of God's agency in the world?[2] These are not abstract considerations that get in the way of the practical work of growing churches and making disciples. They are at the heart of understanding the nature of Christian life in our time

2. See Rowe, *World Upside Down*.

and, therefore, the practice of leadership. The bias of the Scriptures is that we dwell in our everyday lives as signs and witnesses to the fact that this is God's world—God is its primary agent. The struggle for Christians in the late modern West involves how to awaken to the power of those other forms of agency shaping our leadership practices. We are proposing that Christian leadership has been seduced into a forgetfulness that prevents it from grasping the kind of captivity now determining its leadership practices. This chapter proposes ways the modern project has created a situation wherein our leadership functions with little sense of God's agency. Where, in fact, God has been turned into a supplemental, derivative support for the latest leadership models borrowed from other sources.

MODERNITY'S WAGER

Modernity is a huge wager! It is a wager that life can be lived well without God.[3] Human beings are seen as autonomous, self-making individuals whose identities are not given but plastic and, therefore, malleable to all kinds of social administration. We can make ourselves in whatever ways we deem congruent with our experiences or needs. Autonomy, plasticity, and self-making are the marks of Modernity's Wager, and the creation of technocratic elites with the skills to manage and control desired outcomes are the hallmarks of its leaders. This modern world is not the creation of some Maker (even if there is a Maker, this is only a vague reference to a deity who left the field of action in some chided recognition that human beings have come of age, have entered their adulthood, and are now in control). In the place of the Creator has come another entity—Nature—a vast canvas of potential upon which human beings paint and create and materialize their wills. To be human is to be in control with the capacity to make and manage the world into the projects we desire.

The quote from Michael Steinberg that stands at the beginning of this chapter is but one of thousands of comments about the strange, radical shift that happened when, in the West, the modern was born. But it didn't simply all begin in seventeenth or eighteenth century Europe or with the beginnings of the great navigational journeys or the industrial revolutions (the "creation" stories of the modern West have multiple variants and time lines). Long before these astonishing events transformed the world and birthed the

---

3. It was Pascal who first put forth this notion of a wager in his *Pensées*. The phrase was used by Seligman in *Modernity's Wager* and is a key element in the argument proposed by Roxburgh and Robinson in their book *Practices for the Refounding of God's People*.

modern, often to the benefit of human thriving even when there was little sense of its effects on the created world, forces were at work that turned these times of human creativity into Modernity's Wager. The wager is not about inventions but the story that came to drive these inventions; they all derive from human agency. In the modern, human agency becomes the primary force of life, the primary agent of making. To be human is to be the maker, the agent, the shaping and defining force in all creation. The antecedents of this hubris go back a very long way. They are rooted in a powerful story about how force and power are the central energies driving human life.

FORCE AND POWER

The German social theorist Peter Sloterdijk points us in these directions when discussing the issue of power in modernity and its relationship to the new *Anthropocene* age of the planet, wherein "human beings have become responsible for the habitation and management of the Earth as a whole, since their presence upon it is no longer more or less seamlessly integrated." In the scale of human activity, human beings are now *the* agents determining the fate of the earth.[4] Surely, notions of the planet as being one gigantic canvas upon which human beings are free to paint and sculpt, is the barely covered aesthetic of Modernity's Wager. Earth became a construct that humans make, not a gift for which they are stewards. The earth is no longer the foundation within which we live but the vessel in which we travel for our own ends. Parenthetically, this naming of the modern age as the anthropocene has created all its own anxieties. Today the term is used to designate an apocalyptic turning in the natural history of the world, for this hubris of human beings has produced the dire predictions of climate change that will destroy our very way of life. Here we witness the outworking of this modern sense of power as *control over* coupled with its notions of freedom and the radical autonomy of human agency. Together, these forms of the modern imagination are bringing us to the brink of the abyss. Where do we locate a different understanding of power and human agency from outside Modernity's Wager?

In terms of what is involved when we wrestle with notions of power and human agency, Sloterdijk uses the phrase "kinetic expressionism"[5] to describe how these two elements point to how, in the use of fossil fuels and atomic energy, power and agency express an understanding of human beings as free, autonomous agents who make projects in the world. While his

4. Sloterdijk, *What Happened*, 1.

5. Sloterdijk, *What Happened*, 13.

concerns are, like many others, about the environment and the precarious-ness of "spaceship earth," the sources of these concerns go far deeper than questions of fossil fuels or atomic energy, as critical as these are today. The concerns have to do with larger questions of our relationship to power and force (force being part of the meaning of kinetic that is about the forces used to move something) as agents. These are also fundamental questions for a theology of leadership. The words *kinetic* (force) and *kenotic* (a self-empty-ing of God for the sake of the world that calls for the reciprocal response of human beings in doxological relationship to the Creator and creation) are dialectically related to one another. But when, within Modernity's Wager, the conversation about power is limited to one in which God as agent is made absent, this dialectic is emptied. We are left with only one side of the dialectic, a truncated understanding of power as kinetic rather than kenotic within this radically new modern understanding of human agency. This limiting description of the human situation, along with all its hubris, frames the current environmental crisis. The crisis gets expressed as being about the use of fossil fuels. But what has to be seen is the way in which fossil fuels are linked to these deeper distortions in our understanding of power, of the nature of the created world (nature) that has now been turned into a project of human making and power. In the environmental crisis we can clearly see troubling manifestations of Modernity's Wager and recognize the deeper pathologies in our understanding of power and human agency. But what we tend not to recognize is how these very same pathologies are at work every day in the practices and methods of leadership shaping the Euro-tribal churches.

In the genesis of Modernity's Wager, force becomes one of the central drivers of the human imagination. It shapes the challenges confronting a Christian engagement with this culture. Some of the critical questions con-fronting Christian leaders are therefore: What is our relationship to force? What is our engagement with power? What is the nature of Christian lead-ership in a world shaped by these central sources of human life in the *saeculum*?[6] The concept of force that gives to contemporary human beings their understanding of "freedom" as autonomous agents runs through much of the imagination and practice of leadership in our time. This reality has to be factored into any framing of a theology of leadership. Sloterdijk is helpful in pointing out the direction of modernity's central imagination but his

---

6. *Saeculum* refers to the time between the ascension of Christ and Christ's return. It is the ordinary time within which God is present and at work. It is from this Latin term that we derive the modern word *secular*, but we have changed its fundamental meaning. In its modern usage it tends to mean a time and place where God is absent or has been absented. There existed no such sense of the secular before the modern period.

description does not sufficiently express the underlying problematic of agency that confronts Christian leaders and our life together.

Queen Elizabeth I Armada Portrait

The picture of Queen Elizabeth I is an example Sloterdijk uses to illustrate this sense of force present in the West before the birth of the modern. There Elizabeth, dressed in her regalia of power and sovereignty, places her hand over the orb of the earth that lies beside her to symbolize who is in control, who is the agent, the maker and determiner of all things on earth. Sloterdijk points out how this sense of force is echoed in some of the West's finest minds. It is the young Goethe who writes, "I am now entirely embarked upon the wave of the world, completely resolved to discover, to battle, to founder, or to spring into the air with all of my cargo."[7] And Nietzsche in *Ecco Homo* declares: "I am not a man, I am dynamite."[8]

A twentieth-century thinker who saw all this most clearly was Simon Weil. Her brief life (1909–1943) was shaped by the great wars and the great ideologies of the twentieth century. She moved from a secular Jewish, French context toward becoming a Christian within the Catholic Church, and in so doing reflected deeply on the questions of force, power,

7. Cited in Sloterdijk, *What Happened in the 20th Century*, 14.
8. Nietzsche, *Anti-Christ*, 143–44.

and human agency as they had shaped the Western *corpus christianum*. In a series of influential essays and books she studied the presence of what she called "force" in the Western tradition, beginning with an analysis of Homer's *The Iliad,* wherein she proposed that the real protagonists were not the heroes of the Trojan Wars but force itself. She defined it as "That X that turns anybody who is subject to it into a *thing*."[9] In her view, the forms of Christianity that emerge in the West in the medieval period (around the eleventh and twelfth centuries) were characterized by their appropriation of force, or raw power, over all else that opposed it. For her, it was this "spiritual totalitarianism" that would produce the reactions to Christianity in such movements as humanism in the Renaissance (or contemporary liberalism). Alan Jacobs quotes her in this way: "from then onwards, the spiritual life of Europe has diminished until it has almost shrunk to nothing" and goes on to state that for Weil, "it was against this tyranny that the early modern spirit revolted."[10] As Jacobs points out, she saw this Christendom as a "spiritual totalitarianism" or "the rule of force in one place from which force should be exiled."[11] Jacobs acknowledges that in many places, Weil's readings of history can be extreme, but the point being made here is the way she reads back into the story of Christendom in the West the continued centrality of force and power as the underlying shaping mechanism—not simply of the culture at large but of how human agency functioned even from within the churches. In Modernity's Wager the primacy of force and power continues to shape our imagination and, we argue, much of contemporary practice of leadership. In a pithy analysis, Weil proposed that superstition is not a matter of believing in gods but the human propensity to believe that as primary agents we can control the forces (natural or supernatural) at work in the core of social relationships. This superstition, at the heart of Modernity's Wager, drives many of the leadership models shaping the actions of churches with their vision and mission statements, their strategies for making the church central again in culture, their plans for driving change and innovation, their projects for making things happen with their focus on management, control, and outcomes.

9. Weil, *The Iliad,* 3. See also Jacobs, *Year of Our Lord 1943.* Jacobs examines the work of a variety of Christian "humanist" thinkers in the period leading up to and during World War II, including C. S. Lewis, W. H. Auden, Jacques Maritain, and Simone Weil. He gives particular attention to Weil's understanding of force as well as her critique of medieval Christendom as laying the groundwork of a Western Christianity shaped by power and force.

10. Jacobs, *Year of Our Lord 1943,* 98.

11. Jacobs, *Year of Our Lord 1943,* 112.

GOD AS USEFUL

Our habitual choices of leadership tools, models, and methods are expressions of what Charles Taylor calls the *modern social imaginary*.[12] The word *imaginary* refers to background assumptions determining how we see and act in the world. Within the background assumptions of the modern project God has become little more than a useful resource for all the making, planning, and projecting of futures that shape much in current modes of Christian leadership. The primary models and practices of leadership in congregations and denominations tend not to operate from a conviction that God is the primary agent in the life in the world. They live inside the narrative of Modernity's Wager—this radical break from all other forms of human society up to the birth of the modern West.[13] Before, all other societies functioned within the conviction that all of life (including the human) was dependent upon and derived from its relationship to some form of the transcendent or divine. As indicated above, the wager isn't a claim that God does not exist, but rather that as moderns we have entered our maturity, our independence, our capacity to make the world apart from the need for any transcendent meaning. Like a child developing into adulthood, we now have the ability to stand on our own, to create our own kind of world. As mature adults we can work out the shape and directions of life without recourse or reference to God. We are the measure and makers of all things. The world is now the project of human imagination made anew through our innovation. In the wager, our understanding of God shifts from God's being the primary agent in the world to being either absent or merely useful to human making and thriving. Inside this transformation the location of our primary desires shifted from experiencing God to our self thriving. This radical transformation is now the assumed social imaginary and, as such, has become invisible to us. The devaluation of Christian life in the West is not about the disappearance of God but the revaluation of God to a useful construct within human power and self-making. When, for example, we are asked if we know "God has a wonderful plan for our life," or you are invited to a seminar on how God can give you the very best life, the God encountered in Jeremiah, Matthew, Acts, and Ephesians is rendered into a useful conscript for our own ends. Modernity's Wager is a profound forgetting from which the Spirit would invite us to awaken.

12. See Taylor, *Modern Social Imaginaries*.
13. See Seligman, *Modernity's Wager* and Rieff, *My Life Among the Deathworks*.

Method and Control as Central Characteristics of the Wager

Since the Enlightenment, priority has been given to the conviction that truth is derived from a particular method. This method of compelling nature to reveal its secrets lies near the center of the modern imagination. It is the taken-for-granted default understanding of how information, facts, and truth are attained. The point is not that this method is wrong. It has, in fact, resulted in some amazing discoveries that have given life to millions. The point is that this is practically the only method shaping our leadership practices. The pervasive assumption driving leadership within the churches is that with the right techniques, sufficient information, and metrics, we can break problems down into their simplest elements so that we can then design strategies for managing and controlling the outcomes we desire. The presumption is that good leaders must be well skilled in these methods of management, control, and predictability. Good leadership involves this capacity to name reality, create designs, craft plans, and write mission and vision statements that direct and control a preferred future. These methods are expressions of Modernity's Wager. God's agency has become a secondary, attendant, useful presence—baptizing and blessing decisions drawn, for example, from models in the social sciences or business world. As chapter 1 pointed out, the biblical texts invite us into a different imagination. If God is the primary agent in the world then the forms of leadership shaping modernity (management, control, determining preferred futures, and providing certainty) dull and desensitize us to God. An old truism gets at people's sense that something is awry—"If the Holy Spirit disappeared, at least 90 percent of what we're doing would proceed without any changes." We need to be awakened in order to see and discern what this God is about.

Leadership in a Euro-Tribal Imagination

Modernity's Wager is deeply embedded in the Euro-tribal churches. The term "Euro-tribal" describes those churches born from the European Reformations of the sixteenth and seventeenth centuries that then expanded and grew to power from the seventeenth century forward. These churches became, functionally, the sufficient narrative for all Christian life, not just in the West but across the globe through exploration, colonization, and mission and, today, networks and media.[14] These Western peoples conceived of their culture as Christian and understood their religious vocation as exporting that culture as the normative form of Christianity wherever they went. This

---

14. See Willie Jennings's masterful analysis in *The Christian Imagination*.

is the form that "Christendom" took from the sixteenth century forward, replacing the medieval Christendom that ended with the formation of the nation states after the Peace of Westphalia in 1648. In the Euro-tribal mind Christianity was now coterminous with Western structures, ideals, methods, and narratives. This imagination was exported across the world. It resulted, for example, in the *white man's burden*, an imagination shaped by the conviction that divine providence had given to Europe and, by extension, North America, the responsibility to Christianize (Europeanize) the world. Within this global expansion of Western life, the theologies and practices of the Euro-tribal churches were viewed as normative for everywhere else. The Euro-tribal churches viewed themselves as the primary form of a global church. The new Catholicism was the West. The term *Euro-tribal* conveys this meaning. For almost five centuries the imagination of the Euro-tribal churches has been that of being at the center of all things Christian. It's an imagination of ascendance, power, and control.[15]

These notions of power via method, management, and control are now embedded practices shaping the habits and imagination of leadership within these churches. While this imagination is in a process of unraveling, a social imaginary of 500 years is not quickly dispelled. The anxiety for a growing number of leaders in the Euro-tribal churches is that their places of power and privilege are gone; their methods of management and control no longer work. At the same time, numerous leaders still use these frameworks of Modernity's Wager to effectively create successful churches but, even so, fail to understand the underlying framework of human agency driving them. Over the last fifty years, church leadership in North America has been shaped by multiple attempts to fix this unraveling and return the churches to the center of the culture.[16] This effort to regain primacy is pursued through an increasingly intensive application of the methods of management and control, strategic actions of restructuring, the development of new metrics for measuring and assuring success, or the adoption of the latest methods from business schools—all with little or no reference to God's agency, all of them forms of belief in Modernity's Wager.

The Euro-tribal churches need to be distinguished from what is popularly known as Christendom. This term has been used to describe the cohabitation of a specific culture and the Christian faith. There is a tradition that blames "Christendom" for the current woes of the churches. Leaders want to proclaim the "end of Christendom" in order to propose new forms

---

15. This is one of the primary arguments Jennings makes and it underlies his audacious claim that the Western theological imagination lives and moves within a "diseased social imagination." Jennings, *Christian Imagination*, 6.

16. Roxburgh, *Joining God*, 13–37.

of church for the "post-Christendom" world. In point of fact, the end of Christendom started with the Peace of Westphalia (1648) and the birth of nation states. Religion became the prerogative of the king, or prince, not the church. Christendom was birthed in the mass conversions (by the sword and penalty of death) of Germanic peoples under the Frankish King Charlemagne (742–814). In this eighth century context Christendom would come to describe the socio-political reality of Europe. Until the seventeenth century, Christianity was essentially viewed as coterminous with Europe. By the eighteenth century, the West was dismantling its Christendom as a new center of power, the nation state, emerged.[17]

What did not change in this transition was this conviction of the West as the apex of civilization. This conception welded the exportation of Christianity with the territorial expansion of European control and culture. For African historian and missiologist Jehu Hanciles, European nations believed territorial acquisitions were divinely ordained for the spread of the gospel. Power, control, and domination become an axiomatic part of the church's mission, "Thus, the same spirit of nationalist competition that spurred European economic expansion also energized the missionary project to a huge extent. Missionary enterprise was also imbued with the conviction of manifest destiny: the sense that one's particular nation, or tribe, was uniquely called to fulfill divine purposes."[18] This ethnocentric outlook spawned racist ideologies such as "white man's burden," "manifest

17. Several comments about the use of Christendom are important here. First, numerous writers use a more functional definition of Christendom than the one offered here. A functional Christendom has to do with a society's self-understanding. In this sense most people assumed that European and North American states were "functionally" Christian in that a majority assumed that some sort of Christian perspective or values guided their lives. Within this functional Christendom such writers did not assume that Christianity had any form of political power or authority in terms of the state or its making of laws. It has been the case that this idea of a functional "Christian" society has informed the imagination of many. That being said, it might, therefore, be helpful to state that the "idea" of Christianity being a primary influence in society has been the norm through much of the nineteenth and into the twentieth centuries. But to say that this was Christendom is not the case. One suspects that when people write about the end of Christendom in our current context what they actually mean is that there has been lost this loose sense that Christian values shape the understanding and practices of its citizens. Second, there is a narrower sense in which it can be argued that during the later half of the twentieth century there was an ending, or a move "beyond" Christendom in terms of Western missions beyond its shores, the complex ways that globalization has transformed the imagination of people in former "colonies," and the massive migrations that are remaking the West in so many ways. In this sense, Christendom, as the exportation of Western Christianity around the world, is over. See Hanciles, *Beyond Christendom*.

18. See Hanciles, *Beyond Christendom*, 96.

destiny," and "divine providence," all of which rationalized the conviction that the superior values, ideals, and material benefits of Western civilization should be spread around the world. The global expansion of European culture as a normative expression of the Christian faith represents "the most comprehensive attempt in the history of the world to impose the civilization of one race or people on all others."[19] This imagination continues to affect our understanding and practices of leadership. Willie Jennings describes how, for example, our notions of space, place, and even "whiteness"[20] were reframed as projects of our power and control, manipulable for fulfilling the abstracted goals and purposes of the Western imagination. For Jennings, this led to a deformed theological imagination and practice in the West—a distorted understanding of God, one another, and place. It is out of these conceptualities that our practice of leadership has been shaped.

A theology of leadership must come to terms with this now taken-for-granted, pervasive, and embedded self-understanding of the Euro-tribal churches. The disorientation of these churches is about the unraveling of this once dominant story of being at the center of God's movement where the Christian project was driven by methods of management and control that never needed God's agency because the source of the project lay within the autonomous skills of human method and making. These skills were all we needed to guarantee success.

Willie Jennings on a Diseased Theological Imagination

The Euro-tribal churches are no longer dominant, even in their original countries. The narratives of these churches were birthed in the limited contexts of the European reformations.[21] We now recognize that these movements were as tribal and limiting as those of any other group in the world. Tribalism was never unique to non-Western, non-modern parts of the world. The West was as tribal as any other people. The European reformations,

19. Joel B. Carpenter, in Hanciles, *Beyond Christendom*, 3.

20. See Jennings, "Can 'White' People be Saved?" See also Sechrest et. al, eds., *Can "White" People Be Saved?*.

21. Our tendency is to create a shorthand language for what was a very complex set of developments. Hence, people speak about the Reformation as if there was this single movement when in fact there were numerous "reformations" in various parts of Europe. In this way, the Reformation becomes a reification as if it is some objective event. We should, for example, speak of the "Reformed" movements of northern Europe or the "Lutheran" movements of across the German states or the English or the Anabaptist movements and so forth. There was no single Reformation but a series of reformations that interacted with each other in a wide variety of ways.

once seen as representing the apex of all theological and churchly thinking, can no longer be viewed as the center point around which all else is referenced. While this makes sense from the perspective of the early twenty-first century, it's a radically painful challenge to these churches that have lived long in the assumption that these reformations and their churches were the center point of Christian life in the world. The term *Euro-tribal* is intended to relativize what came to be viewed as the central story of Christian life in the modern world. It doesn't mean these reformations are unimportant or that they should be ignored. It means they can no longer be reified and assumed as the starting point, or definitional moment, for understanding the challenges before these churches today. This unraveling is a new situation for most church leaders. As such it is incredibly destabilizing for the embodied self-understanding in which they were formed and to which they want to return. A major question, therefore, confronting leaders of the Euro-tribal churches, is one of how they can gain practices and capacities to perceive and respond to this *de-centering* in order to participate in God's ongoing missional activities in the West.

It is always helpful to have someone who stands just outside the dominant story as a guide to seeing with fresh eyes what has been happening. Like fish in the proverbial water it's almost impossible to see the water in which one swims. African-American theologian Willie James Jennings is such a guide. His book *The Christian Imagination* traces how the West, from the fifteenth century forward, established a theological imagination that still determines our leadership practices. He describes this imagination in language that is difficult to receive: the Euro-tribal churches have a diseased theological imagination. What does he mean?

The answer to that question is present in the book's very beginning, where Jennings describes an encounter he experienced as a boy in Grand Rapids, Michigan—the iconic center of Dutch immigrant, religious culture in North America. As an African-American, he grew up in a Christian tradition different from the city's Reformed majority. He recalls the all-encompassing faith of his parents, Mary and Ivory. As Jennings tells it, Jesus was a member of their family, involved in their everyday conversations. Faith and life were one. On a hot summer afternoon the young Willie was in the back garden with his mother, from whom he had taken into his imagination that "dirt" was the earth and to be attached to the earth was to be attached to place, time, one's history, people, story and hopes. They heard footsteps coming down the side of the house and across the grass toward them. As the two white men approached, Willie's mother stepped between them and her young son. The men were from First Christian Reformed Church, just a few hundred yards down the street. They'd come to talk about their church, especially its activities for kids. They wanted to connect with the neighbor-hood. Best of intentions! Jennings remembers the older man talking for a long time in a formal manner as if giving a rehearsed speech. The younger man looked increasingly impatient until, finally, he bent down to speak to Willie. It struck young Jennings as odd that someone would do this to a twelve-year-old, talking to him like he was a kindergarten child with little intelligence, asking his name, where he went school and if he liked school. This, too, seemed rehearsed.

> The strangeness of this event lay not only in their appearance in our backyard but also in the obliviousness of these men as to whom they were addressing—Mary Jennings, one of the pillars of New Hope Missionary Baptist Church. I thought it incredibly odd that they never once asked if she went to church, if she was a Christian, or even if she believed in God. . . . My mother finally interrupted the speech . . . with the words, "I am already a Chris-tian. I believe in Jesus and I attend . . ." I don't remember his exact reply . . . but he kept talking for quite a few more wasted minutes. . . . I remember this event because it underscored an inexplicable strangeness embedded in the Christianity I lived and observed. Experiences like these fueled a question that has grown in hermeneutical force for me: Why did they not know us? They should have known us very well. . . Why did these men not know me, not know Mary . . ., and not know the multitude of other black Christians who filled the neighborhood that sur-rounded the church?[22]

What Jennings experienced in his backyard was a microcosm of a form of Christianity familiar to a majority of people "enclosed in racial and cultural difference, inconsequentially related to its geography . . . detached from its surroundings of both people and spaces . . . [W]e were operating out of a history of relations that exposed a distorted relational imagination."[23] In *Christian Imagination*, Jennings interprets this distorted relational imagina-tion of the Euro-tribal churches in the form of their narratives of ascendan-cy and control. It goes to the heart of an imagination wherein the leaders of these churches assumed confidence in their capacities, methods, programs and technologies of leadership to control outcomes. Jennings argues that the Euro-tribal churches move within a diseased social imagination about themselves and their place within North American culture, and among the nations of the global missionary movement. Their leadership frames have

22. Jennings, *Christian Imagination*, 3.
23. Jennings, *Christian Imagination*, 4.

been formed within an imagination shaped by methods of power and control that perceive both other people and locations as objects of their ends and outcomes.

In *Christian Imagination*, Jennings explores European colonization and missionary expansion from the fifteenth century forward. A metaphor Jennings uses to frame these colonizations is *displacement*. When Europeans entered other lands and engaged their people, this distorted imagination involved the failure to see the other except in terms of their own European cultural formations. Europeans "establish a new organizing reality for the world—themselves."[24] Displacement worked itself out in several interconnected ways. It meant seeing oneself, as European, as the norm and measure of every other person or group. The dazzling transformations of the West became self-authenticating proof that God had given the world a new center. While Israel had been the central character in God's unfolding story, it was but the prelude to the new people of God. The West had ascended to the role of Israel. From within this imagination, the West saw the rest as the object of its vocation to civilize and Christianize.[25] This was something new—a cultural, global self-understanding wherein the West believed it was the apex and bearer of God's intentions for the world. The future and the kingdom (be it religious or secular) now had its still point in a turning world—the West. From this center the principles for framing society and for understanding nature, economics, politics, and intellectual grounding were set. All else was displaced in the light of this reality. The Euro-tribal churches and their leaders were formed inside this distorted social imagination. They were in control with the skills, tools, and resources to design and operationalize their desired outcomes. All other groups and peoples were, at best, secondary to this metric.

Now the process of becoming a Christian took on new markers (metrics) that were defined by Europeans (whites) within the assumption of the West's ascendency and control. The marker of Christian identity became race (Western superiority).

> Here was a process of discerning Christian identity that, because it had jettisoned Israel from the calculus of the formation of Christian life, created a conceptual vacuum that was filled by the European. But not simply qua European; rather the very process of becoming Christian took on new ontic markers.

24. Jennings, *Christian Imagination*, 58.

25. Jennings describes this critical move as *supersessionist* wherein the church replaces Israel in the mind and heart of God. He describes this imagination as a decisive distortion that has had awesome effects on Christian thinking. Jennings, *Christian Imagination*, 32–33.

> Those markers of being were aesthetic and racial. This was not
> a straightforward matter of replacement (European for Jew) but
> . . . of displacement and now theological reconfiguration. . . . If
> Israel had been the visibly elect of God, then that visibility in the
> European imagination had migrated without return to a new
> home shaped now by new visual markers. If Israel's election had
> been the compass around which Christian identity gained its
> bearings and found its trajectory, now with this reconfiguration
> the body of the European would be the compass marking divine
> election. More importantly, that newly elected body, the white
> body, would be a discerning body, able to detect holy effects and
> saving grace.[26]

The Euro-tribal churches' practice of leadership has been formed
within this imagination. It is, overall, a practice of leadership that operates
from a place of power, control, and management. Inside this imagination
was a new marker for being fully human—whiteness. Whiteness became a
primary form of Western, Euro-tribal self-identity. It involved the perceptions of being in control, of holding the mantle for determining God's future.
For Jennings, it is not that a person or social group is born "white" in this
sense but that the enlightenment culture and the colonizations of the West
are formative of this identity of "whiteness." Within this new kind of racial,
tribal identity there emerged a new kind of gradation about what it meant to
be both human and inside the arena of privilege and control. This gradation
moves from white to black. People groups are placed along this spectrum
to determine the process of becoming and being Christian, or, fully human. In the context of this displacement Jennings argues: "Christianity in
the Western world lives and moves with a diseased social imagination,"[27]
a "theological mistake so wide, so comprehensive that it has disappeared,
having expanded to cover the horizon of modernity itself. "[28]

The discourse of displacement had its sources in transformations
that took place from the thirteenth century forward. A movement known
as Nominalism[29] changed the West's understanding of God's relationship
to the world. A new understanding of God as will, power, and sovereignty
would reshape Western self-understanding and determine how it engaged

---

26. Jennings, *Christian Imagination*, 33–34.

27. Jennings, *Christian Imagination*, 6.

28. Jennings, *Christian Imagination*, 38.

29. Nominalism in this sense came to expression in the writings of Duns Scotus
(1265–1308) and William of Ockham (1287–1349). For a fuller description of Nominalism in relation to the development of the modern West, see Roxburgh and Robinson, *Practices for the Refounding*, 16–21.

with the peoples and places it encountered in its colonizations. In the West this transition into modernity meant turning lands, places, soils, and persons into commodities—ends to be used. This flawed social imagination became the soil within which modern methods of leadership emerged. The transformations in the West from the seventeenth century onward became proof of the superiority of the Western tradition. This was something new! This imagination believed that in its identity the universal principles for truth, method, politics, economics, science, and the making of society had been discovered—the master keys to understanding the world and the making of society. There were counter voices to this story but it is hard to argue that it did not become the dominant, driving narrative of the Western imagination. Nobody could have foreseen the unintended consequences of this incredible outburst of Western creativity and its all-encompassing assumptions. Some of these consequences had to do with the framing of theologies of leadership and perceptions about the nature of the church.

The Problematic Particularity of the Christian Narrative

Modern, pluralist societies shaped by liberal democratic practices operate in a tension between the universal and the particular. This is related to how God's agency disappears from our acting. Liberal democracies are concerned with how people with differing belief systems (politics, economics, social practices, religious beliefs) live together when no particular belief system is privileged. One approach to this tension is to generalize specific belief systems into a common, or universal, set of elements abstracted from the particularities of each. This presumes that those making such determinations have some privileged position from which they can discern these universal principles. The abstractions are then synthesized into the operating truths of a society (for example, have respect for one another, do no harm, love everyone, etc.). These collected truisms then become common, generalized values everyone is (non-coercively) to live by.

This solution creates a tension that is usually resolved by the elimination of God as agent. A group's particularities are often distinguished by how they understand *causality*. So, when a society prioritizes some common universals so that participants can live together, causality is ignored or given meaning inside some vague, generalized notions such as "will of the people." The focus is put on the practical ways differing groups can co-inhabit a space. But to do this these groups must tacitly put away their specific claims about the sources (causes) of their particular virtues. What must not be lost in this is that the particularity that makes a group who they are gets dismissed or deemed irrelevant to the common good. As this happens over time, their very identity, what makes them who they are as a people, disappears into the general amalgam of universal principles. Charles Taylor describes it as "a new, civilized, 'polite' order" that is seen more and more in "immanent" terms. So this "polite, civilized order *is* the Christian order. . . . This version of Christianity was shorn of much of its 'transcendent' content, and was thus open to a new departure, in which the understanding of good order—what we could call the modern moral order—could be embraced outside of the original theological . . . framework."[30] In a pluralist democracy this valuing of a universal, common ground (in, for example, ethics, education, policing, health, and so forth) is generalized to most other parts of life (in, for example, models of change or leadership frameworks). This is another way in which it becomes strange to ask, as Christians, questions about God as agent. We are schooled by a society that plays down particularity in favor of the universal. We are then practiced into applying generalized principles and models, not the particularity that is at the core of our identity (in this case that, as Christians, God is acting).

Once a society has lived for numbers of generations in this way the universal becomes its collective *habitus*.[31] Universal ideals, models, or values get generalized across all forms of life and practices and, as such, particular social groups lose touch with their distinctiveness. This is how any people, group, or tribe loses their identity in modern societies. A tragic illustration of this is to be observed in what continues to happen to First Nations people. There comes a pervasive forgetfulness of the particular, unique stories, habits, and practices that made a group who and what it was. When this happens it's very difficult for a people to embody their story or live out their tradition. They disappear unless they are able to rediscover the practices, the *habitus,* that comprised their core identity. Such practices, in the case of First Nations peoples, are often seen by the settler culture as antithetical to progress or living in a "modern" world.[32]

In a similar way, when groups of God's people seek to address the society around them, by default, they tend to look to universals rather than draw on the particularities of their own tradition. These universals take on the status of unassailable fact, objectivity, and truth. In this situation the abstract universal becomes the arbiter of what is true. As such, leaders become professionalized experts in the technocratic ways of modernity.

30. Taylor, "Foreword," xi.

31. Christian Scharen's *Fieldwork in Theology* is an excellent primer on the meaning and operation of *habitus.*

32. See Simpson, *As We Have Always Done.*

These universal, professional systems have become our default (*habitus*). We turn first to the universal (love, justice, peace, reconciliation, adaptive, innovative, and so on) and the expert (management, therapy, organizational change) for our frames, models, and instructions. In so doing we grow forgetful of our own story, of the peculiarity of the charism and grace out of which we were formed and called to be *God's* people. We cease asking what the particularity of the God revealed in Jesus Christ has to say about our communities or leadership frames. Rather than a theology of leadership, leaders operate out of borrowed, universal, professionalized models over which, from time to time, we do some theologizing.

AN ARCHITECTURE OF LEADERSHIP

The houses we live in, offices where we work, and church buildings in which we worship are constructed around particular architectural imaginations. These architectures presume ways of seeing the world. They assume habits and practices that are important to people in particular times and places. The people who live in these houses, work in these offices, or worship in these buildings are, normally, unaware of the narrative forms shaping the structures within which they live, work, and pray. But these forms are continually shaping their actions and habits and how they inhabit their places and communities where they dwell. In a similar way, the imagination of Modernity's Wager is, itself, an architecture that is shaping the leadership practices of the Euro-tribal churches. Any theology of leadership must understand and address this reality. In our homes, offices, and churches we usually don't, first, sit down and ask why the house, office, or church building has been designed in a certain way: Why pews? Why an offering? Why sing a certain kind of hymn? Why these kinds of worship songs? Why "worship leaders" up front? What makes preaching necessary? What does it do to us when preaching is placed at the center of what we do? Why do churches need mission statements? Who determined the metrics for measuring outcomes? What do we communicate about our understanding of persons when we make statements such as "We worshiped 1500 this Sunday" or that "We are an organic church"? Nor do we usually sit down and reflect on why we practice leadership in certain ways. There are, however, architectures at work shaping how leaders see and act in their world.

This chapter has suggested what some of those underlying architectures of leadership are in terms of Modernity's Wager—issues of power, control, management, and the sense of being able to paint a new future on a blank canvas of our own making and imagination. This leadership architecture of management and control was built upon the rational tools of analysis, assessment, planning, and measured outcomes, and remains a primary characteristic of leadership with the Euro-tribal churches. No matter what specific theological perspective—whether mainline, Pentecostal, evangelical, or local—this leadership imaginary is dominant. It is built around assumptions about the self-making individual of Modernity's Wager where there is little need for God as agent except as a support to predetermined actions. God is continually rendered as a secondary, useful resource to the planning and control of autonomous selves. Much has been lost in this wager, especially the sense of God's agency in the world and, therefore, our identity as human beings. This is the world into which a transformed imagination of Christian leadership must journey. Chapter 3 introduces the location of such a journey in theological terms of God's agency and what we are calling the space-between.

CHAPTER 3

Theological Themes

INTRODUCTION

THIS CHAPTER LOOKS AT key theological themes in the light of our argument regarding the diminishment of God as agent and our use of the metaphor *space-between* as a primary framing for Christian leadership in Modernity's Wager. This chapter offers a theological reading of the metaphor space-between as a descriptor of leadership.

GOD'S AGENCY, TRINITY, AND INCARNATION

Our comprehension of God as Trinity affects our understanding and practice of leadership. The incarnation compels us to confess that the One who encounters us in Jesus is Trinity—God the Father, Son, and Holy Spirit.[1] Jesus' declaration that "I and the Father are one" moves in the direction of God as dynamic relationality. It is not a statement about some singular, mathematical oneness in God, or that reality is, fundamentally, some great singularity, some "One" from which all else emanates from a center. Such a position can only produce a hierarchical view of the world and, thus, our notions of leadership. The weaving dance of the perichoretic Trinity is the foundation for understanding the nature of leadership in God's economy. Leaders are not at the top of some hierarchy from which they commend

---

1. See Newbigin, *Proper Confidence*; Gunton, *Promise of Trinitarian Theology*; Gunton, *The One, the Three*; Jenson, *The Triune Identity*; Weston, ed., *Lesslie Newbigin: Missionary Theologian*.

the right directions to people. Rather, they are shapers of relationality and creativity among the people of God.

Furthermore, this relationality recognizes that difference is constitutive of all creation as an expression of God's own nature. Difference isn't a problem to be solved but the source of the creativity of creation. This dance of relationality, and creativity, occurs in the space-between where we cannot press the other into some plan, strategy, or vision statement. Leadership, therefore, is not about creating alignment around a preferred future or a set of determined outcomes. That kind of leadership occludes a Trinitarian way of life as it shuts down difference and the creativity that comes from being in relationship with the other. The revelation of what God is doing in the world is given to us in these kinds of relational encounters with the other.

Trinity: Relationality, Intimacy, and Risk

This understanding of the Trinity locates the vocation of leadership in what we are calling the space-between. This is not our usual way of understanding either the Trinity or leadership. Most conversations about the Trinity focus on the inter-relationship between God as Father, Son, and Spirit, placing the focus on the social inter-relationality within the Trinity. But there are other implications of this inter-relationality that are seldom discussed when framing approaches to leadership. The emphasis on relationality has tended toward notions of intimacy with God and one another. Notions of closeness and intimacy with God predominate popular interpretations of texts (such as John 10—"I and the father are one . . ."). Intimacy and togetherness are presented as the core meaning of God's relationality. But these passages might also be read primarily through the lens of the incarnation rather than romanticizing categories of self and intimacy. In the context of the incarnation this Trinitarian statement is about the self-giving risk of God as Father, Son, and Spirit in self-emptying for the world. God as Trinity inhabits the risky space-between rather than some notion of closeness.[2]

The term *perichoresis* describes the dynamic inter-relationship between Father, Son, and Spirit in terms of the entwined dance of lovers. The Trinity is a dance of love among Father, Son, and Spirit. Inter-relationship also implies difference from another. The word for this is *alterity*—the state

2. There are important matters of closeness, belonging, and attachment that are needed in modernity (especially for male leaders) that are different than romantic notions that are about (a) confused boundaries, (b) being enmeshed, (c) using power to overrule the other as subject. Closeness for Trinity is about such characteristics as knowledge, collaboration, giving. It involves a kind of vulnerability for which modern manipulation/power is a shadow.

of being different. There is, for example, alterity between God the Creator and creation. But something else is meant here. Alterity is part of the nature of the Trinitarian God. Within the perichoretic Trinity, the Father is not the Son, the Son is not the Spirit, and the Spirit is neither the Father nor the Son. This understanding of alterity within the Trinity is critical for our understanding of leadership given the overstated emphasis on Trinity as intimacy. The dance of difference in the Trinity is the dynamic creativity through which the love of God is expressed. In the Trinity the Three-in-One embrace each other as Other. It is in this difference, this space-between, that God's creative relationality is expressed. Space-between, where we encounter the other and where there cannot be control or manipulations toward someone's ends, is not an accident of creation or history; it is a part of the ontological reality of all things as expressions of their Creator. It may be only when we encounter the other in this space-between that we have a genuinely human, creative encounter that reflects the *imago dei*. It is essential to what it means to be made in the image of the triune God.

This understanding of Trinity means that leadership in the community of God's people is about standing in the space-between—in those spaces where one refuses to control and manage outcomes, where the other is called into the dance of God's creative future. Leadership that turns others into the objects of a goal, program, or strategy fails to discern the nature of God revealed to us in the incarnation and, therefore, the shape of creativity. The role of leadership is to draw people into this space-between where the dance of difference calls forth the ways the Spirit is forming a community of God's future in the places where they live.

God's Agency and the Incarnation

"And the Word became flesh and dwelt amongst us" (John 1:14 NASB).

"What was from the beginning, what we have heard, what we have seen with our eyes, what we have looked at and touched with our hands, concerning the Word of Life—and the life was manifested, and we have seen and testify and proclaim to you the eternal life, which was with the Father and was manifest to us—what we have seen and heard we proclaim to you . . ." (1 John 1:1–3 NASB)

In the incarnation, Jesus is the presence of the incomprehensible One who takes on human form. God comes all the way to us to be God with us in this activity of being both God and human. Brueggemann aptly states,

"There is nothing ordinary about the key claims of biblical faith."[3] The incarnation is outside all our ordinary categories but especially those of Modernity's Wager. If a dominant characteristic of our time is that of autonomous kinetic (movement) power, in the incarnation the primary characteristic of God is as kenosis (emptying)—the humility and self-emptying of God in Christ in and for the sake of the world.[4] For Christians the incarnation is the confession that God became human and dwelt among us in Jesus. In their book *Transformation Theology,* Oliver Davies, Paul Janz, and Clemens Sedmak state:

> At the heart of the Christian gospel and church confession is the claim that God took on flesh for us in Jesus Christ and entered into our world of space and time. It is therefore the claim that God became real to us in the only way in which he can be truly real for us: as a fellow human being, who experiences as we do and shares our mortal fate.[5]

In the incarnation we see God as the one who dwells in the space-between.

This is the revelation of who God is to and with us. In the incarnation we recognize that to be human is to be that creature in all creation who lives in the space-between. A theologically framed praxis of leadership begins here. The incarnation tells us that in Jesus, God chooses not to be in a space of management or control.

Our understanding of the incarnation must be placed within the revolutionary changes in our concepts of the world (the change in language, for example, from *creation* to *nature*) and the sources of human knowledge that emerge from the twelfth century into the modern era. Over this period a new conception of rationality, with its attendant method, emerged, shaped by a new understanding of human agency that placed human agency at the center of Western imagination and displaced notions of God's agency into forms of deism. This new rationality was built on the conviction that autonomous human beings, with the power (kinesis) of method, could manage and control not just "nature" but themselves in ways that would provide their desired outcomes. Herein lies a huge tension for any contemporary theology of leadership. The operative imagination of leadership has taken

---

3. Brueggemann and Floyd, *Gospel of Hope*, 13.

4. This is not to set up kinetic and kenotic as two absolute opposites. It is about the ways in which they are understood and applied in our era. The form of kinesis revealed to us in Jesus Christ is that of kenosis. This is the direction of Christian life, of leadership within the community of God's new creation and, therefore, unalterably, it is about standing in the space-between.

5. Davies et al., *Transformation Theology*, 1.

into itself this basic method of management and control (human agency) so that God's agency becomes little more than a set of moral values that guide these rational methods of control. The kinesis of the autonomous self has displaced the incarnation's kenosis. The tension lies in how contemporary forms of leadership interface with this kenotic nature of God as agent. How does the self-emptying God square with the autonomous individual armed with rational methods of control and management?

The incarnation is dispossession. Philippians 2:1–11 is a focal text for this discussion of the space-between and the kenotic God. It locates the identity of Jesus Christ as he who was in the form of God. Jesus is identified with the creator God who reigns over heaven and earth. The spatial metaphor refers to the heavenly realms in which God dwells beyond access to human beings. Where God dwells is a space that is not human space. It proposes an infinite qualitative distance between God and the created world—God is above, not below. God does not come down or God would cease to be God. The incarnation overturns this distinction. It sets Jesus in the space of one who empties himself of the prerogatives of power and lordly control by taking on the form of a servant, "being found in human form, he humbled himself by becoming obedient to the point of death, even death on a cross."[6]

In what sense, therefore, is dispossession a core element for a theology of leadership?[7] The incarnation manifests the vulnerability of a self-emptying God who in Jesus enters into a space God is not controlling but, rather, has all the potential of being controlled by others.[8] The language of servant is not a posture taken up by one who, in fact, remains dominant. It is, literally, being in the space of non-coercive power. In Graeco-Roman

6. Phil 2:6–8 (English Standard Version).

7. Too often this passage is placed in the service of such models as "servant leadership." But this is to miss the point of what is happening here. In contemporary form, servant leadership is reduced to notions of the values and attitudes one brings to the use of rational models of management and control. In this way, the ways in which God may be present as agent are continually reduced to aspirational values in the existent contexts of leadership by autonomous selves. The incarnation then becomes a reductionstic method inside existing models of leadership.

8. The birth stories are clear about this vulnerability of God in the incarnation. For an expanded exposition of this theme of a vulnerable God see Placher, *Narratives of a Vulnerable God*. Placher points out that the Christian gospel does not start from the place of God as king, all-powerful, omnipotent or the great patriarch. To read the biblical narratives he argues is to first meet a God in Jesus who is vulnerable. His book addresses the question: What sort of God do we believe in if one took the biblical narratives as the place for asking this question? Placher's response is: "God is the one who loves in freedom, and that free love is vulnerable . . ." (xv). See also Williams, *Ray of Darkness*, 231.

cultures to be a servant was, literally, to be without power and to be owned by someone else for their own purposes. It is in this sense that the incarnation is about God choosing to step into the space-between—a space wherein one does not have control and cannot manage the outcomes. Space-between is, therefore, the ontologically real space where God has chosen to be made known in the redemption of creation. It is the central form of leadership in the new creation.

The Palestine into which Jesus came was populated with apocalyptic imagination. Some leaders talked about upheavals and the need for change, others spoke of a universe of angelic and demonic beings competing for power. All were rivalling one another with claims to having the insight into how all the swirling, disruptive chaos would turn out. The New Testament tells of competing groups (Pharisees, Sadducees, priestly classes in the main population centers, along with Zealots, Essenes, and a host of others like John the Baptist) whose claims ranged from having the ability to manage Rome's hegemony, to methods of keeping the Law that would bring forward the great Day of the Lord, to means of revolution that would end Rome's tyranny. All these groups claimed they had the means for controlling a chaotic world.

In the midst of this cacophony of claims and counterclaims were the crowds, that swirl of people whose primary experiences were disorientation, dispossession, and disempowerment in a dangerous political and social climate. Jesus looked at the crowds with compassion. He described them as sheep without a shepherd because he saw what the claims and counterclaims were doing to them. These are the "crowds" of Matthew. They were just trying to get by as other powers taxed them while demanding acquiesce to either Temple, or Law, or Herod, or apocalyptic revolution, or Caesar's peace. Underlying these conflicting, counterclaiming movements lay a presumption: they knew what God (or the gods) demanded and how God (or the gods) was to be served. Each peddled its own method of solution; each had its answer in terms of method and power.

In the incarnation, God is present in a way utterly different from these groups. In Jesus, God is, literally, on the ground, in ambiguous spaces where he refused to take on any of their power claims. In Jesus, God is literally embodied presence among us as a radical counter-narrative to the regnant claims to agency being made by these movements and their leaders. Jesus' pitching a tent among the "crowds" makes clear where and how God is present in the world. The incarnation proposes that leadership is not located in the spaces of technocratic elites nor professionals managing preferred futures. God's being in the world means leadership is dispossession, not control of how things turn out.

Across Facebook pages, blogs, and the latest books there are endless attempts by leaders to propose initiatives, visions, and fixes for churches—rationales for why their forms of community or discipleship-making are the correct ones. There are hosts of proposals for how to plant churches, be more neighborly, or have congregations be more innovative.[9] The Euro-tribal churches have a cacophony of claims and counterclaims shouting in a market square where their goods are bought. Recently, several members of Alan's family were in Florence, Italy participating in an international dragon boat regatta on the Arno. Visiting the famous markets of Florence, they encountered endless stands selling everything from tee-shirts to "genuine" Italian leather products to the best olive oil in the world. Each was marketing their wares as the most unique, best, and above all, the most value to the customer. The market represents something of the world Jesus entered. It parallels the world of the Euro-tribal churches still creating a venue in which their goods are presented as the answer.

Perhaps the incarnation became a central confession of the early church because the God they encountered wasn't presenting a posture of being in control. The God present in Jesus wasn't an elite or a guru spreading a brand in endless tweets. God is utterly different. God in Jesus chose to dwell in the space-between where power, management, and control cannot operate; among the crowds, outside the assumed places of power from which one manages the world. Jesus proposed that this space-between dwelling was where God would be found. The crowds had never heard anything like that before from leaders. If the incarnation tells us that God is known and experienced in this space-between, then it is also a primary location of leaders. In this location the New Testament shows Jesus engaging the "powers" in terms of principalities and powers seeking to control, manipulate, and bind people's lives.

In the incarnation the meaning of being human is infused with a mystery that can't be grasped or reduced to abstractions or formulae. God's embodiment means we only know who we are, where we are, and how we are to live in the riskiness of vulnerable relationality, in reciprocity with the other where there can be no controlling outcomes. This knowing, in the language of St. Paul, is about seeing through a glass darkly. It is a way of knowing that invites humility about all our predicting, managing, proposing of visions, and fermenting of innovations. Leadership in this way of knowing is not about predicting or formulating plans, futures, and strategies but the cultivation of a common life that discerns God's actions in the local. There can

9. See Sax, "End the Innovation Obsession."

be no instrumental rationality that treats the other as a reducible means to some ends. The objectification of the other that informs most vision shaping and strategic planning cannot be a part of an incarnational leadership. Such leadership dwells in the risky, ambiguous spaces where God's creative future breaks forth around, for example, a ruler's table where protocols are disrupted by an outsider, in a street life that challenges the hegemony of the state, in the workplace (fishing) that becomes the locale of transformative learning.

GOD'S AGENCY AND A CHRISTIAN ANTHROPOLOGY

Anthropology: Theocentric and Modern

Anthropology is that body of work that seeks to provide an interpretive meaning for being a human being in the world. What is involved in an anthropology that points beyond a modern framing where a self-making, autonomous individual is the prime agent and shaper of a world? What is a Christian anthropology and what are its implications for leadership? This section first summarizes an anthropological perspective rooted in an understanding that Jesus Christ is the primary revelation of what it means to be human. Second, it sketches the anthropological understanding that emerges in the modern West and is now sedimented into our operating frameworks. Models of leadership in the Euro-tribal churches are largely shaped by this second anthropological frame. What is attempted here is a way of coming to terms with what the Dutch philosopher Peter Sloterdijk[10] describes as the *modus vivendi* of modernity, the taken-for-granted assumptions that shape the everyday habits and values of people's lives, the ways they read and act in the world. A *modus vivendi* is like the metabolism of a culture; it's the way a particular culture operates that, generally, people don't question but assume as basic for doing things together.

An Anthropology Rooted in the Revelation of God in Christ

Questions of what it means to be human, of our place in the cosmos, are given as a revelation from God. In the incarnation we see God's desire for humankind and the creation. Jesus is this fundamental *modus vivendi* for all human life—for a true anthropology. The sin of humanity is the distortion of our desires wherein we turn one another into objects, projects of

---

10. Sloterdijk, *What Happened in the 20th Century*, 14–17.

distorted desires that make life about me and my ends. This desire to have control rather than live in God and for the other reveals the distortion. Jesus reveals another way of being human. In Matthew he speaks of those things hidden "from the foundation of the world" (Matt 13:35 NRSV, see also Eph 1:4–10 NRSV), making explicit that the question of the purpose and meaning of being human is, while once hidden, now revealed in Christ.[11] In Ephesian's doxological introduction (doxology points to the nature of a theological anthropology) it is declared that in the coming of Jesus what's revealed is the mystery hidden to us since the beginning of time, namely, that all things in the cosmos receive their meaning from Jesus Christ and that in him God is acting to bring a broken, fragmented creation into unity. The *modus vivendi* of God's order means being persons in worshiping communities shaped by this teleology.

The Modern Anthropological *modus vivendi*

Graham Ward frames the modern question of being human in this way:

> The foundation had changed: society was now the fundament to be examined by new philosophical methods—empiricism, positivism, naturalism, humanism. In the light of this new foundation and its approaches to understanding, the presence of religion was to be explained (away) by the newly minted social sciences.[12]

An anthropology shaped by the modern West has a fundamentally different *modus vivendi* with profound implications for a Christian understanding of leadership. If being human implies a doxological vocation, then being God's people is being sign, witness, and foretaste of what was hidden but is now revealed. The metabolism of life in the modern West beats in a totally different way. What confronts a theology of leadership is how our desires are so shaped by a modern anthropology that we're hardly aware of its presence or radical novelty.

11. Further, what it tells us is that to know the other is about revelation not power or manipulation or even a long list of clinical studies. Therefore, leadership is about how we form a people who are coming to know, through the revelation of a non-coercive relationship with the other. This is to be the character of the church. Perhaps the best work done on the meaning of knowledge as revelation rooted in relationship is that of Michael Polanyi's *Personal Knowledge,* which Lesslie Newbigin leaned on a great deal in developing his missiology to the West.

12. Ward, *Politics of Discipleship,* 121.

The French anthropologist Louis Dumont framed this challenge when he stated: "In the last decades, some of us have become aware that modern individualism, when seen against the background of the other great civilizations that the world has known, is an exceptional phenomenon."[13] The modus vivendi is the modern conception of the individual: an "exceptional" anthropology that now shapes our thinking, acting, theologizing, and pastoral values. It is now the functional basis upon which practically all frames and theories of leadership operate. It is such a deeply embedded "metabolism of life" that, like a fish in water, we do not experience it as a contradiction to a Christian anthropology. Euro-tribal leaders show little critical engagement with this reality. The modern West produced the now normative modern individual as an autonomous agent. To be human is not about being given vocation but the self-affirming project of making the world its own creation. In modernity, the world is not a creation gifted by the agency of God but a raw canvas, a resource upon which the free human agent makes and creates meaning out of him/herself. A doxological vocation involving humility before creation and Creator is rejected like the spitting out of a bridle. Any kind of heteronomy is an offense. As Ward states, "paralleling this exaltation of the individual was the loss of an ontologically founded community—that is, a community rooted in a sense of belonging to one another, to a social order, a cosmic order ordained by God."[14]

The Project of Order, Mastery, and Its Rationality

This modern anthropology produced a rationality that has affected everything about our understanding and practice of leadership. The modern project is "first of all the project of the mastery of nature. It reverses the taking into account by anthropology of the cosmological context. Instead of the cosmos that gives man his measure, it is man who must create a dwelling to his measure."[15] Rather than viewing our lives as embracing the vocation of being God's image in creation we see life as our project. Everything outside the self is a project to make into an object for some human end. This life-as-project has no source other than the autonomous self. It is a fundamental reversal of Christian imagination. Before the modern, order was attributed to the work of God: "In the beginning God created the heavens and the earth. . ." (Gen 1:1 NASB).[16] In modernity, order is imposed on the world

13. Dumont, *Essays on Individualism*, 23.

14. Ward, *Politics of Discipleship*, 226.

15. Brague, *Kingdom of Man*, 4.

16. As Walter Brueggemann points out, "The theologians who work in a distinctively

(chaos) through methods of rationality. Everything external to the self is an object to manage for a determined outcome. Method is the means of the project.

Contemporary models of leadership are not neutral on these questions of agency. The anthropology that undergirds Modernity's Wager attributes the sources of order within methods of rationality shaped by the autonomous agents. Our praxes of leadership are derivative of and dependent upon this anthropology. They're formed in the assumption of the human agent as the source of order through the imposition of method. Attention is shifted from discerning God's agency in the ordinary (the meaning of the Incarnation) to the methodologies of human agency. This is not to suggest that the use of methods such as strategic planning, adaptive change, or methods of innovation have no place. Rather, it is to argue that for the churches, questions about sources of agency have not been addressed in the adoption of such leadership models. Our primary models of leadership are shaped by assumptions about the sources of agency that have no reference to God's agency in the world. This is where the crisis lies: at the core of leadership praxis within the churches is an anthropology of human agency.

Modernity as a Wager

This modus vivendi is a seemingly ineradicable perception that being human is privileging the autonomous agent. This is what we call Modernity's Wager.[17] The wager is that, whether Christian or otherwise, life can be lived well without God, or, at best, God is a useful adjunct and support of the primacy of the autonomous human agent. Inside this modus vivendi the adoption of leadership theory and practice is based on what gives the leader the best possible methods of managing and controlling outcomes without needing to presume God's agency. When leadership frameworks and practices within the churches are taken up from experts and professionals in a variety of disciplines whose work builds on this anthropological foundation, there's little reflection around God's agency in leadership frames.

Books on leadership often start from either proposals about the character of leadership or certain models taken from the wider leadership

---

Israelite way in Genesis 1–11 want to affirm at the same time (a) that the ultimate meaning of creation is to be found in the heart and purpose of the creator (cf. 6:5–7; 8:21) and (b) that the world has been positively valued by God for itself." Brueggemann, *Genesis*, 12–13.

17. See Roxburgh and Robinson, *Practices for the Refounding of God's People*, for a development of the idea of Modernity's Wager and its implications for the practice of everyday life.

literature. Such models implicate certain kinds of leadership skills (church as movement needs, for example, an entrepreneurial leader; church as community requires a community developer kind of leader; church as innovation center requires a leader skilled in methods of innovation; church as agile band requires a good, non-directive leader of a "jazz" ensemble, and so forth). Often absent is a prior engagement with the question of what it means to be human (a theological anthropology) given the revelation of God in Jesus Christ. Little is written about practices of discerning where God is already present ahead of us in our communities. A theology of leadership must ask: How do leaders form communities whose *modus vivendi* is shaped by God's agency? How do I as a leader awaken to the anthropological assumptions underlying contemporary models of leadership?

The Modern Person—Autonomous, Cut Off

The modern age "portrays a figure of a human being who, on the one hand, is totally cut off—who was designed to be cut off—from all authorities outside of himself, or his self. Cut off from any divine, to be sure, but from a normative nature as well."[18] Leaders form disciple communities that engage the question: What is God is doing in this place at this particular time? But modernity's normative leadership models are designed to ensure that leaders and people are cut off from any authorities outside themselves. Therefore, too often, existent models of leadership undermine, in their very use, the possibility of asking prior questions of God's agency in any kind of normative way. In cutting the human agent off from external authority there can't be a rationality that directs us to God's agency. Within this anthropology our desires are formed by leadership models directed toward an autonomous agent within a telos of creating projects through the methods of management and control. In Brague's words: "the modern project is the technologically armed pursuit of the dominion of human beings over all things, including, paradoxically, their very humanity."[19]

Technique is the *modus vivendi* for the emancipated individual. The state of being cut off is hardly recognized within the ubiquitous power of a technical rationality that privileges human agency. Some of the questions this raises for a theology of leadership are: How do we become aware of those places where the primary energy of leadership is in applying techniques (example: how to "outwardly mobilize a congregation"; how to creatively "innovative responses to adaptive challenges") to predict, manage,

18. Brague, *Kingdom of Man*, viii.

19. Brague, *Kingdom of Man*, viii.

and order desired outcomes? How do we practice a different metabolism present in the scandalous (for Greeks and Jews) God?

An Anthropology of Hope in a Context of Fear and Disillusionment

A Christian anthropology is radically hopeful. It is an alternative story of being human, far more life-giving than the modern story wherein to gain happiness we develop ways of cooperating by forming social contracts. But underneath this contractuality we're still self-seeking creatures with the will to power. While this is not how things were intended, it feels like the inevitability of a modern anthropology. Mistrust and suspicion have become the ways we approach the other, whether in the neighborhood or at work. This pessimistic anthropology turns one another into objects for the purpose of other ends—wealth development, organizational goals, someone's vision for a growing church, and so forth. We internalize methods for managing people to get the ends we desire; we find ways of enticing and offering rewards (bonuses, higher salaries, newer positions, a greater ability to consume) to do our bidding because, at its base, this anthropology does not trust the other, doesn't believe that the other could want to seek the common good.

In Christ is a different, hopeful anthropology. To be human is not to be fundamentally turned in on oneself as a free, unassociated autonomous seeker of freedom and happiness. In the revelation of the mystery hidden from before the foundation of the world, to be human is to be formed and bound in a relationality that makes us the priests of creation to the glory of God. In Christ we have been given the power to be human—to act in ways that enable the other to flourish, to know that no one can be made into an object for one's own ends no matter how worthy the ends may be. In God's economy to be human is to dwell with others for the thriving of the common good and without need to objectify, manage, or control another. Leadership is cultivating communities that live as a denial of modernity's anthropology.

Leadership theory and models of leadership are not conceived as theological questions but that of specialization where notions of God's agency are reduced to supporting text. Models of leadership start from within a basis of human management and control, not with questions of what God is doing in the world.

The creation stories (see below) fill out the relationship of human beings to God, one another, and to the rest of the creation. Here is the fundamental relationality that is encountered in the doctrine of the Trinity. This relationality tells us that as Adam and Eve recognize one another as "bone of bone," they are human only as being-in-relationship. There is no such thing as an autonomous human being; the "I" only has being within a "we," and that "we" is formed in worship—which implies that to be human is to dwell humbly in a heteronomous, doxological relationship with God. We are, by nature, a unity in diversity. Sin is the refusal to receive and live within that unity; it is the breaking of the bonds of relationship with one another, with God, and with the world.[20] The *modus vivendi* of this anthropology is that of being given a vocation within an accountable relationality with all things that is doxologically shaped. This radically different anthropology from that of the modern gives us the clues to what it means for God's people to inhabit a space-between and what it means to lead in such a space. Leadership is both a continual wrestling with the forces that are forever turning us into projects (and, therefore, objects) and a continual inviting of God's people to discern the mysterious ways God is forming them as partners.

ESCHATOLOGY, GOD'S AGENCY, AND BEING THE CHURCH

The eschatological reminds us that the movement of creation to the intended ends of its Creator is not in our hands nor sourced from our projects. We don't make the kingdom come. Eschatology reminds us, in humility, that leaders are not strategists or makers of preferred futures. In a post-Christian West, eschatological thinking is not a category one readily hears when attending to questions of leadership in the church. Other frames dominate our attention. There is a language world of a leadership culture that believes it has been trained and called to build a future to change the world. This perspective replaces an eschatological reading that is about trust and discernment of God's agency. Christian leadership is confronted with two radically different interpretative frameworks, two different anthropologies—*project*

---

20. As Brague points out in *The Kingdom of Man*, in the ancient worlds there is no sense of human dominance over the natural world. It is the cosmos that provides the meaning of the natural world and what it means to be human (4). He states: "It does not seem that the ancient civilizations conceived of a control of nature by human activity. The accent rather was on the supple way that this activity ought to adapt itself to the exigencies of things, for example, by adapting to the rhythms of the seasons. The idea itself of a 'nature' confronting man was not clear. Rather, man was experienced as part of a whole that also embraced plants, animals and the stars" (17), and, "for all these thinkers, man is not the owner of creation. In antiquity some thinkers saw man as the steward of God on earth; the idea constantly reappeared . . . his dominion is itself subject to a condition—namely, obedience to the Creator. For a Christian like Augustine, man is not lord of creation except to the extent that he is son of God" (22).

or *eschatological hope.* In the former, as primary agents, our actions are designed (method) to achieve certain ends and effects in the name of a vision or some notion of progress. In the latter, we are shaping our actions around God's eschatological future that is neither project nor the effect of our control.

Not Private or Projects or Postponed

This is not a mute point for the vocation of leading among God's people. Modern notions of progress are not an equivalent to the eschatological purposes of God. The former does not produce the latter; it deflects Christian imagination from the actions of God toward a future shaped by human agency. Leadership in an eschatological framework begins from the acknowledgment that the telos of all creation is the reconstruction of all things (all the creation in its material and social relationalites) in and through the Lordship of Christ. In this sense, the eschatological is expectation and mystery: the one is the hope that God is continually at work in the world, the other is that we cannot dwell in that hope within assumptions of control. Making all things new comes from God; it can never be a project of human making of some better world. This does not imply there is nothing that we do. To the contrary, as priests of creation we are given an immense, creative vocation. The eschatological brings perspective—God is the agent and we are not. This eschatological realism moderates and relocates our perspectives about leadership in God's economy. It relativizes all the isms of modernity (progress in its many forms whether under capitalism, nationalism, socialism, fascism, liberalism, communism, and so on) along with its romantic, utopian projects which, in the twentieth century, resulted in the deaths of millions upon millions in the mechanization of killing and the devastation of the planet.

The eschatological is not about the transferring of hope out of this world into some unseen future. That only creates passivity toward the horrors of the present, allowing destructive forces to gain strength. On the contrary, the eschatological points toward the One who is in this present time (the incarnation and the pouring out of the Spirit on all flesh), in our concrete, everyday, ordinary lives. It directs us away from dreams of a perfectible, pure future and turns our attention to the everyday where the liturgies and practices of Christian life continually reorient us to this story of the One who is making all things new in the perichoretic dance in the local. Christians are, therefore, the most realistic people in the world. They see and celebrate the ways God's "being made new" are appearing among them in neighborhoods. Christians are freed from pretense, from euphemisms, that cover brokenness and death. Realized eschatology reduces Christian hope to a secularized one built on the projects and techniques of human agency.

In the eschatological frame, leadership is neither the creation of a vision nor the implementation of projects; it is the formation of a people in their local places who are discerning how God is making all things new in the name of Christ. This happens through a community's liturgical life as well as its practices of dwelling with the people of a neighborhood. Leadership recognizes that this liturgical, communal dwelling means learning to practice a radical "*No*" to Modernity's Wager. In such communities, leadership means forming a people in practices of discernment. Such leadership dwells comfortably in the ambiguity of trial and error, knowing that such discerning and acting can never be perfect, "right," or complete because we see through a glass darkly and the times of completion are in God's hands. Leadership is, therefore, both humble and patient;[21] it is about dwelling with and attending to the ferment of the Spirit, suggesting where the Spirit might be filling imaginations and encouraging risk.

This is the space-between where God calls leaders to dwell. A theology of leadership draws its practices and frameworks from this understanding of God's vocation in the world rather than the structures and assessments of the social sciences or the latest research from schools of business. While these sources have a role, they are secondary and derivative from God's agency in the local. The church's vocation isn't that of an instrument in projects of progress; it is the sign, witness, and foretaste of this other doxological vocation toward all creation. It is an eschatological community whose leaders' practices are shaped by the nature of its Lord. It is to be a people who always dwell in the space-between the now and the not yet. Augustine described this as the *saeculum,* the time between Christ's ascension and his return when all things will be made new. It is ordinary time within which the church lives and participates with the Spirit in working out God's purposes. This space-between is not amenable to vision statements defining preferable futures. God's future cannot be managed or strategized into existence.

The implications for a theology of leadership are enormous. So much leadership formation in the North American churches has been directed toward assisting people discover their "god within" or own "inner selves" rather than being opened up to an entirely other road far beyond an inner self. Part of the Euro-tribal church's crisis is that it has defined the gospel

---

21. This is the important point Kreider is making in the title of his book *The Patient Ferment of the Early Church.*

in terms of the self and self-discovery. The eschatological vocation of God's people moves in a different direction in the saeculum. It is a journey beyond ourselves where, on the road like Abram and Sara, we are travelling into— the space-between for the sake of the other. This calls leaders into a new location. It is not managing the inner life of churches; it is found out in the spaces between where God meets us as the other.

Creation and the Eschatological Shape of Leadership

Creation is the story of where all creation is moving—it is an eschatological imagination and, as such, is critical in informing our practice of leadership. The creation stories in Scripture reveal what it means to be human in relationship to the Creator of an unfolding creation.

In Genesis the Spirit calls order out of primeval chaos. God gives order, and, therefore, meaning to the creation. The question of the why and whereto of creation is given by God. Babylon's creation myths background Genesis's creation stories. Babylon confronted Israel with the question of what it meant to be human. Their victorious gods gave an unambiguous answer: beside a selected few with power, all other humans are slaves and others had power over you! Genesis was a radically different response. Creation is God building God's temple. It is the temple of God. The meaning of creation, therefore, is doxological. Being human means being the priests of God's creation. Clarifying, being priests of creation requires a few observations. Humans are created on the sixth and final day of God's creating as male and female. They are at the apex of the creational pyramid. But that place is not about control over, but the work of recapitulating in their bodies and representing in their relationality, creation before God in its doxological movement toward its telos.

Here is the core meaning of being human: that of a priest. Our first parents are dust of the earth and the breath of the Spirit. To be human, creation's priests, is to be, constitutively, the creatures who stand in the space-between in order to call the creation to its telos. We stand between all creation and our Creator. On the one side, to be human means we bear within us all the "earth" in order to recapitulate in our bodies and relationships the whole of creation before our Creator in an unfolding movement toward creation's telos. As that creature made of the mud of the earth, our vocation is to attend to and bring all of creation as a doxological offering to our Creator. We are not distinct, separate monads standing over and outside in splendid isolation as autonomous individuals free to turn creation into an object of our ends. We embody the whole of creation. This is the dignity of our vocation of being human beings. At the same time, we are God-breathed, Spirit-enfleshed creatures. As such, to be human is to re-present to all creation the reality of God's life for all creation.

In this double sense, to be human, in all our inter-relationships and sociality, is to be God's priestly creatures who, for and with all creation, are participating in its God-shaped telos. Priesthood is, therefore, the act of standing in this space-between; it is living in the tension of both/and rather than either/or. In the Christian narrative there is no "spiritual" realm and "ordinary" life. In creation it is one. When this holy priesthood loses connection with its eschatological vocation, its priestly calling is misconceived by being turned into a private work of the soul (inner space) over against some kind of hostile creation (outer space), and it distorts the meaning of being human. We are made and breathed into the amazing privilege of living in the creative, ambiguous, non-controllable tension of the ambiguous space-between because only in this space can we discern the telos of creation, the eschatological form of the common good. In creation, being priests is the church's vocation. Leaders form communities whose priestly life makes them the sign, witness, and foretaste of when all the creation is doxologically brought together in praise before God (Eph 1:1–21).

INTERMEZZO 1

Practical Theology and Discernment

INTRODUCTION

PART I INTRODUCED A way to listen to biblical texts, named contemporary leadership challenges, provided an overview of how we got here as churches in the West, and proposed a theological reorientation for leadership. We gave priority to a theological claim—that God is the primary agent. We have offered a metaphor—the space-between—in order to emphasize a theological interpretation of our context and to provide an imagination that moves us off old maps and toward alternative practices (more on that in chapters 8 and 9). Before we provide a deeper dive into biblical materials, theoretical resources, and specific leadership practices, this first intermezzo names an overall framework—practical theology—and its corollary—discernment.[1] This process explains why we are giving attention to particular resources in our work of reframing leadership.

Practical theology (which we understand to be a mode of corporate discernment) is a continual process of *waking up*[2] so that we can discern what God is doing in our context and determine how we can take steps to participate. For leaders this involves developing practices that help us become aware of the assumptions and habits shaping our activities and thinking. Waking up means observing and describing how assumptions

---

1. The practical theology method is adapted from Branson and Martínez, *Churches, Cultures and Leadership*, 42–44; see also Branson, "Disruptions Meet Practical Theology" and Branson and Martínez, "Practical Theology of Leadership."

2. Sedmak, *Doing Local Theology*, 1–2.

currently shape us. We usually need assistance from external resources and from conversations with others to do this kind of reflective work. Such interactions can enable us to name and hold lightly our current assumptions while giving appropriate consideration and weight to other perspectives and emerging alternatives. In this way, doing practical theology is a process of stepping into the space-between because it begins to create some levels of questioning and disorientation around our assumed, taken-for-granted actions. Stephen Brookfield notes the kind of disruption this involves for us as leaders:

> Becoming aware of our assumptions is a puzzling and contra-
> dictory task. Very few of us can get very far doing this on our
> own. No matter how much we may think we have an accurate
> sense of ourselves, we are stymied by the fact that we're using our
> own interpretive filters to become aware of our own interpretive
> filters! . . . A self-confirming cycle often develops whereby our
> uncritically accepted assumptions shape actions that then serve
> to confirm the truth of those assumptions. . . . To become aware
> of our assumptions we need to find some lenses that reflect back
> to us a stark and differently highlighted picture of who we are
> and what we do.[3]

In practical theology, we are continually moving between acting and reflecting within a posture of listening to God. This mode of action-reflection is rooted in the work of Brazilian Paulo Freire.[4] For discernment to be engaged, all of our actions—all of our experiences among friends and neighbors, in church and work, at home and in civic life—get brought into conversations with reflective practices (including worship, prayer, silence, daily office, dwelling in the Word, etc.) concerning our actions and experiences. This interactive work becomes a continuous spiral: actions, then reflections, then more actions, and additional reflections. Praxis-theory-praxis is a means of *doing local theology.*[5] It is a part of the essential core of

3. Brookfield, *The Power of Critical Theory*, 56.

4. Freire, *Pedagogy of the Oppressed*, 52–53.

5. We actually believe this is theology proper—but in the modern West, with the fragmented interests in universal concepts, the pursuit of certainty, and the academy's approach to disciplines, pride of place was given to systematization, which can tend toward abstract, rational, universalizing modes. Practical theology became a discipline initially to specify activities of clergy and churches, then it was expanded to reintroduce concepts about God into other disciplines—like psychology, sociology, and other social sciences, but even that is inadequate for what we emphasize. Because God's agency is at the center of what we are proposing, we are using the term *practical theology* to name what we believe is the core work of theology—a community's reflective activities of noticing God's presence and initiatives as we continually take steps to participate in

leadership that stands in contrast to a common approach called theory-to-practice, which assumes we or some experts can discover the truth, some set of knowledge, a specified goal, a definitive strategy, or correct theory, and then just apply it. This is an inadequate and often deceptive approach.[6] Rather, we are proposing a process that doesn't begin with theory (or models taken from other disciplines) but with actions and experiences in a particular situation—a local, embodied, reflective engagement. In this action-reflection-action process we become critically reflective practitioners—local theologians. The following is a graphic depiction of what's involved in doing local theology.

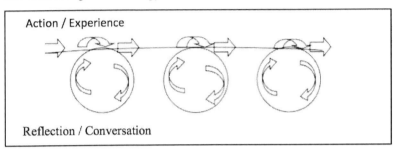

Action / Experience

Reflection / Conversation

OVERVIEW AND MOVEMENTS

We are using five steps in the movement from praxis through theoretical research and reflections then to new praxis.[7] While we will explain the process as a set sequence, it is likely that leaders will often engage alternative starting points and sequences.[8] The five steps we describe are:

1. Name and describe current praxis.

2. Analyze the praxis and context using resources of the culture.

3. Study and reflect on Christian texts and practices regarding the praxis and analysis.

4. Recall and discuss stories relevant to the experiences and analyses.

5. Discern and shape new praxis, then test with experiments.

---

those initiatives. See Sedmak, *Doing Local Theology*, and Schreiter, *Constructing Local Theologies*.

6. See Branson and Martinez, *Churches, Cultures and Leadership*, 39–42.

7. Among authors who have influenced our proposal, see Anderson, *Shape of Practical Theology*; Groome, *Sharing Faith*; and Wimberly, *Soul Stories*.

8. In part III we will provide suggestions and stories that demonstrate options.

Each step requires *individual processes* (like recalling, thinking, praying, studying, reflecting) and *group activities* (including listening, discussing, sharing stories, researching, testing). Also, throughout steps 2 through 4, rather than waiting for step 5 before anything new is tried, individuals and groups frequently engage smaller actions that guide attention and learning. This shows the challenge of providing a comprehensive model—we want to name important elements of discernment in this process, but we believe that rather than walking through one large action-reflection-action cycle, that there are smaller reflection-action-reflection elements within each of the steps.

Another movement that affects each step is a back-and-forth attentiveness to both the past and the future. This attentiveness seeks *explanations* (How did we get here? What influenced our current situation? What assumptions are embedded in our current praxis?) and *imaginations* (What options do we have? What is God inviting us into? How might we imagine a new way of being and acting?). We can get an overview of the method by engaging the question we are proposing: *How do we lead a community of God's people, in a specific context, to discern the agency of God among and ahead of us, in order to join with what God is doing in our community and in us?*

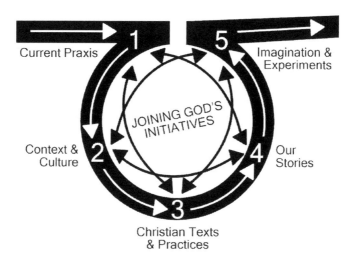

ENGAGING THE PROCESS

1. Name and Describe Current Praxis

A group begins by *naming* and *describing* some specific situation, experience, or cluster of experiences (for example: What are our current activities in terms of the neighborhood around us?). This work of observation and description, with multiple voices, sets in place the thematic center of the inquiry. This initial step includes what the group was already aware of regarding motivations, reasons, assumptions, and consequences.

Regarding our question about leadership practices in discerning God's agency, the group describes leadership positions, activities, and expectations, along with recent changes that may be affecting the situation. If the current activities warrant it, descriptions can connect activities with the conviction that God is active among them and their context. They also describe what they currently understand about the *assumptions* and *consequences* of their leadership practices. Regarding *looking back*, the group provides an initial description about how their leadership beliefs and activities were shaped.[9] Concerning *looking forward*, participants can make some preliminary comments about alternatives, then those new options are set aside so they can be considered in light of the next steps. For example, perhaps participants are aware that their primary assumptions are framed by organizational priorities that give little attention to God's initiatives, so new options will provide that emphasis.

2. Analyze Praxis and Context Using Cultural Resources

In step 2, the learning community looks more carefully at the assumptions, convictions, and contextual factors that influenced what they described as leadership beliefs and practices in step 1. They are seeking to understand the elements of their *culture* that are shaping these leadership activities and consequences. Also, step 2 uses *resources of the culture*, such as organizational theory, the humanities, philosophy, social sciences, media, and education, since these lenses provide ways of reading the influences that are shaping the actions and decisions of leaders and congregations. So step 2 uses cultural resources and it looks for cultural explanations.[10]

While the focus of step 2 is on *reflecting*, there are *actions* that make this step more generative. For example, if step 1 noted that the church's

9. For an insightful account regarding the development of church and denominational organizational structures and leadership modes, see Van Gelder and Zscheile, *Participating in God's Mission,* chapters 3–7.

10. A learning community will benefit if they engage resources within their immediate skills as well as resources beyond their own usual stable of sources. So, for example, if business models are common, then exploring critical theory or transnational studies may make it more likely that sight is improved. Or, if the participants are most likely to include psychological categories, then engaging the framework of social justice or immigration might add perspectives.

leaders have been disconnected from people in the neighborhood (their relational connections are elsewhere and church roles tend to direct attention either inward toward members or toward programs that do not develop real human connections), then participants can take steps so they become aware of their people in these contexts. (This may be about the neighborhood surrounding the church or where participants live.) The focus is just on awareness and learning—prayerfully asking God for connections, conversations, and learning that builds awareness. We will provide more specific practices in chapter 9. In our experiences, these reflective engagements often give very real experiences of what God is already doing.

Regarding the move of looking back, in previous chapters we provided insights into how those of us in the West have been shaped in modernity—with an emphasis on how God's agency has been diminished in our awareness and practices. Also, organizational theory from the last century shaped congregational and denominational forms and structures, so the consequences of those influences are engaged in step 2.[11] And we can tentatively look forward, toward possible leadership practices more suitable to how we can attend to God's initiatives. This might prod us to gain a deeper understanding regarding the perspectives of those beyond our own group. So, for example, an awareness of neighbors who are from other cultures or social locations can lead us to new conversations in which we are learners—and that helps us imagine how leadership could make those activities more likely. The initial work in step 1 plus the new learning of step 2 are held by the group as they next engage step 3.

3. Study and Reflect on Christian Texts and Practices

The group's reflections are next brought into conversation with the beliefs and practices that we find in Scripture and Christian history. The Scriptures are uniquely authoritative—and these narratives, prayers, prophecies, and letters show us how God has already spoken into and worked in specific places so that followers can discern and participate. Our work in chapter 1, where we began this engagement with biblical texts, will receive more attention in chapters 4 through 7. We believe that Scripture, when attended to prayerfully, helps us see our own contexts and discern what God is doing and wants to do among us and through us. For many centuries others have read these texts, prayed, and acted in their own locations. From their

---

11. In addition to the resources we provided in part I, see Roxburgh, *Structured for Mission.*

lives we have rich theological traditions to assist us in our discerning and practicing.

While we will provide more suggestions in chapter 9 regarding practices, participants can consider some activities that could make step 3 more likely to shape awareness. For example, a Bible study of Jeremiah 29 (which we engage in chapter 4) may encourage participants to be more aware of housing or gardening or food in their own neighborhoods. They could seek out those who know more and are engaged with these matters of daily life among neighbors. With a continual prayer regarding attentiveness to the Spirit's presence and work, participants may find that such conversations not only bring awareness of the experiences of neighbors but could reshape how we see and engage with God's initiatives The work of discernment always assumes that only through life-on-life experiences with others can we begin to see what we need to see.

Because we can be unaware of the theology and traditions that we embody, during step 3 our reflective work of looking back can help us name those formative texts. Perhaps our theology formed us to avoid people who are different, or to believe we have the truth so we don't need to listen to others. Another realization may involve recognizing that the theology we *espouse* is not necessarily our *theology-in-practice*.[12] By working to name theology that has been unhelpful, or to name discrepancies between good biblical and theological resources and what we actually practice, we get clearer on the theology that has shaped our actions. For example, Christian theology teaches us that the people around us are subjects rather than objects, yet we may have adopted practices like marketing or other tactics with little attention to how we objectify our neighbors. Looking forward, we begin to see new theologically-motivated options. The church's rich and varied tradition has all kinds of Spirit-given, on-the-ground guidance for deepening our reflection on what it means to form communities that are discerning the agency of God in their communities. In chapter 3, for example, we saw how creation, incarnation, Trinity, and eschatology might reshape our leadership practices in terms of joining God in the space-between. These interactions with Scripture and tradition then assist participants to ask one another: "How will our leadership praxis be changed through reflection on Christian texts and practices?"

12. See Argyris, "Teaching Smart People," 103.

4. Recall and Discuss Stories from Our Own Lives, Church, and Community

Discernment lifts up the journey we engaged in steps 1 through 3 and connects it to local voices. Just as Peter would not have known God's activities if he had not listened to Cornelius (Acts 10) and Paul would not have known how God was working if he had not met and listened to Lydia (Acts 16), we have to place ourselves in situations where stories, questions, and conversations, from among ordinary people in our contexts, are possible. Listening to God through the other (alterity) is essential. In the experience, voice, and imagination of the other (in both our church and in the neighborhood) we gain more access to God's voice and activities. As noted in earlier steps, step 4 includes simple activities with people in our communities so that we demonstrate a confidence that God's Spirit meets us and teaches us through others.

There are many layers to this step. In looking back, for example, the church's participants can provide stories from the church's own specific history regarding connections between leadership practices and capacities to discern God's agency. There may be stories that note some misunderstandings and waywardness along with narratives that are full of wisdom and faith. Personal stories can surface experiences with God, and step 4 calls us to listen to where people are aware of God's activities but don't always have the language for interpreting their stories in this light. Similarly, in our neighborhoods there are a myriad of stories of people's encounters with God where, again, people don't have the language to see God in this way. Step 4 creates room for stories about conversations with a neighbor, a dream about some person or activity, or an intuition—all these are present among church participants, often in informal ways, off the radar from the official plans of churches and communities. But learning to listen and assist people give voice to these stories is critical to how we re-envision the kind of leadership that shapes new attentiveness and practices.[13] These stories need to be brought into conversation with what was learned in steps 1 through 3—as the arrows in the diagram show, the reflections of each step interact with the others steps. And regarding how step 4 might look forward, there will be some tentative comments about how the new conversations around Christian resources and cultural analysis might deepen our understanding of our stories and provide new imagination—which takes us into step 5.

---

13. Appreciative inquiry is a mode of conversations that is shaped by gratitude so that we become more attuned to God's graces; see Branson, *Memories, Hopes and Conversations*. This book contains five chapters describing occasions in which congregations had new and generative conversations with their neighbors.

5. Discern and Shape New Praxis through Prayer, Imagination, and Experiments

Practical theology requires that we engage new actions rather than just perpetually engage in reflection. The work of reflection named in steps 2 through 4 feeds into the specific work of imagining, describing, and engaging some experiments that focus on discerning and participating in God's initiatives. While we noted initial, smaller actions that could be helpful in each reflective step, step 5 provides an opportunity to bring all of that learning and awareness together. Our traditions have many resources regarding the practices of discernment, often with some rhythm of individual and group activities. Given that we want to discern what God is doing, and we've deepened our understanding and imaginations through reflective learning, what are some specific actions we want to take as leaders of our communities? How can we assist each other to take new steps? What experiment can we take (personally and together) that engages us with the people and stories of our context? How can we experiment in order to clarify our seeing and our participation in God's initiatives? In this praxis-reflection-praxis cycle, the goal is not certainty, a large strategic plan, or clearly delineated functional roles. The goal is simply to have some experiments that seem faithful to what is being learned. Sometimes a group's process may include prayer visions (Acts 10 and 16), or reminders about Bible passages (like how Ephesians 4 recalls Psalm 68), or the Spirit's provision of wisdom about possible experiments in a concrete situation (Acts 2).

SUMMARY

The purpose of this intermezzo is to indicate why our chapters are always doing integrative work with Scriptures, contemporary experiences, theology, and diverse cultural resources. We want readers to bring their own experiences and habits and challenges into critical reflection with these chapters. Each step provides specific lenses, and while a group's process will probably not engage each lens in depth and in this sequence, we believe each of these lenses is important for discernment. What we describe as sequential steps are usually messier, with times for looping back to previous analysis or making jumps to some tentative awareness that needs more resourcing. And we want to emphasize what is at the core of this venture: God is already active in our lives and contexts, and our own agency is about discerning how God is inviting us into those initiatives. The practical theology cycle fosters skills for those who work in ambiguous environments, in the space-between, in order to increase the capacities needed to participate with God. Part II shows how this work unfolds in several biblical books—Jeremiah, Matthew, Acts, and Ephesians. A second intermezzo and part III will explore important metaphors and some concrete practices of leadership in the space-between.

PART II: BIBLE & LEADERSHIP

CHAPTER 4

Jeremiah as Interpretive Leader

INTRODUCTION

OUR EARLIER CHAPTERS EXPLORED how North American Christian communities face challenges that are rooted in our theology, cultural contexts, and organizational habits. We have emphasized the theological challenge—that while we affirm God's grace and care, our leadership practices tend not to embody confidence that God is continually initiating in our contexts with our neighbors and us. Chapter 1 introduced four biblical books that provide narratives to deepen our theological explorations and various practices regarding leadership and God's agency.

This chapter, continuing our exploration of the book of Jeremiah, will focus on a context of massive disruption, in which Jeremiah counters all the assumed and official explanations concerning Israel's disruptive situation, how God is involved, and the options available to those who are caught up in these events.[1] In chapter 1, we provided an overview of the historical context of Jeremiah, emphasizing that Jeremiah is working against various forces as he names what God is up to, thus offering to Israel an opportunity to reclaim their primary theological convictions and agency.[2] When a culture or community experiences major societal shifts that bear on their identity and agency, leadership functions need to adapt or the group's identity is at risk. We believe that North American churches and their leaders currently face this challenge; we need to name and interpret our new social

---

1. Much of this chapter benefits from Branson, "Interpretive Leadership."
2. We suggest that readers review the section on Jeremiah in chapter 1.

environment, the fragmenting of our own social cohesion, and the accompanying disorienting challenges. And this interpretive work needs to be done with theology at the center—specifically that God is active. It is expected that leaders might instead work to avoid such challenges, pretend to provide expert fixes, or mangle the tradition in efforts to deflect responsibility. We believe that Jeremiah is an appropriate voice; he holds up a mirror and offers interpretive help and practices that might redeem.

The Context of Jeremiah's Leadership

As the sixth century BCE began, Babylon's forces threatened Israel's existence. Jerusalem officials clung to misguided theological predictions regarding their continued institutional existence. Inside that set of beliefs, Israel's leaders pursued various military options, and Jeremiah called for non-resistance in regard to Babylon. As a backup, Jerusalem officials sought the protection of Egypt, just in case Yahweh was not providing the needed initiative.

Jeremiah, although relationally connected to Jerusalem elites, lacks the kind of power that leaders always seek—he is without a recognized portfolio; he has no levers on governing structures; he is not managing a workforce. But, as we will explain more fully below, leadership is about engaging a group to reshape the meanings they embody as they move through significant challenges.

In 605 BCE, Babylon defeated Egypt in north Syria (during Jehoiakim's fourth year),[3] and soon began forcing Israel to pay regular tributes to Nebuchadnezzar II. This stage of the traumatic disruption included the capture and deportation of those who might have become the new generation of Israel's leaders. Then in 601 BCE, Egypt defeated Babylon's invasive troops, and Israel took advantage of the situation by revolting. This brought a Babylonian siege, significant destruction, and defeat for Israel in 597 BCE. Nebuchadnezzar appointed a puppet king, killed many officials and citizens, and forced other officials, elites, and craftspersons into exile in Babylon. From 597 to 581 BCE there were additional deportations of Jewish citizens into exile.

As we noted earlier, this was a massive theological challenge. While officials continued with their attempts to manage the situation (seeking partnership with Egypt), and various prophets claimed that each stage of the deepening crisis was only temporary, Jeremiah interpreted the theological situation differently.

3. Allen, *Jeremiah*, 400.

Jeremiah 22—Memories of Josiah

An important element of the back-story of Jeremiah is the hopeful but even-tually tragic story of Josiah. King Josiah of Judah, considered among the most righteous of kings, began renovation work on the temple in 622 BCE. These years included the discovery of a covenant scroll, significant renewal of worship, and tearing down of pagan shrines (2 Kgs 23).

These reform actions, a century after Israel (the northern tribes) fell to Assyria, were engaged at a time when Josiah had in effect gained inde-pendence as Assyria waned. With the fall of Nineveh (612 BCE) and Haran (610 BCE), Assyria was defeated by the Babylonian forces. Judah then be-gan several years of tightrope walking between the Egyptian and Babylo-nian empires. As the Babylonians secured territories east and north of the Euphrates (directed by Nabopolassar and his son Nebuchadnezzar), Egypt held sway over Palestine and Syria.[4] After Josiah's death, Jeremiah speaks against Josiah's wayward son King Jehoiakim, who had become a vassal of Egypt, saying, "Woe to him who builds his house by unrighteousness . . . who makes his neighbors work for nothing . . . paneling it with cedar. . . . Did not your father eat and drink and do justice . . .?" (22:13–15 NRSV).

Can Jeremiah use speech to change the misdirected commitments in Judah? Everyone can see these tangible realities—a level of national auton-omy along with an upscale new palace. However, some other observations (concerning cedar and forced labor), once uttered, create a new interpretive situation. Jeremiah is working to shift the interpretive capacities of the peo-ple; he wants them to shift their understandings and behaviors. He works with historical texts and recent memory in order to compare Jehoiakim (who is instigating and collaborating with unfaithful activities) with Jehoia-kim's father, Josiah: "He (Josiah) judged the cause of the poor and needy. . . . Is not this to know me? says the LORD" (22:16, NRSV). This reference to the Josiah narrative connects the hearers with the ancient covenants that had been rediscovered during Josiah's reign. But now Jehoiakim interprets the times (the defeat of Assyria) as an opportunity for palace construction, perhaps in imitation of Egyptian opulence, and in complete disregard for basic kingly obligations. Jeremiah claims, ". . . their houses are full of loot . . . their evil deeds exceed all limits, and yet they prosper. They are in-different to the plight of the orphan, reluctant to defend the rights of the poor" (5:27–28). So Jeremiah's interpretive leadership attends differently to texts and times. He challenges the dependence on a military coalition (with Egypt) for protection from Babylon, and the practices of maldistribution of

---

4. Bright, *History of Israel*, 143.

resources. Jeremiah's interpretation of Hebrew texts and the chaotic context —an interpretation he accredits to God—makes the claim that God has chosen Babylon as a temporary power. Jeremiah's reading of God's involvement led him to call on the national authorities to reject counter-violence and military coalitions. Without this theological interpretation—that God is active, something misread by established leaders—Israel chooses wrongly and the consequences are profound.

Mark saw an urban multiethnic church become aware of an interpretive challenge. They had just completed a year in which they taught and preached through the large, whole biblical story. They were continually observing that, in Scripture, everyday people, old and young, Jews and Gentiles, freely told their stories even when they lacked philosophical or theological sophistication. Storytelling is human, but they'd become hesitant concerning stories about faith and God and salvation and healing. So various church leaders began to tell such biblical stories in sermons, in studies, and at meetings. They were aware that these story-telling behaviors are not strange in everyday lives—around meals, at home, in a school cafeteria, in passing, on the phone. So, with reference to Brueggemann, they began to realize that unless a church tells stories, they will forget who they are and how God has engaged their lives. This focus on story-telling stirred imaginations and led to some experiments. Those who led worship created a sanctuary environment that included a trellis. This was the "green growing season" of Ordinary Time.[5] They asked some of the older members for faith stories, often sitting with them over tea and transcribing or outlining the stories in order to ease the public event. When members brought stories, they were invited to bring something to hang on the trellis. Soon there was a photo of a favorite, faithful aunt, a cane from one whose walking was restored, and onions in memory of parents who farmed as they also gave pastoral care. There were amazing stories, often continued after the benediction, which in turn encouraged other storytellers. These utterances began reshaping the way they lived with each other and among neighbors.

CONTEMPORARY FRAMEWORKS

In each of the four chapters of part II, we name conceptual frameworks that have been commonly used in North American regarding the work of leadership. In each case, we rethink these frameworks in relationship to the

---

5. This is terminology that the children (and some of their parents) were learning through the Montessori-styled "Godly Play" approach to Christian formation of children. See Berryman, *Godly Play.*

theological matters we have been raising. We have named many of these frameworks in chapter 1, and noted that a core matter for all of them is how they are altered when we name God as the primary active agent. The frameworks we work with in this chapter will interweave interpretive leadership, Charles Taylor's theory of social imaginary, and Ronald Heifetz's work on adaptive challenges and holding environments.

Jeremiah and Interpretive Leadership

The leadership triad Mark has written about previously[6] describes the work of leaders in three overlapping spheres: relational, implemental, and interpretive leadership. Leaders need to attend to the dynamics and activities of a group in these three spheres. *Relational leadership* has to do with all the human connections within the group and with those beyond the group. With our priority on God's agency, the work of leadership is to be attentive, and to increase the attentiveness of others, to what God is doing in and through all those relationships. As we wrote in chapter 3 regarding Christian anthropology, God has shaped us to be in community, to be formed by alterity, and to recognize ourselves and others as subjects rather than objects. These are all matters of relationality. *Implemental* leadership is about a leader's work in fostering a group that forms actions, acquires and makes resources, and assembles organizational structures that promote the practical theology goal (noted in intermezzo 1) of discerning what God is doing and participating in those initiatives. A leader prompts a group's behaviors and seeks to structure it toward those ends. *Interpretive leadership* shapes an interpretive community—which means that leaders nurture an environment in which the group gains interpretive competences regarding texts and contexts. The focus in this chapter on Jeremiah is on interpretive leadership.

Interpretive leadership engages a group so that its responses to the on-the-ground realities of its context are interpreted in terms of discerning the actions of God among them. As we noted in intermezzo 1, this work of discernment involves three areas: (a) the written texts of Scripture and tradition along with (b) cultural resources and (c) the stories in the local setting. There are various practices and activities that foster this engagement, such as listening to stories, participating in cultural spaces, and learning about traditions, all with a focus on God's agency. Virtues of gratitude, patience, humility, and kindness are also important. In chapter 9 we will suggest specific ways to develop these practices and virtues. Anne Streaty Wimberly emphasizes this interaction: "21st century Christian faith communities are

---

6. See Branson, "Ecclesiology and Leadership" and "Forming God's People."

called to an imperative vocation of listening in face-to-face contexts as a necessary counterbalance to the social separation and the 'listening at a distance' that occurs in cyberspace."[7] In all of these activities, the interpretive capacities of the group are increased, particularly toward discernment and joining God.[8] This is what makes a new social imaginary possible[9] (as explained, below). Practices that create this focus, this awareness, are at the core of interpretive leadership.

Interpretive Leadership, Discontinuous Change, and Holding Environments

Expectations and scenarios for leadership are significantly different when the interpretive community faces discontinuous changes in its context (external), or in its own makeup, experiences, or sense of vocation (internal). Many changes that a group faces are somewhat predictable and expected; during these changes, the work of a group and its leaders will always continue to be that of discernment and engagement regarding God's initiatives. But there are other times when the changes are larger and more unexpected. A discontinuous change is one that requires that a group reconsider basic beliefs, assumptions, values, and practices; without DNA-level adaptation, the group would be incapable of embodying its core identity and agency. This requires what Ronald Heifetz calls adaptive leadership. In these situations, there is no clarity about goals and paths, and management priorities on announced vision and strategies are misleading and defeating. When such challenges are present, leaders must provide reality testing, a reconsideration of values, and a shift in learning activities.

Key to such leadership is a shift from standard views of leadership that encourage control and management to, instead, the work of shaping an environment in which an increasing number of participants are mobilized for experiments, discernment, shaping new social arrangements, testing practices, and reflecting on what is being learned.[10] Ronald Heifetz and Marty Linsky use the term "holding environments" for this kind of group atmosphere.[11] They explain how leaders can create an environment—through

---

7. Wimberly, "Called to Listen," 331.

8. This was noted in chapter 3; in the next chapter on Matthew, social construction will be examined as a theoretical resource for this interpretive work.

9. Branson, "Interpretive Leadership," 29.

10. Heifetz, *Leadership Without Easy Answers*, 22–27; Roxburgh and Romanuk, *Missional Leader*, chapter 5.

11. Heifetz and Linsky, *Leadership on the Line*, 102–7. This theory is rooted in

their practices and words—that makes alternative convictions and behaviors possible by giving the adaptive work to a larger group of participants.[12] This is not a mode of strategy, command, or control, but rather work that connects with the background and current context, distributes leadership more broadly among participants, and prompts experimental steps.

We have both written about the benefits of these concepts—adaptive leadership and holding environments—and believe they can help leaders better embrace disruptions and find alternative forms of leadership that contribute to the ways interpretive leaders cultivate discernment among their people.[13] However we have also experienced problems when leaders adopt this language but, because of their own deep habits, they simply continue with forms of power and control even though their language shifts. Further, this theoretical material requires a fundamentally different frame in light of our emphasis on God's agency. While Heifetz and Linsky do not posit God as a prime agency, or discerning God's initiatives as the core of learning, we believe their frameworks can be suitable for that work.

Heifetz posits that leadership is not primarily about character traits and positional authority but rather about what a leader says and does.[14] The habits that leaders inhabit—which are formed by technocratic rationalism with God-talk attached—are inadequate for these challenges. The adaptive changes that we want to foster will impinge on churches, including the practices of groups and individuals; such changes will require leaders creating something like a holding environment for the explicit purpose of fostering experiments and learning among all participants. What is critical is that this kind of holding environment work be done from within the basic frame of the community's focus on discerning the ways God is present and active. As stated in chapter 2, we believe North American churches are in a context of discontinuous change. The holding environment required, therefore, is one that embraces an action-reflection approach (as we noted in the intermezzo) in the new space. And, because of our theological praxis regarding God as the primary agent, this shapes the community toward the new realities of God's initiatives in the changing context.

Winnicott, *Maturational Processes*.

12. Heifetz and Linsky, *Leadership on the Line*, chapter 6.

13. Roxburgh and Romanuk, *The Missional Leader*; Branson and Martinez, *Churches, Cultures and Leadership*; Branson *Memories, Hopes, and Conversations*.

14. Heifetz, *Leadership Without Easy Answers*, 20.

Taylor and Social Imaginaries

A significant part of interpretive leadership work is forming what Charles Taylor calls a new social imaginary. Any group has a shared imagination about the world we live in that causes it to understand what is real, how the world functions, and what roles people have. Taylor posits that disruptions to a group's imaginary are the opportunity for them to test their assumptions and practice new actions. The disruption becomes an opportunity to reshape the group's meanings and in so doing create a new coherence or wholeness within the group's culture.[15] Taylor assumes that we all live in the midst of false imaginaries that are "full of false consciousness," noting that "what we imagine can be something new, constructive, opening new possibilities, or it can be purely fictitious, perhaps dangerously false."[16] One cause of such false consciousness is a group's tendency to conjure continuity even when it is not present.[17] A church's imagination, for example, can be shaped by years of mental, emotional, and behavioral habits that have been formed from within its own internal life but have become quite out of touch with the forces that are forming them, as well as with what is occurring in its surrounding context. The result is that the congregation's relationship with its context is made up of this kind of conjuring rather than any real engagement or attending (reflective work) to what is going on. This becomes apparent when activity patterns are perpetually repeated even when the desired outcomes have long ago ceased. Interpretive leaders have the work of fostering a group's capacity to perceive this situation then to reflect on its social imaginary and the places where it is only "conjuring" meaning in the midst of discontinuous change. As we posited, especially in chapter 2, a key element in creating this conjuring, or false imaginary, is when churches and leaders fail to develop these habits of interpretive reflection in their thinking and acting that have God's current agency at the center.

As claimed in intermezzo 1, texts and situations, old and new, are the critical background in the formation of an interpretive community. Taylor writes that "the background that makes sense of any given act is thus deep and wide."[18] We see Jeremiah leading by engaging such background, showing contradictions between the espoused beliefs of the palace (unmasking their "conjuring") and what they actually practice.[19] They claim the texts of

---

15. Taylor, *Modern Social Imaginaries*, 23–30.

16. Taylor, *Modern Social Imaginaries*, 183.

17. Cormode, *Making Spiritual Sense*, 9–14.

18. Taylor, *Modern Social Imaginaries*, 28.

19. See Argyris, "Teaching Smart People."

the covenant but their words and actions contradict those claims. This has parallels in North American churches.

Noting the space that times of transition provide, Taylor describes how "people take up, improvise, or are inducted into new practices" in ways that background meanings and the current context are mutually reinterpreted: "new understanding comes to be accessible to the participants in a way it wasn't before."[20] This is at the interface of interpretive and implemental leadership—shaping a space and suitable practices for new life. As the situation in Judah deteriorates, and Jeremiah is eventually trapped in their negotiations with Egypt, he begins to prompt new practices among those captive in Babylon (see below). The new interpretive frameworks that Jeremiah has provided are inadequate without activity patterns (actions) that make the interpretive work visible and promising.

The prophet Jeremiah can help us see and interpret discontinuous challenges, and learn how new social imaginaries might be formed. Those who had positions of authority—the royal household, the priests, the court prophets—read and interpreted the covenant and their context in certain ways. They made assumptions about God, goals, neighbors, actions, and what it meant to be God's chosen people. This was the shape of their social imaginary—the assumptions that they brought to bear on how they exercised authority. They interpreted their historical context, their texts and traditions, and, as recognized authorities, they prescribed how their community should respond. Jeremiah countered their interpretive work as he shaped an *interpretive community*.

HOW JEREMIAH SHAPES AN INTERPRETIVE COMMUNITY

Jeremiah 36—Texts, Options, and Avoidance

Jeremiah, in responsiveness to God, shapes an interpretive community in Judah through the use of texts[21] (God's instructions, promises, and the

20. Taylor, *Modern Social Imaginaries*, 29.

21. It is impossible to know precisely what texts Jeremiah had or what history and traditions were being passed on, though there are numerous assumed references. Second Kings 22 notes the discovery of a "covenant book" in Josiah's time, possibly a form of Deuteronomy; Allen notes allusions to Deuteronomy (Allen, *Jeremiah*, 137). W. L. Holladay notes that Jeremiah draws on the Psalms and that some Psalms are dependent on Jeremiah; see Holladay, "Indications of Jeremiah's Psalter," 245–261; see also Allen, *Jeremiah*, 5–6. Other references include Micah (quoted directly), Obadiah (but who borrowed from whom?); see Lundbom, *Jeremiah 37–52*, 334–35.

liturgies of Israel), the offering of options (surrender to Babylon), and by creating a situation in which the authorities retreated to avoidance. With the Babylonian victory over Egyptian forces at Carchemish (605), Judah felt the increasing threat. Nebuchadnezzar returned to Babylon upon the death of Nabopolassar (604), creating a brief sense of relief, but he soon resumed his southern march. As Babylonian victories increased, a fast was observed in Jerusalem.[22] This is the occasion in which Yahweh directed Jeremiah, with the assistance of Baruch, to commit his oracles to writing. The messages repeated throughout the book (e.g. Jer 21) were probably the essence of the scroll, naming bad behavior with the hope for repentance: Judah, like Israel earlier, has betrayed the covenant; Babylon is God's tool for judgment; Judah should surrender to Nebuchadnezzar in order to preserve lives and options. The fast provided an occasion for reading the collection, and that task fell to Baruch. Subsequently, members of the pro-Jeremiah Shaphan family arranged for the scroll to come to the attention of the king, and for Jeremiah and Baruch to be safely in hiding. (This episode indicates the importance of relationships and leaves us curious concerning the nature and history of these who value Jeremiah's words even as they took risks. Leadership needs to be alert to kin and neighbors who are trustworthy and to those who are deceitful [9:4–6].) Then, in the midst of the protests of several officials, "As Jehudi read three or four columns, the king would cut them off (qara') with a penknife and throw them into the fire in the brazier, until the entire scroll was consumed. . . ." (36:23 NRSV). This is in contrast to the reception Josiah had provided when a Deuteronomic scroll was found in temple excavations—he tore (qara') his clothes and deepened his leadership toward faithfulness (2 Kgs 22:11). The Jeremiah text notes that "neither the king, nor any of his servants . . ., was alarmed, nor did they tear (qara') their garments" (Jer 36:24, NRSV).

This text makes it clear that all fasting is not equal. "Although they fast, I do not hear their cry, and although they offer burnt offering and grain offering, I do not accept them" (14:12 NRSV). Fasting is not a technology for controlling supernatural powers; rather it is intended as a means of deepening attentiveness, perception, and cooperation with Yahweh. As a practice of the faith community, fasting serves interpretive work—it can serve the forming of a holding environment. God's grace through Jeremiah, Baruch, and a web of relationships, was the provision of a text. Jehoiakim's rejection was consistent with the nation's enduring trends toward alienation from Yahweh. Had Jehoiakim forgotten that God had supplied provisions and

---

22. The text does not state the reason for the fast, but Babylon's sacking of Ashkelon occurred in that month, increasing the danger for Judah; Allen, *Jeremiah*, 398.

protection even when Israel was not a sovereign nation? Could he not remember the clan life of the patriarchs, during the desert sojourn, and in the decades of the Judges? Evidently, having lost that imagination, Jehoiakim had no capacity to receive Jeremiah's words. Jeremiah's interpretive leadership remained within small boundaries, a very limited community in a dangerous environment. However, this episode of the narrative indicates how Jeremiah's hermeneutics would eventually shape a much larger community.

Interpretive leadership includes not only preserving, reading, and interpreting a community's texts but also creating texts as God's agency is discerned. This was an appropriate time to increase the diffusion of particular words, so the oracles of Jeremiah were collected and transcribed and eventually (slowly) made more broadly available. Technology and social networks make access possible. As the scroll was relayed, leaders connected with Jeremiah and Baruch properly interpreted the signs of danger and decided to protect God's intermediaries prior to the royal audience. They were preserved, but the scroll was not. The text was a means for creating an alternative reality, offering an option to Jehoiakim other than a doomed coalition with Egypt or the full and total destruction of Jerusalem. It was Jehoiakim's job to receive the text and live into the alternative, but he stopped the text's intent and even sought to stop any chance that the text would shape Judah's reality. Walter Brueggemann explains how interpretive work, especially when written, shapes options:

> The prophetic tradition provides something like a scripting of reality, not in totalitarian ways, but in ways that seed and authorize an alternative imagination. . . . This textual tradition, over time, has provided the endless authorization of a counter-existence in the world. . . . It is now clear that written utterance has a kind of freedom from context that spoken utterance does not. And this written utterance explodes always again in odd, energetic, and transformative ways.[23]

After the first scroll was destroyed, Yahweh prompted the creation of a second and longer scroll (36:32) that was likely the basis of the collection we read over two millennia later.

The pressures on Jehoiakim (externally from Babylon, internally from the dominant pro-Egypt party) made him resist the thoroughgoing adaptive change proposed by Jeremiah. Jehoiakim could not fathom a social imaginary that included the end of Judah as a nation, and he clung to a belief that cooperation with Egypt would allow Judah's continued existence. Heifetz's

---

23. Brueggemann, *Texts That Linger*, 9.

perspective on work avoidance is telling, especially for our current North American situation:

> [P]eople fail to adapt because of the distress provoked by the problem and the changes it demands. They resist the pain, anxiety, or conflict that accompanies a sustained interaction with the situation. Holding on to past assumptions, blaming authority, scapegoating, externalizing the enemy, denying the problem, jumping to conclusions, or finding a distracting issue may restore stability and feel less stressful than facing and taking responsibility for a complex challenge.[24]

Jehoiakim was in denial concerning the contingencies of Yahweh's covenant; the stress level created by Jeremiah's alternative (surrender to Babylon) was too high. In this way, Jehoiakim was clutching past assumptions that desperately needed new theological work. But it was too easy to use Jeremiah as a scapegoat ("Jeremiah is causing trouble") and too hard to embrace the change that would allow a degree of protection (surrender) that would also come with God's presence in a new location.

Jeremiah 29—Texts and New Practices

In Jeremiah's contentions with the royal prophets and the huge disorientation of those in exile, the prophet provided two things: first, a different interpretive grid for texts and contexts of Babylon, and, second, a radically counterintuitive set of practices for life together and with their neighbors in Babylon. By 603 Jehoiakim had become an unwilling subject of Babylon. Nebuchadnezzar's southern drive was initially successful, but after intense and indeterminate battles in 601, Nebuchadnezzar returned home. The assault was reengaged in 598, probably resulting in Jehoiakim's death. His son Jehoiachin was on the throne for only three months before he surrendered in 597 (2 Kgs 24:8), leading to the first deportation of thousands of officials and citizens to Babylon. Zedekiah (another son of Josiah) was installed as Babylon's vassal, while some assumed that exiled Jehoiakin was still king.[25] The prophet Hananiah provided Zedekiah with his interpretation of these events and the expected outcome (Jer 28). Prophets are to serve the king and the nation by providing a word from Yahweh; Hananiah's claim "thus says the LORD of Israel" was consistent with this job description but contradicted

---

24. Heifetz, *Leadership Without Easy Answers*, 37.

25. Oded, "Judah and the Exile," 471.

by Jeremiah and by events. These various accounts tell of the ongoing and collaborative opposition that clerics and rulers perpetuate against Jeremiah.

Notably in the book of Jeremiah, prophets were usually lumped with priests and seen as part of the problem, "For from the least to the greatest of them, everyone is greedy for unjust gain; and from prophet to priest, everyone deals falsely" (6:13 and elsewhere, NRSV). Hananiah claimed that the deportation was a temporary setback. Claiming to speak for God, he predicted, "Within two years I will bring back to this place all the vessels of the LORD's house . . . and all the exiles" (28:3–4). In Heifetz's terms, this was work avoidance: "the pain will go away." Jeremiah admitted that he wished it were true, and then he departed the conversation. But later God sent Jeremiah to address Hananiah, again emphasizing that he (Yahweh) was behind Nebuchadnezzar's lengthier reign. Then it got personal: "Listen, Hananiah, the LORD has not sent you, and you made this people trust in a lie." Hananiah's demise is predicted, and realized within a few months (28:12–17 NRSV). Hananiah could not see beyond the political imaginary of relative national autonomy, the maintenance of those with Jerusalem portfolios, and a textual rendering that required Yahweh to always serve those ends. Only a more thorough and less self-interested look at the texts could provide a new imaginary.[26]

The grieving and restive exiles, deported in 597, were dealing with conflicting interpretations of their situation. Babylonian documents indicate that Jehoiachin was identified as king even though he was part of the exile community; Zedekiah's claim to legitimacy was apparently challenged, and seen as temporary at best. The words of exiled prophets, including Hananiah's colleagues Ahab and Zedekiah, predicted a brief exile and quick return. These interpretive positions needed to be challenged. In these contrasts, the challenge to the community is not an imaginary in which God has been excluded as an agent but rather two parties claimed they could identify God's agency. The interpretive community had work to do regarding discernment: What was consistent or inconsistent with how God has previously spoken and acted? What behaviors of Israel's leaders were consistent or inconsistent with what God had previously revealed? What current experiences favored the perspectives of which prophet? Whose words could explain the disruption they were experiencing? Jeremiah, in conversation with Hananiah before a temple audience, recalls that earlier prophets provided oracles of both salvation and judgement, and clarified that "the prophet who prophesies

26. The texts embraced by Josiah were available to Hananiah and Zedekiah, but they chose to stay inside a narrative that proved to be false. Old Testament theologies include both the perpetuation of a Davidic dynasty and the need for Israel's faithfulness (rooted in Deuteronomy); these differences are at play in Jeremiah.

peace is recognized as one who is actually sent by the LORD only when that prophet's message is fulfilled" (28:9). Interpretive claims need collaboration; as Leslie Allen writes, "The test of authenticity for a prediction of peaceful restitution can only be its eventual fulfillment, before which judgement on its validity must be suspended.[27]

Jeremiah continues his counter to Hananiah's views with a letter to the exile community: "Thus says the LORD of hosts . . . [they] are prophesying a lie to you in my name" (29:21 NRSV). God's role was interpreted as a partnership with Nebuchadnezzar (!): "Thus says . . . the God of Israel, to all the exiles whom I have sent into exile" (29:4 NRSV). The exiled prophets who prompted a revolt against Babylon were quickly squashed (29:21 NRSV). Instead of revolting, or just hunkering down in enemy territory in expectation of a quick, violent rescue by God, the exiles were instructed by Jeremiah's letter to "Build houses . . . plant gardens . . . take wives and have sons and daughters; take wives for your sons, and give your daughters in marriage, that they may bear sons and daughters . . ." (29:5–6 NRSV). This does not fit the expectation of an immediate rescue. The enemy and this city[28] of exile were being interpreted in ways that were profoundly disorienting. God was/is acting, but official interpreters had perpetuated bad theology, wrong expectations, and unfaithful activities. Jeremiah writes that the exiles had an alternative: turn toward a different interpretation and some basic communal, neighborly practices. In those practices they would enter a new imaginary.

The commended activities reflect two preceding biblical tests.[29] First, as Daniel Smith observed, the Deuteronomic restrictions regarding warfare list these activities as reasons for not soldiering: house building, vineyard-planting, and engagement (Deut 20:5–7).[30] Second, when Deuteronomy warns of disobedience and resulting judgement, the specific curses are, "You might get engaged to a woman, but another man will have sex with her. You might build a house, but you won't get to live in it. You might plant a vineyard, but you won't enjoy it" (Deut 28:30). God's disruptive activities and these instructions provide a reorientation for a generation that had lost its way; a faithful community can live amidst God's initiatives even in Babylon.

Not only were the exiles to settle in for a few generations, their relationship with this new context was beyond their imagination: "seek the shalom

27. Allen, *Jeremiah*, 317.

28. Lundbom notes, "This is not necessarily Babylon or Uruk, but whatever city or town in which the exiles happen to be. Settlement was not all in one place." Lundbom, *Jeremiah 21–36*, 351.

29. Allen, *Jeremiah*, 324.

30. Smith, "Jeremiah as Prophet."

of the city where I have sent you into exile, and pray to the LORD on its behalf, for in its shalom you will find your shalom" (29:7 NRSV adapted).[31] The social imaginary promulgated by Jerusalem's leaders—the Davidic paradigm—was profoundly contradicted by the Babylonian conquest. This meant that their convictions about God's presence and actions had to be reconceived. This disruption created a space in which an alternative interpretation of texts and contexts could emerge, one that might provide a way to reconnect with Yahweh and thereby allow a pathway toward a new imaginary. John Howard Yoder describes the shift: "Babylon itself very soon became the cultural center of world Jewry, from the age of Jeremiah until . . . the Middle Ages. The people who recolonized the 'Land of Israel' . . . were supported financially and educationally from Babylon, and in lesser ways from the rest of the diaspora."[32] In this way, the faith community gained a new way of life, based in texts, with distributed leadership, gathered into synagogues for recitation, singing, varied cultic activities, and support for life among the nations.[33]

The innovative and jarring work of creating a new social imaginary will challenge the best leadership. The depth of the contextual discontinuous change can serve a community's availability to God's continual priority on shaping a faithful shalom community as a light to the nations, although such situations will also surface reactionary forces. As victims of a violent empire, and as a community with a poor track record of attending to God's words, the exiles did not recall interpretive resources concerning good will for an enemy as a mode of social resistance. As noted, they could be encouraged toward violent rebellion, and probably even thought this might bring God's participation. But Jeremiah provided a different interpretive grid for texts and contexts, along with practices concerning life together and life with neighbors. These two elements—texts for reflection, practices for engagement—become mutually interpretive. As we outlined in intermezzo 1, and as will be revisited in our chapter on Matthew (chapter 5), this is Paulo Freire's emphasis concerning praxis: an action-reflection cycle that leads to a genuine learning community.[34]

When churches face major challenges, whether brought by the accumulation of incremental changes or by more rapid discontinuous change, their responses are often embedded in the behaviors of resistance and

31. This is the NRSV text with our inclusion of the original Hebrew *shalom* for the English word *welfare*.

32. Yoder, *For the Nations*, 57.

33. Yoder, *For the Nations*, 71–73. This missional life, according to Yoder, uniquely shaped Jewry for life among the nations.

34. Freire, *Pedagogy of the Oppressed*, 52–53.

denial.[35] Common leadership approaches in such situations employ top-down work where leaders try to fix the unraveling with such techniques as vision statements, large strategies, and programmatic answers—all modes of technocratic rationalism. Instead of these approaches, interpretive leaders learn how to give the work to the people. Such leaders, recognizing the profoundly disruptive nature of the situation, seek to form learning teams who are testing out how to engage with God and neighbors. It is in this mix of interpretive leadership and learning communities that a new imaginary emerges as congregational conversations help reshape meanings and practices.

While Jeremiah had significant problems creating a learning community in Palestine, it can be argued that such a community took root in Babylon. In this letter (Jer 29), Jeremiah drew on the Torah to reinterpret how they were to relate to this city, its people, and its normative violence. Four specific ways this was done are noteworthy: houses, gardens, family, and neighbors. The first three community-building activities are cited in Deuteronomy as restrictions on soldiering (Deut 20); thus it can be argued that Yahweh is prompting the creation of a nonviolent community that can survive, increase, and be prepared for their eventual return as a faith community giving witness to a God of shalom. And mutual caring among neighbors, also signaled by Deuteronomy in reference to aliens and sojourners, while reversed in this setting (Israel is now the sojourner) is still consistent with their sacred texts. So texts and context were given new meanings, and familiar practices were commended in an unexpected way.[36] At issue here is that Jeremiah was shaping an interpretive community that began to live in a reality that did not exist until his words arrived, that is, the instructions from God via the prophet. It was this contrary text that enabled the exiles to embrace a new social imaginary when all they could see was just an ethnic barrio, on enemy turf, awaiting God's violent rescue. With these new words their relationship to their context changed—they could recognize despised Babylonians as neighbors with whom they could seek shalom; they could imagine a future in which God's ways were embedded in their hearts and, therefore, in their practices (31:33). The "holding environment" of exile creates an opportunity for generativity. As the exile community absorbed Jeremiah's words and entered into these practices, they began to form an environment for interpretive work concerning God, and their own texts seen from a new context. When avoidance is no longer an option, the old social

---

35. Heifetz et al., *Practice of Adaptive Leadership*, 71–73.

36. Smith, "Jeremiah as Prophet," 95–107; and Smith-Christopher, *Biblical Theology of Exile*.

imaginaries are discredited. The events as interpreted by Jeremiah, given time in the practices he prescribed, were recast as the people engaged their daily work and their reflective work.

The texts of Jeremiah, and probably much of what we call the Old Testament, began to receive renewed attention in Babylon, which led to editorial work and preservation. There was serious theological work to do about the exile (and the preceding experiences) and what it all meant for them as a people. Such work required an interpretive community that became freed from the partisan fights of their generation and from the despair of their situation. Somehow they found and created laments, the Torah came alive, they attended with reformed knowledge to prophets past and present, and in life with each other and with neighbors they lived through probably the most important interpretive work the community had ever experienced. Brueggemann emphasizes this phenomenon: "Exile did not lead Jews in the Old Testament to abandon faith or to settle for abdicating despair, nor to retreat to privatistic religion. On the contrary, exile evoked the most brilliant literature and most daring theological articulation in the Old Testament."[37] This is what we refer to as Jeremiah's interpretive leadership: his corpus, picked up by a community that was being formed in the hermeneutical space created by the letter and its practices, funded the larger work of a community that was rethinking, reimagining, praying, and (with neighbors) practicing its way into a transformed identity and agency.

JEREMIAH AND OUR SOCIAL DISLOCATION

The activities of an interpretive leader during discontinuous change must be rooted in attention to the powers that have shaped/are shaping the situation. In the North American context, if we are to work by analogies,[38] is our work closer to that of Jehoiakim and Hananiah (maintaining the recent interpretive paradigms and securing the prerogatives of institutionalized power) or that of Jeremiah and Baruch (drawing on older texts to reinterpret the current situation, and to provide suitable practices that form an environment for that alternative)? The former option could be framed in a more positive light by asking if our situation (and leadership priorities) are more like David's and Hezekiah's, in which the leadership framework is that of stewarding a governing institution in a context with fewer discontinuous challenges. But this is about something more than choosing textual interpreters; it is

37. Brueggemann, *Cadences of Home*, 3.

38. This mode of working analogically between texts and contemporary community is served well by Hays, *Moral Vision*.

about recognizing God's agency. We do need to be asking: In what ways are the gospel story and the church's story available and formative and powerful for us, and in what ways (per Jeremiah) have we lost essential narratives and meanings? And we need to be asking: In what ways is God on the ground in our communities and neighborhoods, and how are we to practice our way into that generative life?

Jurgen Habermas, in his work on detecting false narratives, notes that a social entity may have imaginations that are colonized, and that communicative action (forming an interpretive community for truth, justice, transparency), rather than strategic planning, holds promise.[39] We believe this framework could be generative for us. The work that Jeremiah began under protest and duress in Jerusalem became uniquely powerful in Babylon. The small learning community, gathered around the texts of Jeremiah and Baruch, became more substantive as they engaged the specified practices in the relocation, and their interpretive activities gained a larger hearing. Conversations and other activities evidently brought Jeremiah's texts and their background into the community's identity and imagination; our Old Testament (even its very existence) bears witness to the new hermeneutics that preserved the ancient texts. Even Jesus' call for a non-governing community of faith, giving witness to God in our lives and words, is funded by Jeremiah's message.

Israel faced (as we must) primary questions about God's initiatives among and around them, and about the vocation generated by God's presence and invitation. Do we know God better when we give up national governance and military options? Is the reign of God better understood if we are taking initiatives concerning the shalom of the other? How can we shift our attention from security and acquisition toward humility and the provisions of God? The chaos of discontinuous change is an opportunity, and the disruption brought about by ecclesial disestablishment is such for us. We also can adopt basic practices of loving God and neighbor, of studying and praying with texts, and of meals and communal labors. Then we can enter demanding work of hermeneutics—concerning context, texts, and our own social agency—and find a provocative and empowering source in the gifts of Jeremiah.[40]

---

39. Habermas, *Reason,* 284–88.

40. Mark notes that colleagues Rob Muthiah and Scott Cormode offered insightful comments and conversation during the writing of this chapter, and Old Testament professors Leslie Allen and Robert Hubbard offered expertise on Jeremiah.

CHAPTER 5

Matthew and Learning Communities

INTRODUCTION

THE YEARS IN WHICH Jesus lived in Israel, and the later years when Matthew wrote what we call the Gospel of Matthew, were shaped by massive social disruptions. Chapter 1 began our engagement with this Gospel.[1] We noted that these economic, religious, and governance circumstances created a disequilibrium that Jesus' listeners and Matthew's readers experienced. What we have in this disequilibrium narrative teaches us a lot about what it means to live and lead when we hope to attend to God as the primary agent. As Jesus speaks and acts, and as Matthew shapes this narrative, they are claiming that God engages human disruptions and that God is a disruptive agent who is continually upending presumptions about how things ought to work in the kingdom. Also, they are making clear that in the disruptions created by Israel's leaders and by the Roman Empire, God is continually present and active. In the Lord of the Rings, the nine members of the traveling fellowship journeyed into encounters, challenges, and provisions that they could not have imagined—and Matthew, knowing the world of his readers, tells the Jesus story in a way that helps them see their own situation more fully—they, too, had entered a world they had never imagined. In their post-Jerusalem fall context they were going to need very different ways of reading themselves, God's agency, and their context, if they were to make any sense

---

1. These materials on Matthew are built on an earlier article, Branson, "Matthew and Learning Communities." Several colleagues have provided important feedback on various drafts: Love Sechrest, Tommy Givens, Susan Maros, and Carson Reed.

of what it meant to be followers of Jesus. From their perspective, how do you make sense of Jesus and Christian life when Jerusalem just got laid waste? Matthew wants them to see that, as people and leaders, they were going to need a new way of going about learning as a community if they were to make sense of their world. This is what we refer to as "learning communities"—specific groups of people who together, through various experiences, modes of leadership, and reflection, become perpetual learners in a manner that attends to God's agency.

The Context of Matthew's Learning Communities

In order to understand how Matthew is shaping learning communities in the midst of disruptive events, we will explore some contextual matters regarding this Gospel's socio-cultural setting and the priorities of the author.[2] At the time of Jesus' earthly ministry, Israel was largely a diaspora people living in communities of faith across the spread of the Roman Empire as well as to the east. These dispersed communities, through festivals, Torah readings, synagogue gatherings, and the practice of Sabbath, nurtured the expectation that God would take up again the promise of restoring Israel in her homeland. Diaspora would end with return. But Rome had occupied their homeland for many years. Empire made the kingdom a distant dream with little possibility of change. Within this narrative there were trade-offs. Alongside the frustration and not infrequent rebellions, Israel had a certain amount of religious and social freedom. These allowances were the trade-offs for compliance in matters of politics, trade routes, taxes, and commodities. Under Augustus, Herod's (d. 4 BCE) realm rivaled David's and Solomon's.[3] Upon Herod's death his realm was divided among his sons. During this later period, including the primary years of Jesus' ministry, Judea was governed by what were called prefects.[4]

The perpetuation of Roman occupation led some Jews in Israel to understand their condition in terms of a continuing exile (paralleling earlier

2. A summary of contextual matters and some background footnotes are in chapter 1.

3. Ferguson, "Herodian Dynasty," in Green and McDonald, eds., *The World of the New Testament*, 64.

4. When Herod the Great died, Archelaus was appointed over Judea, Samaria, and Idumea, but his brutality led to a quick dismissal and the subsequent rule by prefects in those regions, including Pilate during Jesus' ministry. Antipas's tetrarchy included Galilee and Perea, and Philip ruled to the north and east of the Sea of Galilee, so they became players in the Gospel narratives.

captivity in Babylon).[5] Jewish consciousness was, therefore, shaped by some bitter realities: the conviction of a continuing exile wherein God had not yet brought release,[6] the continued diaspora where more Jews lived across the empire and beyond than in the promised land, a vassal relationship with Rome that required the paying of taxes and the giving over of goods to Rome, significant limitations on self-rule, and a growing agitation with the compromises of the Jewish ruling elites around matters that many believed to be central to their self identity, such as the temple and the priesthood.[7]

The Jewish people responded to these realities in a number of ways. Some groups collaborated with Rome, others adopted a stance of minimal cooperation; for some the only option was withdrawal, and for others, up-risings. All of these responses and the tensions they produced are present in Matthew's Gospel, where Jesus is shown continually negotiating all these expectations and behaviors. The Hebrew Scriptures, always present in Je-sus' teachings and Matthew's writing, shaped the imagination, the language world, and the meanings people placed upon their experience of empire in tension with the promises of God.[8] Matthew's Gospel seeks to demonstrate that Jesus is the fulfillment of Hebrew Scripture's expectations while also clarifying that nationalist expectations were misguided. For Matthew, Jesus' teaching aims to reorient and make sense of discipleship in the particularity of these complex, conflicting expectations around what God is doing in a time when the empire seems firmly in control.

We will refer to the author as Matthew, following tradition, and our work here assumes that this Gospel was written in Antioch in the late seventies or early eighties.[9] Antioch was the third largest city of the empire,

5. See Nicholas Perrin, "Exile," in Green and McDonald, eds., *The World of the New Testament*, 25–37; that earlier exile was under consideration in our chapter on Jeremiah.

6. For example, when Jesus preaches from an Isaiah text in the Nazarene synagogue, the word for *release* of prisoners and *to liberate* the oppressed is *aphesis* (Luke 4:18), which can also be translated forgiveness, cancellation of debts, and pardon. See Green, *Gospel of Luke*, 209–13.

7. This is related to their concepts of sin and other topics that Jesus (and Matthew) engage. For example, N.T. Wright engages a major theme: "The most natural meaning of the phrase 'The forgiveness of sins' to a first-century Jew is not in the first instance the remission of individual sins, but the putting away of the whole nation's sins. And, since the exile was the punishment for those sins, the only sure sign that the sins had been forgiven would be the clear and certain liberation from exile." Wright, *Christian Origins*, 273; see also Perrin, "Exile," in Green and McDonald, eds., *The World of the New Testament*, 26–29.

8 This is especially true in connection with the book of Daniel.

9 We are using the author's name according to tradition. Concerning the context of the Gospel's origin, while some recent commentators propose Galilean cities like Sep-phoris or Tiberius, we agree with a substantial number of Bible scholars that the author

with over 200,000 residents shaped by Roman government, trade, military force, and a diverse population. Over the centuries a Jewish diaspora community had grown up there. It had received varied treatment ranging from being favored to experiencing persecution. Christians, as they came to exist shortly after Jesus' resurrection, were an admixture of Jewish and Gentile converts. Like other Christian communities in Roman cities, they were working out their identities as Christians in this relationship between their Jewish origins, including the cultural diversity of those communities, and the increasing cultural diversity shaped by the gospel. These decades featured the expulsion of Jewish believers from synagogues (and from their families).[10] In the midst of this struggle came the news that Rome had violently destroyed Jerusalem and laid waste the temple. This created a new crisis as large numbers of Jewish people and Christian believers fled Titus's legions and the dislocations of Jerusalem. It would have been disorienting not just to those fleeing but also to the Antiochian church. The new arrivals were traumatized. They had lost all their possessions, their communities, geographic roots and practices, livelihoods, and (for many) any vision of a future. What could all that mean for their core narratives, practices, and beliefs? We will look at Matthew's opening texts before we reflect on implications for a theology of leadership.

Matthew 1:1—4:25: Genealogical Framing

The Antiochian learning community brings these recent experiences (new cross-cultural churches, expulsion of Jewish believers from their synagogues, the Roman destruction of Jerusalem), and their Jewish-rooted disappointment regarding God's lack of interference in the empire's aggression, to their reading of Matthew's text. For those with a Jewish heritage, the genealogy of Matthew 1 is both familiar (their own story) and disruptive (for Jews who are not Christians, because it ends with Jesus). Matthew's formation of the three-part genealogy—the three groups of fourteen, rooted in Moses, David, Exile—is a reminder that God saves, provides, and accompanies them. Also, since Jewish believers in Antioch felt the impact of their expulsion from synagogues and the recent destruction of Jerusalem, Matthew's writing helps them see something new that God is doing. They are experiencing the loss of Jerusalem just as they're formed into a church with diverse peoples. Therefore, in the narrative of Jesus' birth, Matthew recalls Jesus' family's flight to Egypt to avoid Herod's slaughter, indicating

had been resident in and was writing to Christians in Antioch, Syria.

10. Brown and Meier, *Antioch and Rome*, 48–49.

an intersection with those in Antioch who had recently fled violence caused by Rome's sacking of Jerusalem. But the Antioch church also hears that this is not just a Jewish story. For non-Jewish readers, the inclusion of Gentiles in the genealogy and the story of the magi show the particular ways that God has previously initiated beyond Jewish ethnicity and nationhood. Also, the magi provide a quiet but unmistakable counter to Roman imperialism. Matthew's craft is a perceptive gift to this church.

Notice what Matthew does not do. Matthew does not avoid the difficult topic of powers and empires and violence. He does not hedge his vocabulary to separate God's initiative as if it does not concern Herod or Rome. He does not give politics and governing to an earthly set of concepts and then bracket something else for God. After the birth passages, in the narrative of the temptations (4:1–11), Matthew wants to show us that temptations regarding bread, power, spectacle, and fame are also relevant to Jesus' purpose and practices. In these brief chapters, Matthew has drawn his readers into a complex matrix of narratives, underlying forces, and an initial glimpse of what it looks like when God engages with new initiatives. Matthew is saying, "Wake up! Are you Jewish? Gentile? Roman? A migrant? Oppressed? Sick? You are in this story!"

Finally, Matthew does not present Jesus' initiative as a solo enterprise—the first four disciples[11] (with others to come) show Jesus' priority of the formation of a learning, action community. Our work below will provide more details on this approach to learning and leadership. These opening four chapters of Matthew communicate that the Antioch church needs to hear that God's initiatives in Jesus are directly engaged in their current context and lives. If Matthew's learning community, by hearing these chapters, has ears and eyes and imaginations opened by what he has written, then they have a framework for receiving and understanding what the following narrative provides.

Before continuing our work on Matthean texts we want to name some important frameworks that help us in this interpretive work, especially in relationship to our questions about leadership. We noted in the first intermezzo that the resources of our own culture can help us in our work. In our brief look at the Beatitudes in chapter 1, and in the above engagement with Matthew's genealogy, birth narratives, and opening comments on Jesus' ministry, we are using various theories about learning communities.

---

11. See Matthew 4:18–22 for the calling of Simon (Peter), and Andrew, plus James and John (sons of Zebedee).

CONTEMPORARY FRAMEWORKS FOR LEARNING COMMUNITIES

In this chapter, as we read Matthew, we will use *learning communities* as the overall framework, along with the related lenses of *social construction* (about how meanings are shaped) and *action-reflection* (as a primary way that we learn). Our engagement with these theories is guided by our own theological commitments, especially our focus on God's agency, the work of leadership in a space-between, and an understanding that humans are subjects rather than objects.

Because we know that our own experiences shape how we understand and engage theories, we begin with a story that reshaped Mark's most basic ways of understanding what it means to be a teacher, a leader of people. During a trip to Nicaragua, Mark met a Christian public health nurse who worked among impoverished villages. She told Mark about what she had learned from Paulo Freire's work in Brazil.[12] Freire, who had a government post focused on adult education, worked with marginalized men and women. He had critiqued what he described as the "banking" approach to education—a standard method in which teachers, acting as experts, deposited their knowledge as content into students. Freire brought a Christian bias for working against oppression, and he fronted a goal of helping these marginalized men and women become "culture creators."[13] As a result of Freire's work, men and women, out of their own experiences and knowledge, were able to understand and change some of the forces at work in their contexts. Freire assisted them to become agents rather than pawns in the midst of powerful economic and political forces. Learning had to involve raising people's consciousness concerning what was happening to them by learning to discover things for themselves through testing and experimenting with actions. The banking method only provided predigested words and definitions for memorization, thus participants would seldom make significant connections with their own experience, and they would not gain new options for living. Instead, Freire saw marginalized people develop concepts for themselves and they engaged collaborative actions for the shaping their own lives. A decade after her training with Freire in Brazil, the nurse had retained only a slice of what she had learned, namely, to work on behalf of the poor citizens of her country and learn about local resources. However, she had resumed her earlier habit of being an expert—she did the research and then passed the information on to the villagers. As a result,

12. Freire's work is described in Freire, *Education for Critical Consciousness*, and *Pedagogy of the Oppressed*.

13. Freire, *Education*, 4, 100n8.

these Nicaraguan villagers never learned *how to learn* about these medicinal resources; they remained dependent on her and other experts, and those she taught would pass on this expert-oriented mode of knowledge. The tragedy was that, despite all her good intentions, her students did not learn to be agents who created local knowledge.

This experience was disorienting for Mark because he saw himself in that nurse. He realized how frequently as a teacher he operated out of the banking model as a deliverer of content. Mark knew Freire's theories, but in terms of the key elements of Freire's work (students are agents of their own learning; learning happens in a repeated sequence of action and reflection; and change occurs through experiments that produce a new consciousness among people[14]), Mark's actions as an educator had remained unchanged. This experience caused Mark to reflect on the practice of what is called Christian education, discipleship, and formation. He started to see why most Christian education and formation programs seldom change much. This insight connects with some of the ways Matthew sought to address the disorientation that had happened to the little Christian communities in Antioch after the destruction of Jerusalem.

Learning Communities

The concept of a community of learning, or *learning community*,[15] is contemporary language that has much to say about how any group of people engages disruptive space, or, in our language, the space-between. It is a learning method for groups to engage the realities of their *context*. We would argue that in disruptive spaces, one of the primary roles of leaders is in the cultivation of a *learning environment*. These terms are important— there is both a larger social environment (the context of life and disruptions in which the group finds itself) and the smaller group space or environment (in which the group and its leaders share experiences and learning).

14. See Freire, *Education*, 101: "Knowledge . . . necessitates the curious presence of Subjects confronted with the world. It requires their transforming action on reality. It demands a constant searching. It implies invention and re-invention. It claims from each person a critical reflection on the very act of knowing."

15. We are influenced by the work of Peter Senge, who emphasizes certain disciplines for learning organizations: "The 'stake' I wanted to put into the ground would establish systems thinking, mental models, personal mastery, shared vision, and team learning and dialogue as inescapable elements in building learning organizations." For Senge, team learning is the fifth and most comprehensive concept; see Senge, *Fifth Discipline*, x. He wants to shift organizations from their preoccupation with *controlling* to an orientation around *learning*. See also Senge, "Leader's New Work" and Senge, *Fifth Discipline Fieldbook*, 351–441.

The leadership work of shaping this group learning environment is about both processes and content—which means that *how* a leader shapes and resources a learning community is as important as *what* the leader wishes for that community to encounter (in experiences and knowledge). Also, it should be noted: this kind of learning often requires unlearning; it involves sustained personal and group reflection; it does not happen without risk. Much more will be said about this in part III of this book. Here we point out the ways in which Matthew's Gospel is working at creating such communities of learning in the radically disorienting space of Roman-occupied Israel and later in Antioch after the fall of Jerusalem.

Even though many of us believe that Christian education is intended to transform lives and churches, we witness such outcomes too infrequently. Our own experiences have led us to see that books and lectures and seminars and curriculums, while requiring significant amounts of time and money and expertise, seldom bring transformative change. But there are notable exceptions—when minds and hearts and imaginations and hands all seemed to move in some new direction. Even more amazing are the times when such moves are more than temporary—when new habits, new ways of being, the overall character of a church and its people, display transformation. This is what we care about—and we will investigate a theological engagement with some contemporary leadership theories in order to reread Matthew in pursuit of the practices that might transform our lives and churches.

Matthew's Gospel presents us with two learning communities: those surrounding Jesus and the believers in Antioch.[16] Jesus and Matthew are engaging the way language is used—how the social constructs of early Judaism and imperial Rome are being challenged by the alternative presented by the presence and articulation of the gospel. We provided examples of this in chapter 1's discussion about the Beatitudes: Rome shapes a social environment with particular understandings concerning provisions and peace, and Jesus counters those meanings with alternatives that are present in God's reign. Social construction is about those uses of language and the consequential activities of those who are formed by the contested meanings. Kenneth Gergen writes about this social construction of our worlds and Paulo Freire describes pedagogy as an action-reflection process. We will

---

16. We are assuming some academic approaches such as narrative, audience, and redaction criticism while not engaging details regarding those methods. The various commentaries we note work with their own mixed methods. With Carter, we believe that much about the audience is "assumed by the text but not made explicit in it." See Carter, *Matthew and Empire*, 5.

briefly summarize these frames as a preface to engaging more deeply with the communities that Jesus and Matthew address.

Gergen and Social Construction

According to social construction theory,[17] we live in a world that is constructed by communities and their words.[18] Gergen writes, "as we communicate with each other we construct the world in which we live."[19] Our words shape how we see; our vocabulary is shaped as it is used in relationships, and it is sustained if a group finds that a world so described is useful. Our conversations and our thinking take shape in the midst of words and the meanings, metaphors, narratives, and grammar that create connections.[20] Members of churches, for example, live inside a world made by language that has been developed by their social locations, sacred texts, and traditions.[21] Conversations and actions are shaped by this construction of a world. Language about "going to church," for example, incorporates the meaning of church as a place or gatherings or events. This indicates that participants believe that church exists when someone travels from elsewhere to the location where church is. Even though teachings in many traditions seek to emphasize that "church" refers to people, no matter where they are, "going to church" remains an understood and common expression regarding reality.[22] Similarly, in North America we are constructed by a meaning

17. Gergen, *An Invitation to Social Construction*; see also Berger and Luckmann, *Social Construction of Reality*.

18. Regarding other perspectives that ask about what is Real, Gergen explains, "constructionism doesn't try to rule on what is or is not fundamentally real. Whatever is, simply is. However, the moment we begin to articulate what there is—what is truly or objectively the case—we enter a world of discourse, and thus a tradition. . . . Even to ask whether there is a real world 'out there' is already to presume the Western view of the person, with a subjective world 'inside' the head and an 'objective' world somewhere outside." Gergen, *Invitation*, 161. This modern framing of object vs. subject is part of the problem that we described in chapter 2.

19. Gergen, *Invitation*, 4.

20. Gergen, *Invitation*, 32–43. Also, see chapter 8 below for some examples of how certain language worlds (such as inside/outside and public/private) have created the ways we act in the world and how leaders see their work in congregations.

21. Alan Roxburgh writes that "beside, or beneath, our public declarations and theological confessions about the nature of the church, there lies a wholly different imagination about who we are and how we act in the world. . . . [S]ome call this a 'social imaginary' while others use the phrase 'language house.'" He emphasizes that we are shaped by particular social constructs "that are largely out of our sight, even while we are articulating another set of beliefs." Roxburgh, *Missional*, 57, 61.

22. Similarly, at least in the West, "mission" has emphasized (a) excursions by

of education that frequently focuses on classrooms, lectures from experts, and students as passive objects of those teachers.

Social construction as a theory highlights the importance of collaboration, of personal and conversational reflection, and of experiments toward learning that makes a difference in lives and contexts.[23] We believe that social construction gives us a way to better understand Jesus with his group of disciples, and Matthew with his Antiochian church. Jesus and Matthew are engaging the way language is used—how the social constructs of first-century Judaism and imperial Rome are being challenged by the alternative presented by the presence and articulation of the gospel.

We also believe that this work with meanings is related to contemporary matters of leadership in light of challenges that churches face concerning social contexts, ecclesial life, and participation in God's mission. Previous chapters have proposed how language and experiences of the last few centuries have powerfully shaped our ecclesiologies and our approaches to leadership. While we are convinced that social construction is a valuable framework, we believe it is critical that it be set within the context of a theological imagination, in this case, that God both works with societal and local meanings while also disrupting those meanings. Therefore, as we read Matthew we must continue to ask questions about what God might be disrupting and creating (in Israel and Antioch) in regard to language and meanings. We will also ask how God might currently use the Gospel of Matthew in our own contexts and churches to disrupt meanings and provide new knowledge and imagination concerning social contexts, ecclesial life, and participation in God's mission.

Freire's Action-Reflection Pedagogy

While certain kinds of learning can occur through books and lectures, most significant learning takes place in the pedagogical cycle of what Paulo Freire called action-reflection.[24] As noted above, Freire described the inadequacy of banking education in which information is deposited from the teacher to the student. Drawing on Aristotle's concept of praxis, Freire saw the need

---

specialists to other lands or to challenging social settings, (b) local programs developed by church experts that on occasion require others to provide money or some volunteer time, or (c) short-term trips for youth or adults that focus on helping some who are "needy" while enhancing personal discipleship. Our conversation is being reframed to prioritize God's missional agency and the vocation of all churches to discern and participate in that mission as it is already on the ground in their contexts.

23. Gergen, *Invitation*, 124–28.

24. Freire, *Pedagogy*, 36, 52–53.

for learners to be fully involved in activities that were directly related to the situation and information in play. He wanted learners to reflect on their own lives and contexts (rather than on disembodied ideas) and as a group they then would engage in reflective work that would lead to experiments and new information.[25] Freire saw the need for learners to be fully involved in their own learning—as subjects rather than as objects. He wanted them to reflect on their lives and contexts and, as a group, experiment, reflect, and act on new learning. As people reflected on their lives, new questions arise that challenge the cultural forces sapping life.[26] Freire observes, "what happens to a greater or lesser degree in the various 'worlds' into which the world is divided is that the ordinary person is crushed, diminished, converted into a spectator, maneuvered by myths which powerful social forces have created."[27] A leader cultivates the spaces that, through action-reflection, increase the capacities of participants to be subjects rather than objects.[28]

Freire was a Catholic layman, spent several years working with the World Council of Churches, and displays a Christian humanism concerning humans bearing God's image and the need inside societies for those who are oppressed and marginalized to be freed. However, his work does not specify our theological emphasis on God's continuing agency—rather he emphasized human responsibility to enact God's priorities. As we emphasized in chapter 3, we believe such an emphasis on humans as subjects—and as being shaped by and shapers of communities—is important for Christian anthropology. We add attention to God's agency as we employ Freire's framework of action-reflection. Specifically, that means our actions take us into contexts and encounters where God is already ahead of us. In our view, personal and group reflections need to give priority to observations and reflections concerning where we see God and what we see God doing.

25. Much of Freire's work was in the context of a military dictatorship in Brazil; and the vocabulary of oppression and liberation was especially useful. He insists that real learning only takes place when the learners are not just acted upon: "It is absolutely essential that the oppressed participate in the revolutionary process with an increasingly critical awareness of their role as Subjects of the transformation." Freire, *Pedagogy*, 121.

26 His proposal was developed in the context of adult education, in which he demonstrated that men and women did not just need to gain literacy that perpetuated their oppressed situation; rather, reflection on their lives would raise questions as vocabulary increased their capacities to understand and challenge the cultural forces that sapped life. His work is engaged by Christian educators, including Groome, *Sharing Faith*, 54, 179; and Pazmiño, *Latin American Journey*, 28–54.

27. Freire, *Education*, 6.

28 Alan Roxburgh notes that by definition, strategic planning objectifies people—they are pieces in a plan. Roxburgh, *Missional Map-Making*, 59–72.

These contemporary authors demonstrate the connections between leadership and learning. Underlying these theories, and specified in the language of *learning communities*, is the assumption that learning is a social activity.[29] This is a lens for how we engage the Gospel of Matthew and the two relevant communities of learning: Jesus and the disciples and the Antiochian Christian communities for whom Matthew is composing his book.

THE GOSPEL AND CONTEXT: GOD'S DISRUPTIVE PRESENCE

We have noted the diversity of Matthew's audience in Antioch. There are Jews who believe in Jesus, some from the diaspora and some from Palestine, including those who have fled the recent Roman destruction of Jerusalem. There are Gentile believers who are beginning to get a perspective regarding God being king in place of Caesar. This Gospel crafts a catechesis (which is a mode of social construction) that speaks into these realities. Matthew helps these Christians gain interpretive capacities for understanding what had taken place so that they can become subject-actors in and of the gospel in Antioch. He does this by connecting the time and place of Jesus' ministry and the time and place of these Antioch realities. Matthew will show that while there are forces at work over which these Christian's have no control, and that these forces work to turn them into the objects of situated powers (example: obey Caesar as Lord), at the same time, they are also subjects or agents of their own lives. In the midst of this context filled with tension, ambiguity, and confusion, he wants them to see that God is present and active. Matthew's Gospel shows that Jesus understood that everyone had capacities (and responsibilities) to engage what he was speaking and embodying, which meant that this mixed young church also had both capacity and responsibility to engage the challenges of Antioch.

Disruptive Tensions Requiring New Interpretive Perspectives

Mark's encounter with the nurse in Central America, and his realization that Paulo Freire's work on learning could be easily lost, give us insights into how

---

29. Other theoretical frameworks, as developed in these chapters of part II, are also worth connecting to our work on Matthew. Most relevant here would be Ronald Heifetz and Marty Linsky's work on *holding environments*, which received attention in the preceding chapter on Jeremiah. See Heifetz, *Leadership Without Easy Answers*, 103–113; Heifetz and Linsky, *Leadership On the Line*. They note their debt to D. W. Winnicott, *Maturational Processes*.

Matthew is framing the story of Jesus' ministry. In Freire's language, Jesus is working with those in Palestine who are on the margins of that society. They are identified as the "crowds," something we observe, for example, in the Sermon on the Mount discussed in chapter 1. They are outside the circles of those who seem to be the real agents, including Rome and the local elites of their society. Here the Sanhedrin, the leaders among the divergent Pharisees and Sadducees, and the scribes and the soldiers are all on the scene as actors who persuade and coerce. They all perpetuate the worlds in which they live—they see and understand and construct and relate in ways that fit the worlds to which they have allegiances. Within these perspectives the crowds had come to see themselves as the objects of abstract forces controlling their lives. Jesus addresses them and their situation in a radically new way. He doesn't teach as one who just provides new content, asking hearers to bank new information and concepts. As the Sermon on the Mount proceeds, Jesus addresses their experience of loss and marginalization by giving them images and stories that assist them to name the forces that are work upon their lives ("you have heard it said to you . . .") and other stories that invite them to become subjects, agents of God's disruptive word ("but I say to you . . ."). Having been overly objectified by the established interpretation of the law, they could now be participants and agents in this new kingdom. Jesus is offering his hearers a social construct that is an alternative to other contextual identities. God has made humans as subjects. Jesus' words and actions invite these crowds to become subjects and agents—not just abstract objects—who can give allegiance to God's reign.

In Antioch, Matthew's readers find themselves cast into a world outside their control. Over a period of years, Jewish believers have been increasingly scorned and dismissed from their synagogues.[30] Now they learn of the destruction of the temple and they experience the massive dislocation of those fleeing Titus's legions. This would have been disorienting not just to those fleeing but also to the Antiochian church, as new arrivals were traumatized and in need, having lost possessions, communities, geographic roots and practices, livelihoods, and (for many) any vision of a future. How can they manage a crisis of these proportions that has fundamentally disrupted not just their everyday lives but the very narratives upon which those lives have been built? It felt like they were bound up in a world of fate over which they had no control. The Gentile believers, having embraced the gospel, still had to face the prejudices of some Jewish believers while also pulling away from the popular religions with their frequent links to whichever Caesar was

---

30. Brown and Meier, *Antioch and Rome*, 48–49.

ruling.[31] For all of them, the forces of Rome appeared infinitely greater than the gospel of Jesus Christ. These Antiochian Christians had been propelled into the space-between. These stories Matthew tells of Jesus' teaching to the crowds in Palestine were not intended simply to give succor but to point to the ways in which these Christians could resist the narratives of fate and embrace a gospel that invites them to become agents in God's kingdom. This was a different imagination and a different way of living in the space-between. Matthew is helping his readers become aware, to gain interpretive capacities, and to be actors in and of the gospel in Antioch.

The Telos of Learning for Matthew

The telos for Matthew's narrative—the end for which he is writing—is the formation of a people who participate in God's present and active reign as revealed and extended in Jesus ("I am with you always" Matt 28:20 NRSV). By crafting a Gospel (a narrative about the good news) regarding Jesus' actions and words, and describing various responses of those who previously encountered Jesus, he is promoting the embodiment and articulation of an alternative social arrangement. This is the work of leaders, in Antioch and today—shaping learning communities, in action-reflection, that help people to continually be attentive to how God's Spirit is constructing the new social world. In this way of addressing the crises of Antioch, Matthew's Gospel emphasizes that: (1) God is the prime initiator, rather than the powers of Rome or Israel's rulers; (2) God's covenant with Israel is clarified and fulfilled through Jesus; (3) a new emphasis on God's initiative beyond Israel to the Gentiles; (4) followers are invited to join with God; (5) God's reign, the eschaton, has begun.

These actions of God are bringing about an alternative social reality that does not yet displace challengers. In Matthew, the "kingdom of the heavens" (plural) and "heaven and earth" denote God's on-the-ground reign and its ongoing ripples. This is a counter not only to imperial Rome, but economic and power collisions with Rome among Jewish elites, and nationalist initiatives among both zealots and other leaders in Israel.[32] These forces must now be seen from God's point of view. This is what Jesus offers

31. Uncertainty was also increased because of civil war within the empire as the Julio-Claudain dynasty was losing to the Flavian dynasty with Vespasian—and that chaos was no doubt felt in Antioch. Johnson, "Roman Emperors," 970.

32 Note the plural "heavens" in Matthew's writing, which is often not translated, and the pairing with "earth"—both forms that denote our explanation but differ from Matthew's use of "kingdom of heaven," using the singular. See Pennington, *Heaven and Earth*, 8, 132, 324–30, 336–48.

his hearers and the Christians in Antioch. Matthew's Gospel is continually reminding its readers that Rome and its elites aren't the primary story. In the disruption, a space-between is constructed. But it will require a Christian imagination that is able to read the world from God's point of view.[33] God's initiatives call for response. As Carter states, "Of supreme importance is that God's 'will be done, on earth as it is in heaven' (6:10). This is to be the central focus of the human heart, relationships, actions, and social structures."[34] Those who respond must shift identity, allegiances, vocations, and actions. But such a response relocates them in this space-between.

READING MATTHEW AS COMMUNITIES OF LEARNING

Our earlier work on the Beatitudes of Matthew 5 (chapter 1), our study of Matthew's writings on Jesus' genealogy and the birth narratives (above), and the foregoing theoretical frameworks prepare us to engage three other passages. The Beatitudes (5:3–8) were a startling announcement. They contradicted much of what Jesus' hearers (and Matthew's readers) assumed. As we explored in chapter 1, Jesus announces blessings on the persons who are not receiving the blessings of Rome (or of Rome's Sanhedrin collaborators). These few verses are a jarring invitation to see the world through God's eyes in the new situation of the incarnation. Jesus is taking familiar language and contradicting the common perception of its meaning. This is social construction. He is, literally, remaking the world through language. From that point in the text, the narrative describes just *how* these blessings are made concrete in Jesus' words and actions. As Jesus acts, and as he calls others to listen and to act, Freire's theory regarding action-reflection as the mode of human learning becomes obvious. Both social construction and action-reflection, understood inside Matthew's emphasis on God's agency, help us see how learning communities are formed. The following three passages give us different elements of what Matthew believes to be critical for those who are learners of God's kingdom as made present in Jesus.

33. Carter writes, "Here it is suggested that the audience of Matthew's gospel quickly learns, and is frequently reminded through a variety of conventions, that the author tells the story from God's point of view. This point of view evaluates all actions, characters, and perspectives." Carter, *Matthew: Storyteller,* 106.

34. Carter, *Matthew: Storyteller,* 232.

Matthew 7: Hallowed be Your Name

In the Sermon on the Mount, following the Beatitudes, Jesus continues to counter the voices of both the Jewish establishment and the Roman Empire. An important element of these teachings is his re-articulation, and clarification, of traditional piety in terms of prayer, fasting, and alms. This is where we have "the Lord's Prayer" (6:7–13) which expresses the social construction of the new space of God's presence and initiatives. This is a prayer of radical in-between space. Many of the words and phrases of this prayer are explicit articulations of language in use by the Romans in order to cement their power and control over people. The first line of the prayer, for example, "Our Father who is in heaven," is far more than just an intimate name for God in order to express care for people. Further, "Bring in your kingdom" is not about some inner, private space of closeted affections. If you were a Christian in Antioch, with the full force of Rome's destructive power in your face, the language of "father" and "kingdom" was radically political. On Jesus' lips it was a language thrown in the face of Rome's claim over their lives.[35] This prayer locates and confesses the primary spaces of contestation for these Christians in terms of their belonging and allegiance. When this is understood in the socially constructed context of Rome where Caesar was king and claimed the right to be known as "father," then the radicalness of this language would call into being these learning communities which, in figuring out the implications, found themselves in the space-between. Furthermore, the "Father" of Jesus' prayer is not in a distant heaven. Jesus is naming and embodying the presence of the Father and the resulting kingdom on earth, in Israel; and Matthew furthers that claim to include Antioch. The Father was right in the midst of the disruption and disorientation; Jesus and Matthew confront all the claims of Rome to have the final word.

Another phrase connects directly with the work of leaders. The second line of the prayer (6:9) emphasizes: "hallowed be your name" (NRSV), or "uphold the holiness of your name" (CEB). In language that may make us uncomfortable, the pray-er is commanding God to become visible and recognized. While some Jewish leaders claim God's authority and Roman rulers even claim God's status, Jesus instructs the learning community to engage God directly by calling on God "to act and thus reveal himself to be the God he is, to make known his exclusive personage."[36] In other

---

35. *Pater Patriae* (Father of the Fatherland) was a title given to some for major military victories as well as to many Roman emperors, including, among others, Julius, Augustus, Caligula, Claudius, Nero, Vespasian, Titus, and Domitianus. Purcell, "Pater Patriae."

36 Malina and Rohrbaugh, *Social Science Commentary on the Synoptic Gospels*, 272;

words, this is not a spiritualizing request to have some special beatific vision disconnected from life on the ground, but the opposite. Because others work to co-opt God, to claim God's place, and to manipulate God's image through actions and words to their own ends, Christians are called upon to pray that God distinguishes God's presence and status and actions from all claimants and misrepresentations right here in the ordinariness of everyday life. The Sermon on the Mount (and subsequent teachings) addresses many behaviors regarding social arrangements, money and property, power, and piety, and this one request for God to reveal God's presence and actions is the center of it all.

This is a prayer that invites the learning community into the disruptive spaces in which God is already acting. In this sense, these Christian communities are learning how to appropriately desire God's name (meaning God's person and actions) so that God is made visible for them (and others) in various geographic, socio-political contexts.

Matthew 9:35—11:1: Calling and Sending the Twelve

In Matthew 9, Jesus names his primary learning community—now constituting the Twelve (10:2–4)—who are called as subjects into the action-reflection sequence. Matthew describes how Jesus views the crowds: "he had compassion for them, because they were troubled and helpless, like sheep, without a shepherd" (9:36) and that this situation, to switch metaphors, is a plentiful harvest (9:37). These metaphors (sheep and harvest) shape the world in which Jesus' disciples and Matthew's Antiochian church live. The multiple crowds, so described, lead to Jesus' naming of the Twelve, and we assume they have already been schooled in Jesus' praxis because they are immediately sent to do what they have been observing and experiencing in the presence of Jesus. They have listened, followed, and observed (actions), had times for conversations and consideration (reflections), and are now sent into new action. This work of Jesus is now the work of the Twelve.[37]

The instructions to the Twelve form what is considered by some commentators to be the "sermon" of this teaching. The Twelve now need to not only announce the kingdom of heaven, they are to do the same works that Jesus has been doing. God has hallowed God's name (see above) and now they participate. This affirms their agency. And as preceding chapters affirm,

---

this quote is about the same wording in Luke 11:2.

37 As the section progresses, it is obvious that the text has much to do with Matthew's audience and its disruptive context; see Luz, *Studies in Matthew*, 144–9; Davies and Allison, *Critical and Exegetical Commentary*, 179.

there is more to Jesus' inauguration than words; the brokenness that God is addressing includes bodies, powers, politics, and economics. They enter villages and homes; they work and eat in the local context, listening to the stories and observing the environment. They heal and exorcise demons and tell stories about what they have seen and heard in their experiences with Jesus. In the instructions, Jesus is making them dependent on people they don't know; he even now calls the Twelve "sheep" (10:16). Their dependence, which requires a shift in the power arrangements, makes it more likely that others will listen to them.[38] And Matthew, after earlier and later indications about the inclusion of Gentiles, emphasizes here that Jesus sent the Twelve to "the people of Israel," even though they are in Samaria and the mixed countryside of Galilee. The new emphasis on inclusion does not mean jumping over the Jews—the new community in Antioch needs to hear that Jewish and Gentile believers belong together.

Jesus' words stress dangers in their context—they are among wolves. These learning communities (the disciples/apostles around Jesus and the Antiochian church) are to be under no illusion about the world they work in. Those who are suffering floggings or expulsion from synagogues, as well as those arriving in Antioch after Titus's conquest, hear these words of Jesus in that horrific context. A strange comfort arises in knowing that this is not a surprise; Jesus' teaching included how to continue in the midst of such trauma, and Matthew's instructions refer more specifically to the challenges familiar to those in Antioch (10:16–31).

In this kind of learning community, leaders need to give work to the learning team in a way that encourages numerous small experiments.[39] While the Twelve in Palestine might not grasp this quickly, the Antiochian church has already witnessed the kind of boundary crossing that reveals God's initiatives. Their speaking and acting among neighbors (locally and elsewhere) is with the conviction that God's grace is for all *ethnoi* (something that is foreshadowed in Matthew but not specifically named until in chapter 28). It is in this action-reflection that these learning communities are continuing to become the new reality that Jesus names and embodies. The benefits and costs of being subject-agents are emphasized; these learning teams might have seen themselves as oppressed objects, but Jesus and Matthew place their role as agents with God right in the middle of this action-reflection sequence.

38 See Roxburgh, *Missional*, especially chapters 9–11; Roxburgh is working with the parallel passage in Luke.

39 As noted earlier, this kind of learning, in contexts of disruptive challenges, is what Ronald Heifetz and others name as requiring "holding environments"; we also noted this framework in the preceding chapter on Jeremiah.

Matthew 28:1–20: Disciples Suitable for Disruptions

Where is Matthew going with his narrative? What does he want from the Antiochian Christians? If heard and received, what does the text do with and among them? This final chapter (28) provides a focus. Chapters 26 and 27 have narrated the arrest, crucifixion, and burial of Jesus. The account features the assertive work of some Jewish leaders, the betrayal of Judas, the banality and violence of Roman bureaucracy, mockers, a centurion who correctly identifies Jesus as God's son, faithful women, a wealthy follower who provides a burial, and guards posted to prevent any body-stealing scheme.

For Matthew, Mary and Mary are key agents in the resurrection narrative (28:1–10). An angel, after scaring the guards into trances, shows them the empty tomb and says that Jesus will meet them in Galilee, which has been a primary geographical context for Jesus' words and actions. As they ran to tell the disciples, Jesus met them, received their worship, and commended them to tell "my brothers." Then Matthew provides a brief note about the real attempt at a scheme—some priests and elders paid the soldiers to spread a lie about what happened. Notice here the opposing attempts at social construction—the angel, Jesus, and the women tell one story about a resurrected Jesus and the coming meeting in Galilee; the soldiers, paid by priests and elders, spread an invented account.

In 28:16–20, Matthew further shapes a trajectory. With Mt. Sinai and Mt. Carmel in the background, these threads reach back into previous chapters; for example the mountain may be a reminder of the early sermon (5:1) and/or the visit with Moses and Elijah (17:1–8); baptism was significant at the beginning of the story; and authority regarding peoples and events have been themes throughout. The lenses of social construction and humans as subjects/agents make numerous connections between Jesus' learning community and the Antioch church. What reality has been constructed and revealed? What does it mean to be agents along with Jesus/God?

Concerning authority, the disciples had experienced Jesus' actions and teachings as often countering the existing authorities. His resurrected presence with them now demonstrated that what these authorities deemed their ultimate weapon (death) was not effective. So the response that listeners had voiced to the Sermon on the Mount—"he was teaching them like someone with authority and not like their legal experts" (7:29)—becomes an understatement. The disciples are now told how comprehensive Jesus' authority is ("all authority in heaven and earth"—28:18), and this word translated "authority" (*exousia*) can also be translated as "power." Now they are commissioned to live into that authority; it is power that is to be shared.

For the Antiochian Christians, authority was experienced as the systems of the empire, the workings of synagogue life, the Jerusalem council, and apostles (Barnabas, Paul, and others itinerating as prophets and teachers). With the destruction of the temple, the questions of authority are no longer Jerusalem-centered. Jesus' authority has been experienced in Antioch in healings, prophetic words, and the sending of missionaries. Now, even though Roman violence is real, it can no longer be decisive—Jesus has all authority, Rome does not. Just as the crucifixion and Titus's troops seemed to demonstrate the finality of Rome's authority, Jesus' resurrection and his authority have become definitive. The social construction of Christian identity in the disorienting space-between was being shaped around a reorientation of authority vis-à-vis synagogues, governors, rulers, and Rome. Jesus' claim to "all authority" at the end of Matthew is critical for living in the space-between.

The grammar of the text is revealing—there are three participles in Jesus' commissioning ("having gone," "baptizing" and "teaching") and one imperative (usually translated as "make disciples" but perhaps better translated with the command "mentor"). "Having gone" indicates Jesus' assumption that his followers will be in new geographies. So, in Matthew's account, Jesus assumes the learning community is already distributed, whether in Antioch or elsewhere. The imperative "mentor" is to be an engagement with *ethnos* ("nations")—which is not an individualistic focus but life in and among communities that does not erase those communities. "Baptizing," as a reference back to John the Baptist, is about changing "hearts and lives" (3:11). The focus is on changed allegiance[40]—to Jesus' teachings and the new community formed as participants in the Father, Son, and Holy Spirit—which is a powerful reorientation for Antiochian believers in their chaotic situation. "Teaching," with reference to all that Jesus has said, works against the idea of spreading a crafted minimalist collection of affirmations. Among various peoples, in differing circumstances, he had acted and spoken in light of the presence of the kingdom and, from Matthew 10, includes learning from those they teach. He had spoken life into the wounds, injustices, illnesses, and despair. He had noticed and commended faith. He had located blame for sorrows and bad leadership. He spoke of alternative lives for listeners and opponents. Mentoring is to include this full array.

So how does this narrative move forward? How does Jesus' authority find expression in new geographies? In the modern West, discipleship tends to be about structured programs that manage knowledge (doctrine) and behaviors (conforming to the group that is delivering the goods). So a

---

40. Carter, *Matthew and the Margins*, 552.

disciple is one who thinks and acts "like us," which fits the "banking" model of education that Freire critiques. Something far more challenging is happening in Matthew. The book is not about Jesus making a *learned* group; rather he is shaping a *learning* community; he wants new habits rather than just new doctrines. Without the capacity to observe, remember, and discern *in situ*, they cannot be learners—because that is the essence of discipleship. Their learning from Jesus does not stop here on the Galilean mountain—he promises to be with them in the diffusion of the gospel into new places. In his teaching and actions, he has drawn attention to and engaged those whose current praxes that are expressions of life with God—generosity, justice, humility, kindness, faith—which indicate availability to and a witness to the kingdom of God. A disciple, a learner—someone with the habits of perpetual action-reflection—will notice that God's name is hallowed (when God's presence and ongoing actions are revealed) in every new context. This is a new space in which Jesus continues to initiate and followers are commissioned to shape learning communities that discern and participate in new geographies in coming days and years. Matthew quotes Jesus' emphasis regarding this core reality: "I myself will be with you every day until the end of this present age" (28:20).

SUMMARY AND CONCLUSION

This exploration of Matthew's Gospel emphasized specific elements of leadership: learning communities (the work of a leader regarding a group of people so their behaviors, beliefs, and allegiances are changed), social construction (how a leader engages a group in order to create meaning), and action-reflection (how a leader focuses on experiences and reflection as a group learns). In Jesus' leadership with the disciples, and in Matthew's leadership with the church of Antioch, they agreed to several activities in the midst of social disruptions and dehumanizing power dynamics. God's initiatives provided the substance of what needed to be learned. Jesus and Matthew were tuning their communities to pay attention, listen, engage, and reflect. These communities needed to be fully reoriented around the announced presence of God's reign. This learning is disruptive and creative, and leaders have the role of resourcing an environment with attentiveness, activities, and modes of reflection that increase each group's competencies for discerning God's initiatives so that participation increases.

CHAPTER 6

Acts: Luke's Narrative on God's Disruptions

INTRODUCTION

LUKE'S TWO-VOLUME PROJECT HAS sometimes been read as an evangelistic apologetic for the gospel, or as a message to Rome that the church is not a threat to its power, or as a play-by-play documentary, or as an account about the triumph of the gospel against all odds. Our engagement tends toward a more prosaic reading. As a skilled listener, observer, and theologian, Luke is engaged with large contextual matters (the Roman Empire, the Jewish roots of the church, and the mashup cultural elements of Greek philosophies and various mystical religions) and with particular, local experiences of both itinerant and residential Christians. For Luke, this is all about theology—not as an effort toward a system of belief but as a practical matter of recognizing God's ongoing presence and initiatives ahead of the church and in service of nurturing believers toward discernment and participation.[1] As Luke Timothy Johnson notes, "human agents of this expansion had to struggle to keep up with God's initiative and understand it."[2] That is what Luke is narrating.

---

1. Johnson, *Acts of the Apostles*, 7: "Luke's Apology is rather in the broadest sense a theodicy. His purpose is to defend God's activity in the World."

2. Johnson, *Acts of the Apostles*, 8.

Setting Up Luke's Narrative in Acts

In Acts chapter 1, Luke names the context and sets his narrative in motion. After the resurrection of Jesus, on a day we now celebrate for his ascension, the apostles asked about the timing for restoring Israel as a kingdom. Leading up to this, Jesus had been "speaking to them about God's kingdom" (1:3)—so their question leads Jesus to make the theological connection with the Holy Spirit: "It isn't for you to know the times or seasons that the Father has set by his own authority. Rather, you will receive power when the Holy Spirit has come upon you, and you will be my witnesses in Jerusalem, in all Judea and Samaria, and to the end of the earth" (1:7–8). Jesus' reply is not about *when* but *how* they will live into the kingdom. In the turmoil of Jerusalem, under the persecution of Roman agents and the collaboration of Sanhedrin rulers, and then throughout the following decades that Luke will be describing in this book, he frames his narrative in answer to those who interpret their circumstances as undermining their legitimacy and power. There were numerous imaginations in Israel, and among these early believers, concerning expectations regarding God's promises. Prophetic texts shaped their hopes: swords into plowshares, every man sitting under his own vine, and leaders who would judge with equity (Isa 2:3–4; Mic 4:4; Isa 11:4). Some hoped for Jewish leaders who would be more attuned to Israel's Mosaic heritage; others assumed that the kingdom would include a militaristic god who would counter Rome. Willie Jennings reflects on this chapter from our own modern contexts by paraphrasing the disciples' question: "When will we rule our land and become self-determining, and if need be impose our will on others?" He finds parallels with current ethnocentric desires, which arise from vulnerability along with histories of wounds and loss. Jennings describes this as a fantasy "of being self-determined and wielding power over others, and power to control our own destiny. It drives the creation of walled communities, border patrols, and checkpoints."[3] God is initiating something else.

The prophetic tradition connected the coming of the Spirit with God's promised coming; Peter preaches on these texts in Acts 2. So Jesus emphasizes that, rather than presiding over changes framed by various views about restoring Israel, such as a governmental regime change, he promises God's continuing presence (as the Holy Spirit) and thus authorizes their ongoing embodiment ("power") and messaging ("witness") far beyond Israel. Jennings explains two meanings of *witness*—that of being storytellers regarding what they have seen and heard in their experiences with Jesus,

---

3. Jennings, *Acts*, 17.

and continuing to be witnesses of God's ongoing presence in the actual places that are named. In Judea and Samaria and to the ends of the earth, as Jennings writes, Jesus "goes ahead of his disciples into the real places of this world."[4] Instead of embracing the various visions of Jewish partisans, including the hope of some for a theocratic state to disempower Rome in Palestine, the new way is that of becoming a people who are continually engaged with God on the ground, "to the end of the earth," as Jesus announces.

As we wrote in chapter 1, Luke is aware that many churches have reasons to be discouraged. The traveling teams and many local churches have experienced suffering, both from Roman powers and from synagogue leaders. Perhaps they wonder just what Jesus meant concerning the promised power when their experiences, noted in Acts and in Pauline letters, describe violent opposition, rejection, and discouragement (e.g., Acts 7:51–60, 9:4–5; Rom 8:16–17; Gal 6:12; Phil 1:29–30; 1 Thess 2:14–16; 3:3–4; 2 Tim 1:8; 2:3; 3:12). They longed for an end to the suffering, sought to be engaged in the promised Holy Spirit power, and believed that Jesus' return could happen at any time. They were confused when many Jews and Gentiles did not accept Jesus as the way for Israel's restoration and the recreation of the world. They wondered how, as a marginalized band, they could be faithful witnesses. Luke meets their confusion and despair with a theological reading that, without denying their very real experiences, posits an interpretation of these stories, and majors in God's apocalypse (God's continual self-revelation). Their imagination is not adequate. God *is* being revealed continually, in town after town, and at the center of the empire. This is not a triumphalist reading set on conquering the empire or on displacing Judaism—rather Luke is insisting that careful theological attention will provide confidence and wisdom toward faithful, energized, discerning participation in God's mission.

Acts 2: Pentecost & Praxis

Our work in chapter 1 with the story about Peter and Cornelius began to explore how the framework of improvisation might help us understand Luke's narrative in Acts. This approach, with additional conceptual frameworks, will now begin at an earlier place in Luke's text, with a focus on Acts chapter 2. After the eleven apostles received holding instructions in Acts 1, they continued in prayer with over one hundred other men and women, and they selected a twelfth member.[5] On the day of Pentecost they had gath-

---

4. Jennings, *Acts*, 18–19.

5. After deciding to replace Judas, they attended to both ancient and recent

ered in a home. This Jewish feast had become a celebration of the giving of Torah,[6] and the book of Jubilees made connections with the covenants with Noah, Abraham, and Moses.[7] As described by Luke, this first Pentecost after the resurrection of Jesus, in addition to being an audio-visual spectacle, focused on languages, borders, ethnicities, power arrangements, belonging, and agency. Israel was literally an occupied country; some Jews saw that as a problem while others were aligned with that arrangement.[8] Green writes, "Luke's account constitutes a profoundly theological and political statement displacing Babel—and Jerusalem—and Rome-centered visions of a united world in favor of an altogether different sort of community."[9]

The Festival of Shavuot (Weeks), unlike Pesach (Passover), was only one or two days long. (God knows that when a farmer begins a grain harvest in late spring, and leaves home to sacrifice the first sheaf, it is not the time for a week of picnics or liturgies.) Jerusalem likely had pilgrims who could either make the walk or were not tied to agrarian work, but this festival was not a major attraction for international pilgrims (though some from Rome are noted). That contextual reality may serve to clarify our reading of the Acts text. After recounting that believers were in prayerful waiting, Luke describes a roaring wind, a visual anomaly akin to flames, and a cacophony of diverse languages. Then Luke tells us about the people.

> Now there were devout Jews from every nation under heaven living in Jerusalem. And at this sound the crowd gathered and was bewildered, because each one heard them speaking in the native language of each. Amazed and astonished, they asked, "Are not all these who are speaking Galileans? And how is it that we hear, each of us, in our own native language? Parthians, Medes, Elamites, and residents of Mesopotamia, Judea and Cappadocia, Pontus and Asia, Phrygia and Pamphylia, Egypt and the parts of Libya belonging to Cyrene, and visitors from Rome,

---

traditions, the number twelve, a prayer for guidance, and a traditional form of hearing from God (casting lots).

6. Perhaps this connection had not yet been made, per Witherington, *Acts of the Apostles*, 131.

7. Chilton, "Festivals and Holy Days," 374. For further descriptions, including length of holidays and conversion to modern calendars, see Rich, "Jewish Holidays."

8. This gospel challenge to power arrangements is noted in Acts 4. Luke writes, "the priests, the captain of the temple guard, and the Sadducees confronted [Peter and John]" because their preaching that the resurrection had occurred meant the restoration of Israel—something that messed with the institutional arrangements that these players wanted to perpetuate. Johnson notes this as a contest about Israel regarding leadership—the Sanhedrin or the Apostles. Johnson, *Acts*, 80–81.

9. Green, *Luke as Narrative Theologian*, 133.

> both Jews and proselytes, Cretans and Arabs—in our own lan-
> guages we hear them speaking about God's deeds of power."
> (Acts 2:5–11 NRSV)

These people of the diaspora represented a significant geographic spread, far beyond weekend treks. Based on grammar ("living in Jerusalem" rather than "visiting")[10] and the shortness of the festival, it is likely that many of these Jews (including proselytes) were senior citizens who had relocated to Jerusalem, perhaps with other family members, for their retirement years.[11] They brought their diverse languages with them and probably set up life in neighborhoods so they could maintain regional customs and conversations.[12] Like other residents of Palestine, they were accustomed to the empire's language of Greek, and everyone could function in that common language. They were "bewildered" to hear their regional, parochial languages from these Galileans—this perpetuated their own resistance to the empire. Luke credits the entire event to God's Spirit, which is consistent with how the Spirit makes concrete the life and mission of God.[13]

This account specifies that God is initiating, but not in a way that would indicate that God is solving Israel's problem with Rome. So, in Luke's account, believers have the role of paying attention before trying to discern some subsequent steps (more on improvisation, below). In addition to clarity concerning God's agency is the priority on alterity. This transitional and defining event places emphasizes (1) the naming of many locations and cultures of the diaspora; (2) the recognition that cultural diversity was embodied in these groups as they settled into this geographic setting; (3) the use of diverse languages even when a dominant language is available;

10. Green, *Luke as Narrative Theologian*, 138n22; also see Johnson, *Acts of the Apostles*, 43.

11. This situation becomes even more explicit when the poverty of Hellenist widows surfaces as a challenge in Acts chapter 6. This makes clear that some immigrant couples suffered the death of the husband, and the widows, without the resources they may have had in their previous location, were needing new networks of care.

12. Language is a mode of group life, often to counter oppression. Joel Green writes that "Pierre Bourdieu [observes] that the adoption, extension, and maintenance of official language are bound up with the genesis and social uses of the state," so the Spirit's engagement with parochial languages is a form of rearranging such powers. Green, *Luke as Narrative Theologian*, 144.

13. Even though some theological perspectives indicate that the Holy Spirit is primarily ethereal, Craig Van Gelder posits, and we agree, that the Holy Spirit's presence in the Bible indicates concrete, located, specific activities of God on the ground. This is especially relevant to our topic because a key role of leadership is that of discerning, with a group, how they can participate in God's initiatives. See Van Gelder, *Ministry of the Missional Church*, 23–46.

and (4) the inclusion and potential agency of senior citizens.[14] As Jennings writes, "This new world order begins with collapse."[15] Social arrangements are to be redefined in this post-resurrection coming of the Spirit. The gospel will not be preserved inside prescribed borders, languages, generations, or ethnic groups—rather, this confounded group, awakened to God's new work, begins to engage each other regarding "what does this mean?" (2:12). Peter's interpretive work, rooted in prophetic teachings about the Holy Spirit, names the otherness that God is engaging: sons, daughters, young men, old men, slaves, women, all who are far away (thus emphasizing the geographic and cultural scope). As Luke continues to show, over the coming months and years, Peter will struggle with that trajectory.

As we explained in intermezzo 1, practical theology is the work of a community as it pays attention to experiences and reflects on those experiences by engaging stories ("here's what I heard"), and noting cultural elements ("those Galilean men were speaking in our languages"), while also looking to the community's texts (like Peter's quoting of the prophet Joel plus the Psalms). So Peter's sermon plays the role of weaving in previous Scriptures while also naming God as the initiator of something new. Then Luke describes the community's actions: devotion to gospel teachings (obviously a new curriculum), time together (evidently across parochial boundaries), "the prayers" (probably traditional prayers like the Psalms), sharing material goods,[16] worship in the temple (as before or perhaps more frequently), shared meals in their homes (with attention to gratitude), and giving praise to God. This is a notable mix of new and old—traditional enough to be recognizably Jewish (thus "having the goodwill of all the people") but different enough to draw attention and welcome converts. It is obvious, though, that this is not a normative strategy but an appropriate improvisational response by those who were in this place and at this time.[17]

Leadership, other than Peter's preaching and the note about the "teaching of the apostles," seems to be dispersed. The leadership of gathering, study, sharing, prayers, and meals is widely diffused. Peter's sermon sanctioned diversified participation (sons, daughters, young, elders) in witnessing and prophesying as the Holy Spirit's activities continue. Luke's work is descriptive and interpretive rather than imperative. Readers can ask important questions about what activities might merit adopting (studying?

14. Witherington, *Acts of the Apostles*, 135.

15. Jennings, *Acts*, 35.

16. This sharing receives more attention toward the end of Acts 4 and following. The connection between the gospel and property/money is developed throughout Acts.

17. Johnson connects this description with the wide use of idealized "foundation" stories; Johnson, *Acts of the Apostles*, 62.

praying the Psalms? selling extra homes?) but we are left with what Luke narrates: God initiates and we engage with discernment and improvisation. Some with authority are often tempted to prescribe or control, but this early sequence challenges any moves that focus on rules and regulations. Leaders, those with initial authority and those scattered in the neighborhoods, apparently shaped spaces for conversations and discernment and witness, and experiments at embodying the gospel.

CONTEMPORARY FRAMEWORKS

As readers of Acts who are formed by the habits and frameworks of our own contemporary organizations (churches, schools, non-profits), we want to promote competencies for being aware and intentional about when and how we adopt theoretical resources for reading Scripture, interpreting our contexts, and taking steps of leadership. Our first three chapters began the work of naming our resources—Scripture, cultural studies, and theology. Then in the chapters on Jeremiah and Matthew, we engaged theories regarding learning communities, social construction, the sequence of action-reflection, and interpretive leadership. All of these theories continue to be helpful in reading Acts, and theories regarding improvisation, diffusion, and alterity will now receive explicit engagement.

Improvisation

Studies regarding improvisation in organizations have been underway for several decades.[18] Some authors note that improvisation can be valuable when habits of planning cannot provide adequate maps and control. Just as important, we believe, improvisation is not just for exceptional times— rather it is important during normal, less stressed, more mundane times of Christians loving God and neighbors. Sam Wells writes about improvisation as a practice for "how the church may become a community of trust in order that it may faithfully encounter the unknown of the future without fear."[19] At the core, improvisation "diverges in some way from prior plans and habits."[20]

---

18. For an extensive collection of authors and chapters, see Cunha et al., eds., *Organizational Improvisation*.

19. Wells, *Improvisation*, 11–20.

20. Fisher and Amabile, "Creativity, Improvisation and Organizations," 42.

The literature on improvisation and organization frequently draws on improv theater and jazz regarding group interplay and actions. Improv requires both tradition (the practices and texts of the art) and spontaneous engagement (as a group engages collaboratively with a specific situation). Most descriptions of improv include four actions: (1) be present, including being aware of your surroundings or context; (2) say "yes" to what is offered to you by another participant; (3) say "and"—which means you are to add to what you received; and (4) release the situation to others. For example, actors are on stage with wooden chairs and tables, then one actor says, "Jean, why are we in a meeting while the whole city is partying?" Jean cannot say "no" by changing what she received (by ignoring key elements of what was handed to her); instead she moves the narrative forward, "Party? What party! Bill, no one told me about a party!" Participants need to be attentive at all times, ready to engage with "yes . . . and," and to release whatever is shaped for others to form. There is no script; no one is controlling; no one is passive; the end is not known. As is true regarding all of the conceptual frameworks we are using, we consider God to be a prime active agent in these sequences—participating in all aspects of the context, people, actions, and consequences. God is initiating regarding what is offered to the group; God is active in the group's receptivity and discernment; God is engaged in the subsequent steps. As we already noted in the Peter-Cornelius-God story (chapter 1), we have a narrative of how Peter responded to what he received (from God, from Cornelius, from those gathered at Cornelius's house), and he continues to reference God in what he perceives and how he acts.

Patricia Shaw and Ralph Stacey, authors of *Experiencing Risk, Spontaneity and Improvisation in Organizational Change,* focus on the framework of "working live."[21] Ken Kamoche, Miguel Pina e Cunha, and João Vieira da Cunha, key researchers regarding improv and organizations, name key elements: (1) the concept/ideas and execution happen simultaneously—this disallows assembling expert theories that are then applied in a situation; (2) improvisation is deliberate—humans are genuine agents; (3) it is extemporaneous—scripts and detailed plans are foregone; (4) it happens in the midst of action—the improvisation is attentive to and connected to a fabric of contextual activities; (5) appropriateness can only be evaluated in hindsight; rather than power and control, improv is about risk and experiments. There are important elements of bricolage—making do with what is at hand—in

---

21. Shaw, "Introduction." Shaw and her coauthors build on the earlier work by Cunha et al., eds., *Organizational Improvisation.*

improvisation, which emphasizes the organizational knowledge of and capacities to work with existing resources.[22]

As leaders shape a learning environment that is suitable for improv, Cunha, et al. specify some conditions.[23] First, for an organization to foster improvisation, it needs to promote experiments. Risk-taking must be promoted and rewarded, which can be encouraged by "an aesthetic of imperfection." Leaders need to promote storytelling about risk for this trait to be diffused in the organization. Second, rather than detailed regulations and restrictive silos, improv thrives if scripts and structures and controls are minimal. Third, space for improvisation is more generative when there are few controlling routines, so rather than inheriting traditions of tight structures, the improv group thrives with memories that provide stories and imagination supportive of experiments. In our modern context, as we noted in chapter 2, organizations and leaders foster an "emphasis . . . on predictability and the removal of uncertainty. This exclusive focus renders rationally invisible the unpredictable, emotional, responsive, and spontaneous aspects of what people are doing in organizations."[24] Leadership that fosters becoming aware of God's initiatives and receiving those initiatives, as they arise in everyday life with neighbors and each other, will tend to improvise with what is already occurring while nurturing this "working live" as normative.

This mode of activity is not about exceptional individuals or experts.[25] Just as important as the resulting next steps, leaders and participants will be changed in the process.[26] Friis emphasizes that if a participant is not being changed, then they are not really present.[27] Thus among the positive

22. Cunha et al., "Organizational Improvisation," 309.

23. Cunha et al., "Organizational Improvisation," 318–21.

24. Stacey, "Complex Responsive Processes," 124–39. Stacey is proposing an alternative to the more common systems theories that he sees as too mechanistic. This parallels Kant who, in introducing systems as an interpretive option, warned against its helpfulness when dealing with humans. In this theoretical work, Stacey notes that humans are both subjects and objects, that meaning is developed in gestures and responses, that communication is both predictable and unpredictable, and continual learning is valued over staid habits.

25. Friis and Larsen, "Theatre, Improvisation and Social Change," 29.

26. Cunha et al. refer to Robert Greenleaf's proposal of rotating leadership, which is based on the assumption that participants are changing in the midst of the ongoing creative processes. This helps a group avoid conforming repeatedly to one person's expectations. See Greenleaf, *Servant Leadership*; Cunha et al., "Organizational Improvisation," 312.

27. Friis, "Presence and Spontaneity in Improvisation," 89–91.

outcomes of improvisation are flexibility and learning,[28] and this flexibility is about thinking, seeing, relating, and testing. Theologian L. Gregory Jones emphasizes this relational aspect of improv—with an emphasis on diversity in horizontal connections.[29] Learning means more skills and more capacity that arise because of alterity—the diverse participants and their contributions.

Sam Wells notes that the Christian script (Scripture) requires more than repetition or even interpretation: "When Christians, whether scholars in a colloquium or parishioners in a house group, whether bishops in a retreat house or aid workers in a field station, gather together and try to discern God's hand in events and his will for their future practice, they are improvising, whether they are aware of it or not." So the key question is not *whether* we improvise but *how well* we improvise. Well's description of how communicative participation builds in the midst of the activities gives us a picture of listening and engaging in collaboration with the prompts of the Spirit.[30]

Diffusion

Diffusion theory is about how an idea, practice, or object is communicated and adopted throughout a social system or across social networks.[31] For example, a process (or a practice) for precise timing of crop irrigation spreads through rural families and tribes in a drought-stricken region, or a newly invented cell phone (object) penetrates the market of a society. The most thorough research, along with interpretive insights, has been featured in five editions of Everett Roger's *Diffusion of Innovations*. Such diffusion always includes both uncertainty, as the new option is weighed, and social change,

---

28. Cunha et al., "Organizational Improvisation," 327–30.

29. Jones, *Christian Social Innovation*, 69. Jones's book is mainly about organizational innovations; a brief section on improvisation as a needed step toward innovation emphasizes continual learning that is sustained by practices and always interdisciplinary, a bias toward accepting rather than "blocking" (in improv terms) while also being aware that some gifts ("offers") need to be recognized as problematic, and relational connections that are with the past and with a wide contemporary diversity (65–72).

30. Wells, *Improvisation*, 65–70. "There is trust and respect for oneself and the other actors. There is alertness and attention. There is fitness and engagement. . . .There is an aptitude for altering and playing with status roles, for relating to others, remembering, sustaining, and developing character, and sensing the shape of a story" (80). Wells uses the word *play* to emphasize the freedom what participants have when they don't have a predetermined outcome and there is real receptivity to each other's contributions (128).

31. Rogers, *Diffusion of Innovations*, 5, 12.

as it achieves acceptance.[32] In Acts, the diffusion concerns how the gospel spreads so that individuals and their social groups adopt the beliefs and practices of God's reign as exhibited and proclaimed by Jesus Christ and his followers. In our work in leadership development, we are also interested in how beliefs and practices about God's agency, discernment, participation, and the work of leaders is diffused through churches and their networks. Obviously, Rogers does not attend to how God is already on the ground, ahead of any human initiatives. The Spirit is engaged in experiences, relationships, opportunities, and the consequences of decisions and steps. Those stories, in biblical texts and in our own lives, give witness to the diffusion of the gospel.

For diffusion to take place, Rogers noted that four elements are needed: an innovation (an idea, process, or object that is new or significantly reconfigured), channels of communication (including senses and all the dynamics of human interaction), time (for movement of information and for the impact of experiences), and the diverse members of social systems (within and between various groups).[33] While the word *innovation* is inadequate for the gospel, we can see the new expressions of God's initiatives as they are articulated in some passages we have examined. In the Acts passages we have examined so far (Acts 10–11 in chapter 1 and Acts 2, above) the diffusion of something new is a priority for Luke. In the Pentecost event and in the story of Peter and Cornelius, these elements of diffusion are all part of the narrative—the new actions of God, the diverse modes of communication, the narrated time sequence, and the diverse players.

Rogers summarizes the steps that lead to an innovation becoming part of the lives among a new social group: knowledge (of various types, as explained below), persuasion (the formation of positive attitudes), decision (a mix of cognitive, affective, and social elements), implementation (steps, sometimes experimental, into the beliefs and actions of the innovation), and confirmation (personal experiences and the witness of others that affirm the decision). During all of these steps, participants create and share information.[34]

Throughout the diffusion process, several types of knowledge are at play: awareness knowledge (that the innovation exists), how-to knowledge (how to engage the innovation), and principles knowledge (the concepts and perhaps the history that underlie how the innovation works).[35] The

32. Rogers, *Diffusion of Innovations*, 6.

33. Rogers, *Diffusion of Innovations*, 11–31.

34. Rogers, *Diffusion of Innovations*, 20, 80–97.

35. Rogers, *Diffusion of Innovations*, 172–73.

weight of these types of knowledge, and sequencing, can vary. Rogers explains that as the innovation is being considered, there are some general factors regarding whether it will be adopted: relative advantage (when considered alongside the current life of participants), compatibility (with current life, needs, values, priorities), complexity versus comprehensibility (not so complex that it gets dismissed), trialability (allowing others to test ideas and practices), and observability (the innovation and its consequences can be seen).[36] Peter has a tradition and life experiences that emphasized the disadvantages on non-kosher behavior, so only by being convinced of God's role is he able to acknowledge the advantages of the new reality. These other factors—compatibility (with his experiences and Jewish texts), comprehensibility, trialability, and observability—are all displayed in Luke's narrative.

Rogers work covers many other factors in diffusion, including our theme of leadership. Two of Rogers's leadership roles are especially relevant: (1) the work of *change agents*, and (2) the role of *influence leaders*. Change agents are those who bridge groups as they promote diffusion. They need awareness and skills that forward the various kinds of knowledge—and they need to do so with an awareness of each context. This is a key area where our emphasis on God's agency makes a difference, because much of this is about tactics for Rogers while, for our work, God's agency means there are frequent surprises as leaders face their own continual encounter with new initiatives from God (like Peter's encounter with God via Cornelius). Influence leaders are persons in groups who, for various cultural reasons, are trusted by participants regarding change. Rogers notes that there are problems when change agents or influence leaders are themselves innovators; innovators tend to be disruptive, often lessening trust, or they cast an image of being uniquely skilled and competent, which means that others are not able to emulate them.[37] God is the primary disruptor in biblical texts—both in new settings but also in regard to believers. A key reason we write about improvisation as a work of leaders and churches is that innovation tends to promote human agency, which can easily distract focus from God's initiatives.

One final key for diffusion, heterogeneity of relationships, provides a link to the following section on alterity. Rogers is dealing with a challenge: "Homophily can act as an invisible barrier to the flow of innovations within a system."[38] Basically, without communication beyond homogeneity, the new beliefs and practices will remain in a fairly proscribed system. Further,

---

36. Rogers, *Diffusion of Innovations*, 222, 229–66.

37. Rogers, *Diffusion of Innovations*, 318–19.

38. Rogers, *Diffusion of Innovations*, 306.

as Rogers states, "weak ties" are essential because they are the channel along which communication can be diffused.[39] So those strong ties are important for diffusion in a homogeneous system, but weak ties are needed for further diffusion. This is conceptually related to alterity, the importance of how we relate to *the other*—who makes it possible for us to see beyond ourselves.

Alterity

Missiology and ecclesiology have frequently emphasized homogeneity— noting the advantages of working with groups of people who are culturally alike.[40] When European immigrants, from varying locations and cultures, came to North American, they brought their cultural habits and familiar churches with them—German Lutherans, British Anglicans and Methodists, Scot Presbyterians. For centuries, habits, familiarity, predictability, perceived security, organizational systems, and existing associations perpetuated this homogeneity. Even as some participants sought to alter these habits of homogeneity, the norm was still powerful. Even when there is a push for diversity, the imagination is that of helping "them" join "us." More recently, in missions and church planting, training has emphasized the efficiency of communicating with people who are similar, who can be met in their comfort zones of homogeneity according to their consumer preferences. Sometimes a new pursuit of racial diversity is given some emphasis, and even to be commended, but the diversity seldom moves toward thick relationships or significant life across cultural norms.[41] Our priority on alterity challenges these habits.[42]

As already noted in our work on Christian anthropology (chapter 3), humanness includes difference—that is part of God's design, and it is a reflection of difference in the Trinity. Participation with God requires that we know the *other* is a subject, an agent in creation, and someone with whom God is already taking initiatives. More—God intends that we ourselves are to be changed by engagement and mutuality with others. Our engagement with others—our need for habits regarding alterity—is not just for the sake of the other; rather alterity is the frame in which we learn about God, about

39. Rogers, *Diffusion of Innovations*, 339–41.

40. The "Homogeneous Unit Principle" is described in McGavran and Wagner, *Understanding Church Growth*.

41. See Branson and Martinez, *Churches, Cultures and Leadership*.

42. Other important works include Rah, *Many Colors*; DeYoung, *Coming Together*; Emerson, Yancey, and DeYoung, *United by Faith;* and McConnell, *Cultural Insights for Christian Leaders*.

the gospel, about ourselves, about love and grace and vocation. Without alterity, our capacities to discern God's presence and activities are limited to a myopic imagination (thus rendering us blind).

The concept of alterity, like the related terms *alternate* and *alternative*, provides a way for us to understand a major theme throughout Luke's two volumes. Alterity is about difference, otherness, the stranger. By using alterity as a lens for reading Luke's works, we become aware of the emphasis Luke places on geography and languages in Acts 2 (above) and on the lengthy account regarding Peter and Cornelius (Acts 10, in our chapter 1). If for Peter, the *other* (Cornelius, a Gentle) is just an object, defined through the self-understanding and values of being a subject or actor (Peter, a Jew), the fixed beliefs, judgements, and practices of the self-defined subject remain in place. By God's grace (by which we mean God's initiative), Cornelius is a subject, an actor, whose life and activities show him to be participating with God, and Peter can only participate with God if he allows himself to be changed in this subject-to-subject event. Peter does not set the terms of the relationship; Peter is not the prime agent of the encounter. As he allows himself to be changed, as God's disruption shapes his awareness, questions, and tentative steps, Peter is moved toward new understandings and practices regarding God, the gospel, himself, and the early church. This is what we mean by a narrative regarding alterity.

There have been decades of development in the social sciences and social philosophy regarding alterity. Researchers realized that objectifying the other led to a profound inability to understand either the other or the self; the frames and questions and capacities of the researcher are always inadequate, even distorting. Various scholars,[43] working with diverse approaches, speak to the profound importance of life with others, and they name critical challenges of objectification and ethnocentrism. In our own North American contexts, these challenges have become disturbingly obvious in the xenophobia, racism, and intolerance that are embedded in daily social habits.

Luke frequently writes about cultural and economic boundary-crossing, calls attention to women who are among Jesus' followers and early church leaders, points to surprising inter-generational features of the Spirit's work, and emphasizes God's grace among Samaritans, Hellenists, and Greek non-believers. These narratives emphasize being a guest of the hospitality that others offer as well as being hospitable to others. The sheer diversity of those who are included in the Acts narrative, following the initial list

43. Various disciplines have key voices: for theology, see Buber, *I and Thou*; for social philosophy, see Bourdieu, *Logic of Practice* and Habermas, *Autonomy and Solidarity*; for cultural theory, see Baudrillard and Guillaume, *Radical Alterity*.

of Acts 2, is noteworthy: women and men, young and old; scribes, priests, and elders; Jewish proselytes and God-fearers; those who are poor, crippled, and sick; persons with wealth and influence; Roman military personnel and local jailers; local rulers and merchants; worshippers of all kinds; laborers in craft households and in Roman royal households; travelers from numerous points of the empire. Human interactions across these diverse peoples include conversations, collaboration, mob fights, abuse of workers, compassion, heroic actions, cowardice, and conversions. Luke wants us to pay attention to these people and actions, because God is assumed to be in the mix, sometimes prompting, sometimes hindering—and we are participants "on the way"[44] with these early believers. Alterity is noted throughout, indicating how key the other is to how we discern God's initiatives. As we previously noted, diffusion gains new channels through alterity.

READING ACTS AS LEADERS

In chapter 1 we explored the game-changing narrative regarding the Jewish Peter, one of the Twelve, and the Greek, God-fearing centurion, Cornelius. They are both leaders in their contexts, and God initiates with both of them in order to shape the meaning of the gospel and the subsequent social arrangements. These men embody centuries of opposition; alterity is met with the gospel of reconciliation. Throughout the narrative, they had to improvise in response to God's actions. The diffusion of the gospel must be on these terms—the bodies of Jews and Gentiles in a new body.

In Acts 2 (above) God's agency among Jewish and Hellenist Jews was so overwhelming and public as an experience of stories and sensory surprises that Luke narrates it as a defining event. The following paragraphs continue to show the improvisation of believers. The lenses we are using regarding Acts—improvisation, diffusion, and alterity—assist us in noting God's agency and imagining our own participation.

Acts 6–7: The Spirit Disrupts Leadership

The early Jerusalem community of believers, in the midst of healings, exorcisms, and arguments with the Sanhedrin, also faced matters that seem more quotidian, though they demonstrate the transformation from old to new regarding the gospel and social arrangements. The fact that Hellenist widows

---

44. "The Way" is a common term in Acts to designate the way of Jesus: 9:2; 19:9, 23; 24:14, 22. We will engage the metaphor in part III.

lacked food indicates that alterity was a problem; the evidently common discrimination in Judea against Hellenists (those Jews of the diaspora who had relocated to Jerusalem) was now experienced among followers of Jesus. For Luke, this is not a management challenge but a theological one. There was awareness and provision for widows, but not for Hellenist widows: "Hellenists complained against the Hebrews because their widows were being neglected in the daily distribution of food" (6:1). As Green writes, "this failure of . . . economic koinonia must be read as a disruption of the Spirit's work. . . . For widows to be overlooked in this way, then, signals a theological (not just a practical) failure within the community."[45] The complexities of the diaspora, introduced in Acts 2, come to the front in this event. An initial improvised response by the Twelve is shown to be inadequate, and the violent reaction of the freedmen brings both tragedy and another unexpected initiative of the Spirit.

The text names the response of the Twelve: "And the twelve called together the whole community of the disciples and said, 'It is not right that we should neglect the word of God in order to wait on tables'" (6:2 NRSV).[46] Here is the immediate sequence, beginning with the Twelve's instructions,

> "[S]elect from among yourselves seven men of good standing, full of the Spirit and of wisdom, whom we may appoint to this task, while we, for our part, will devote ourselves to prayer and to serving the word." What they said pleased the whole community, and they chose Stephen, a man full of faith and the Holy Spirit, together with Philip, Prochorus, Nicanor, Timon, Parmenas, and Nicolaus, a proselyte of Antioch. They had these men stand before the apostles, who prayed and laid their hands on them. (6:3–6 NRSV)

So, the apostles said, the complaints that have reached them deserve recognition, and a solution needs wider involvement. But their improvisation, which might be commended for a participatory approach and a public recognition that others have (limited) authority, will quickly be corrected by the Holy Spirit (because God's initiatives continue to disrupt). Their instructions specify a division of labor that would leave ethnic divisions in

---

45. Green, *Luke as Narrative Theologian*, 155–56.

46. Johnson emphasizes that the Twelve called for the discernment of a wider assembly, which indicates a changing pathway as modes of discernment are being developed. Johnson, *Acts of the Apostles*, 106. But Green emphasizes that splitting "service" of the word from service of tables is a theological problem: "Their [the apostles'] failure is measured, first, by their neglect of Hellenist widows and, then, in their attempt to fracture the singular ministry (διακονία) modeled for them by Jesus. . . . This is not 'good news to the poor' (Luke 4:18)." Green, *Luke as Narrative Theologian*, 158.

place: the apostles attend to study and prayer—"serving the word"—and the seven Hellenist men are to attend to Hellenists tables. God doesn't settle for that arrangement.

This provision was celebrated and Luke tells us of the growing circle of believers, including a note that "Even a large group of priests embraced the faith" (6:7). But, with attention to alterity, improvisation, and diffusion, the narrative focuses next on Stephen, one of the table waiters, and how the Holy Spirit empowers and redirects. First, Stephen does not accept the splintering of *diaconia* and goes beyond the sanctioned work and authority: "Stephen, who stood out among the believers for the way God's grace was at work in his life and for his exceptional endowment with divine power, was doing great wonders and signs among the people" (6:8) and then he faced arguments from non-believing Hellenist Jews, the freedmen who had also been shaped by the troubles of diaspora living. So, Hellenists against Hellenist—all of them have experienced the marginalization of the empire in which survival always challenged them to the core of their identity.[47] The freedmen, clinging to their Jewish identity, fearful of anything that would mess with their hope of a somewhat better existence in Judea, could not tolerate God's agency as expressed in Stephen: "they couldn't resist the wisdom the Spirit gave him as he spoke" (6:10).

The freedmen spread rumors to discredit Stephen and he is brought before the council. In these venues he continues to do what the apostles had indicated was preserved for them regarding "serving the word"—we then get the longest sermon so far in Luke's narrative. Evidently the Twelve were improvising short of what God was offering. And in this disruptive space we have the first martyr. It is intriguing how the social distinctions play out. "At that time, the church in Jerusalem began to be subjected to vicious harassment. Everyone except the apostles was scattered throughout the regions of Judea and Samaria" (8:1). Obviously the account of this tragedy mimics the turmoil, treachery, and violence surrounding Jesus' death. God's initiatives—preceding and alongside believers—do not serve our preferred plans. But we then learn how the gospel is diffused: "Those who had been scattered moved on, preaching the good news along the way" (8:4). God's initiatives are narrated: "By way of resolution, Luke portrays the authorization of fresh leadership, with this leadership drawn from among the minority of the Jerusalem community."[48]

As that diffusion occurs, we learn of certain practices and characteristics of the embodied gospel. Leadership by the apostles gives way to others.

---

47. Jennings, *Acts,* 7.
48. Green, *Luke as Narrative Theologian,* 159.

Beyond the plans of the apostles, after Stephen, Philip (another Hellenist assigned to food distribution) improvises on the situation by preaching, healing, and doing exorcisms in Samaria—a matter of alterity that Luke signaled earlier in his account of Jesus healing a Samaritan (Luke 17). Diffusion requires adjustments for earlier authorities and structures, and the apostles send Peter and John to observe and participate. They not only observe, but they pray and God enrolls them in this work by an obvious outpouring of the Holy Spirit.[49] Next, because they are awakening to this new work by God, as they return to Jerusalem they imitate Philip by preaching to other Samaritans. So after the problematic response of the Twelve regarding the Hellenist widows, Stephen preaches and is welcomed by angels into heaven, and Philip's improvisation in the midst of persecution leads to diffusion of the gospel in Samaria and new leadership practices by Peter and John.

Acts 16: Alterity & Improv in Philippi

Each chapter of Acts continues to illustrate improvisation, diffusion, and alterity, with God's activities as the center. As Paul and his traveling team become central to Luke's telling, converts in new locations gather into learning communities that engage the developing practices. We witness what Kavin Rowe describes as the gospel's challenges to cultures. In the various cities there are similarities and differences regarding contextual local practices and how Paul, his team, and local believers engage those environments. Alterity continues to be a challenge, especially regarding which Jewish practices should be adopted by Gentile believers. Paul's improvisation of inclusion is not immediately affirmed by some Judean believers ("Unless you are circumcised according to the custom we've received from Moses, you can't be saved"—15:1). An energized debate, in which the apostles note what they've observed and how they discern the Holy Spirit's activities, leads to a less cumbersome set of restraints for new Gentile believers, regarding diet and sex.

After this word is delivered to Antioch and we are told of some changes in the traveling teams, Paul and Timothy revisit some churches and consider new places:

> Paul and his companions traveled throughout the regions of
> Phrygia and Galatia because the Holy Spirit kept them from

---

49. This account also introduces Simon, a sorcerer, and what will become an element of Luke's narrative—the clash of God's initiatives vis-à-vis the gods and demons that are necessarily contested in the coming of God's kingdom. As God continues to initiate, followers are always called on to improvise just as others counter God's graces.

speaking the word in the province of Asia. When they approached the province of Mysia, they tried to enter the province of Bithynia, but the Spirit of Jesus wouldn't let them. Passing by Mysia, they went down to Troas instead. A vision of a man from Macedonia came to Paul during the night. He stood urging Paul, "Come over to Macedonia and help us!" Immediately after he saw the vision, we prepared to leave for the province of Macedonia, concluding that God had called us to proclaim the good news to them. (16:6–10)

Matters of the Holy Spirit's agency, along with improvisation, are apparent in this passage. First, it is interesting to note that when they left Antioch they did not have a full itinerary. They travel through the regions of Phrygia and Galatia, visiting places they had previously engaged. Then, without telling us how this discernment was experienced, Luke focuses on the Holy Spirit's check on their assumed directions. Western Asia? No. Province of Bithynia? No. How might they know that the "Spirit of Jesus" is stopping them? There are other times when Luke reports physical impediments or circumstances, or visions (that get varied interpretations). In this account Luke just writes that "the Holy Spirit kept them from speaking" and that "the Spirit of Jesus wouldn't let them." We learn that discernment can include the Spirit's involvement to block plans, but, other than the already known elements of how to pay attention to God—allegiance to Jesus, practices of worship and prayer and praise, and attention to circumstances—we don't know how this conclusion was reached. According to Johnson, Luke is making something clear: "On one side there is the role of human calculation. . . . On the other side, there is the divine intervention and guidance, now more direct and urgent than ever."[50]

They proceed to Troas, which could be seen as a likely city for their purposes. But Paul has a vision—which might have had less weight if they had already become entangled elsewhere. A man in Paul's vision said, "Come over to Macedonia and help us" (16:9), and because they were convinced that this was God's message (16:10)—a note that indicates reflective conversation—"we prepare to leave for the province of Macedonia." Luke begins using the pronoun "we," probably indicating he joins the team, which might increase the team's competence in Gentile settings. After a couple of days sailing they land in Philippi, a Roman colony where Paul's own credentials carried weight—something that influences the outcome when their preaching is countered by cultural norms that connect commerce and local religious practices. But prior to that conflict narrative are some key details

---

50. Johnson, *Acts of the Apostles*, 290.

that Luke provides concerning Paul's team and their initial practices that met with God's prevenient grace.

Several days after arriving, days perhaps spent looking for a Jewish synagogue or testing opportunities in civic settings (where later events would transpire), they went outside the town to a stream, assuming there would be a traditional place of prayer. Sabbath practices, unique to Jews, could include such prayer practices outside a city if that city had too few Jews for them to have adequate civic standing.[51] Finding a group of praying women (probably "God-fearers" who respected the Jewish faith and participated in some practices),[52] they sat down and the conversation led to Lydia's baptism and the baptism of her household. Lydia was a businesswoman from Thyatira who had a home in Philippi and, "she urged, 'Now that you have decided that I am a believer in the Lord, come and stay in my house.' And she persuaded us" (16:15). Alterity is noted regarding the team's engagement with a group of women, including a wealthy woman, who was formerly a pagan but now engages in some practices of Jewish rituals. Luke describes Lydia as a woman who traded purple cloth, which would indicate a significant social status[53]—and the narrative includes her household (whether family or laborers).

As with the Cornelius narrative, Luke is disrupting the societal narrative. Concerning these scenarios, both recounting baptisms in households, "each of the instances of household baptism appears in the Lukan narrative at points where the 'household' is masterfully juxtaposed with what one would normally regard as the authentic 'active center of social order,' those institutions that serve a world-ordering function, exemplifying and radiating divinely sanctioned dispositions and behaviors, namely, Jerusalem . . . and Rome."[54] These houses were the center not only of economics, production, employment, but they held the meaning of what it meant to belong in the society. As Green argues, "the same way the Cornelius episode establishes the household as 'culture center' over against a Jerusalem/temple-centered ideology, so what takes place in Philippi undercuts the unqualified power of

---

51. As Johnson notes, Luke leaves it unclear whether this is the Jewish prayer gathering that Paul's team sought or if it was some other group that they encountered while still on the way to a Jewish gathering: "The most obvious reading of the story would be to see this as a separate encounter on the way to the synagogue (see 16:16)." Johnson, *Acts of the Apostles,* 292.

52. See Witherington, *Acts of the Apostles,* 493; missiologists Bevans and Schroeder commend this kind of attentive listening in *Prophetic Dialogue.*

53. See Johnson, *Acts of the Apostles,* 292–93.

54. Green, *Luke as Narrative Theologian,* 172.

Rome."[55] God is disrupting more that religious beliefs—because the house-hold was "Rome in microcosm,"[56] the gospel is transforming people and systems at the core of human arrangements.

Luke continues to show the importance of traditions and improvisa-tion—a team of Jewish men experiments on a Sabbath morning by inves-tigating a local stream, enjoins a discussion that leads to converts, and is then welcomed into the hospitality of the business woman's home. After a subsequent disruptive encounter in the city, Paul and the team are in and out of jail, and they "made their way to Lydia's house where they encour-aged the brothers and sisters. Then they left Philippi" (16:40). This makes it clear that Lydia's home had been the gathering place as the gospel had been embodied and uttered in the city. Paul's later letter to the Philippians displays notable affection and appreciation. His visit and the church's con-tinued embodiment and narration of the gospel are evident in that letter. The diffusion of the gospel is noted in Philippians, with specific comments on how they embodied generosity and bear suffering, and these traits are paralleled by diffusion of leadership, especially among women. In his let-ter to the church Paul commends four persons, including two women who "struggled together with me in the ministry of the gospel" (Phil 4:3).[57]

LEADERS AMIDST DISRUPTIONS OF THE SPIRIT

Throughout these Acts passages, God is disrupting expectations. Many Jews, Hellenists, Samaritans, and Gentiles, around Judea, Galilee, and Samaria, then throughout the empire, are being made into a new body. Just as Jesus' actions and words were a threat to the powers—Roman and Sanhedrin—God's mission into the empire deepens the challenge to the empire. That threat is not on the empire's terms; rather it is an encounter of a patient and persistent God who will constantly surprise and disrupt. Johnson writes, "The mission . . . is willed, initiated, impelled, and guided by God through the Holy Spirit. God moves ahead of the other characters. But at the human level, Luke shows how difficult and intricate is the effort of the Church to keep up with God's actions, follow God's initiatives, un-derstand the precedents being established."[58] While strategies and experts

55. Green, *Luke as Narrative Theologian*, 178

56. Witheringon, *Acts of the Apostles*, 488.

57. Most church disagreements in the New Testament lack names, and those with names focus on leaders—Philemon and Onesimus, Paul and Barnabas regarding Mark; Paul and Peter; Euodia and Syntyche.

58. Johnson, *Acts of the Apostles*, 15.

will not gain traction, awareness of the Spirit among others and ourselves, experiments regarding perceived holy prompts, and life-on-life engagement at prayer, in civic places, and in homes, will mark the diffusion of the gospel beyond previous imagination.

CHAPTER 7

Ephesians and New Social Arrangements

INTRODUCTION

OUR LATE MODERN CHURCHES, notably the Euro-American ones, can easily miss Paul's[1] message in Ephesians because of our deeply embedded habits. Our individualism, for example, blinds us to God's priority on covenantal love and interdependence. Our fears lead to avoiding (or managing for our own ends) those who are different. As we have already pointed out, our default confidence in experts, management, and control lead us to find those traits in Paul's words on leadership even when he emphasizes paying attention and walking in response to God instead of finding expert formulas. Our desires for simplistic solutions result in misdefining and subsequently missing out on the wonder of Paul's words about spiritual life, heaven, power, calling, and gifts.

Chapter 1 began to explore Paul's theological engagement with the Ephesian context. We encourage a rereading of that introductory material as a way into this chapter. Because modernity tends to proscribe "spiritual life" to personal inner life, albeit with some overflow, Christians often misread Scripture to fit that modern "spiritual" narrative. Ephesians can help us recover. We pointed out how the word *spiritual*, when read as a disembodied element of reality, leads us to miss how profoundly God's initiatives are engaged with us and our world. We indicated that the telos of God's activities—that in Jesus Christ, *all* things are coming together—has major implications in Ephesus and for us. In the earlier intermezzo regarding practical

---

1. On authorship, see Fowl, *Ephesians*, 9–27, 31–32.

theology, we commended the importance of paying attention to our cultural contexts, including the resources and challenges they bring to our reading of texts. As we've noted, Paul is aware of the contextual challenges from the larger society (the Roman Empire) and the local powers (the temple of Artemis). God is engaged with the people of Ephesus in ways that are directly relevant to those forces. Because God is engaging something specific, concrete, and local, we understand what God is doing as we seek to gain clarity on what's happening on the ground, in the local contextual features. That way of seeing—for the Ephesians and for us—will guide our attention in this chapter.

The Context of Ephesians

Paul is offering a profound alternative for the Ephesians. He clarifies that the world is not accurately described by either the Artemisian cult or by the Roman Empire. Rather, God's self-revelation in Jesus Christ, and the subsequent collaborative relation between church and Christ, is proclaimed as the abundant, active grace of God. Matters of God's presence, authority, power, and telos are all settled, and Paul's opening prayer focuses on how the church gains the capacity to see what God has provided and what God is doing. Ephesians is shaped by this clarity about God's agency and Paul's plea that the church see and engage God's grace (initiatives). In part III we will take on specific matters regarding how our churches might embody this vocation.

Ephesus and Artemis

During the first century, Ephesus was the largest and most influential city of Asia minor.[2] The temple of Artemis[3] was central to its identity and life. Jerome Murphy-O'Connor writes, "Artemis permeated the consciousness of the Ephesians to the point that it was a rock-bottom element in their collective and individual identities."[4] Even the etymology of the name con-

2. For a brief background on Ephesus, see Trebilco, "Province and Cities of Asia," esp. 506–9; and Arnold, "Ephesians," 249–53.

3. Also known as Artemision or the Temple of Diana, twin of Apollos. Even though the initial audience of the letter may have included Laodicea or other Asian cities, Artemis's influence, though less central, was still present. Also, these brief comments about religion, civic life, and the formative elements of human life hold throughout the region.

4. Murphy-O'Connor, *St. Paul's Ephesus*, 16.

veys the meaning and power of this relationship—"secure and healthy."[5] The first temple was built during the Bronze Age (perhaps eighth century BCE), and the building present during Paul's ministry (four times the size of the Parthenon of Athens[6]) was begun in 323 BCE. The worship of Artemis went beyond Ephesus—as far west as the known world. In this manner, the Ephesians knew themselves in covenant with Artemis; they were the divinely appointed custodian of the temple. They were secured from "the foundations of the world,"[7] at the center of an inclusive religion that "is thrown open to all who would sacrifice, or offer prayers, or sing hymns, to suppliants, to Hellenes, barbarians, free men, slaves."[8] These beliefs and practices help us see the context that Paul engages. This totalizing worldview, when linked to the imaginary of the Roman Empire (below), is not dissimilar to that in the modern West, a *habitus* of the Enlightenment, consumer capitalism, and neoliberal economics that we described in chapter 2.

The temple was also a major regional bank—known for honest preservation of deposits. Around 110 CE, Dio Chrysostom wrote, "The immense prestige of the temple of Artemis at Ephesus made it a magnet for deposits" from "kings and commoners."[9] While these funds were securely preserved, and not available to others, the temple had its own funds and held the city's deposits, which were used for numerous matters of personal and civic purposes. Interestingly, concerning the mid-eighties BCE, after "the first Mithridatic War the financial situation in Asia was so desperate that the council of Ephesus, in order to maintain its population, was forced to pass a decree canceling debts to the city and to the temple."[10] Paul's words about inheritance, redemption, down payment, and seals are all related to this world of banking.

Ephesus and the Empire

The Roman context of Ephesus, and its impact on the social imaginary of citizens, is a key to understanding Paul's letter. The empire encompassed

---

5. This meaning is favored by Strabo (in his *Geography*, usually dated around the birth of Jesus). Murphy-O'Connor notes other possible meanings, including "strong limbed." Murphy-O'Connor, *St. Paul's Ephesus*, 14.

6. Trebilco, "Province and Cities of Asia," 508.

7. Murphy-O'Connor, *St. Paul's Ephesus*, 200.

8. Apollonius of Tyana, Letter 67, quoted by Murphy-O'Connor, *St. Paul's Ephesus*, 21.

9. More a depository than a bank per Murphy-O'Connor, *St. Paul's Ephesus*, 64–65.

10. Murphy-O'Connor, *St. Paul's Ephesus*, 65–66.

much of what is now Europe and northern Africa, and from Spain to the Caspian Sea—creating a political entity through military might and economics.[11] In order to manage this vast empire, and thereby to collect taxes, there were clear regulations regarding territorial units (provinces), who was authorized to appoint those who governed, and how tight the controls were. The priority on control also meant establishing and maintaining clear borders, at the edges of the empire and between provinces. The military not only secured new lands but also constructed roads and had policing authority regarding the maintenance of order, protection of transportation routes, and the security and movement of resources and money.[12]

Concerning the more troublesome emperors, the province of Asia generally escaped the "grandiose ideas" of Caligula (37–41 CE) and the "cruelty and folly" of Nero (54–68 CE).[13] In general, Asia experienced steady development during these decades, especially in the cities. At the junction of important land and sea routes, and given the title of "the first and greatest metropolis of Asia," Ephesus received significant resources.[14] As the prime city of Asia and the gateway to Asia and farther east,[15] Ephesus played a key role in the Roman Empire's presence, governance, and economics. Even more than the managerial functions that Ephesus came to have with being a principal city, Rome conveyed through Ephesus and other key cities its power to create and sustain a social imaginary. Any citizen knew that Rome defined reality—that life was subject to the provisions and regulations and military forays of the empire. Like other cities, Ephesus sought to pay homage, and increase its own honor, through buildings. Alongside the State Agora—in the midst of trade and governance—was a temple, dedicated in 29 CE to divine Caesar and Dea Roma (the goddess and mythology of Rome).[16] Also in that area is a courtyard dedicated to Augustus and Artemis, indicating the empire's embrace of the local (regional) religion as a means to signal citizens that they were aligned. It is the power of this imaginary that gets challenged by the gospel.

Anyone living in Ephesus (or in other cities of the empire) could not escape the ways that the power and provisions and promises of Rome were experienced in daily life. Rome and Artemus created a cosmic scope—all of

---

11. Hatina, "Rome and Its Provinces," 559; Garnsey and Saller, *Roman Empire*, 12–19.

12. Hatina, "Rome and Its Provinces," 560–61.

13. Trebilco, "The Province and Cities of Asia," 503.

14. Trebilco, "The Province and Cities of Asia," 507.

15. Murphy-O'Connor, *St. Paul's Ephesus*, 56.

16. Murphy-O'Connor, *St. Paul's Ephesus*, 190; chiseling shows that markers were changed as rulers changed.

life was of one fabric, under the authority and agenda of these powers. The drama of life was cast by this larger drama—that is what social imaginary means. But as we began to note in chapter 1, Paul challenges this imaginary. Caesar is not their father; rather they are adopted by God through Jesus Christ (1:5). Their blessings don't come from Caesar and Artemis but from "the God and Father of our Lord Jesus Christ" (1:3). Their peace is not from the empire but from "God our Father and the Lord Jesus Christ" (1:2). And the "mysteries" that can provide a narrative for wisdom and guidance are not hidden in Artemis's cult but rather were revealed in Jesus Christ and are continually revealed and enlivened by the Holy Spirit. So Paul is directly countering the Ephesians' narrative regarding the source, substance, and telos of their lives.

Ephesians 1: Churches and Powers

The opening paragraphs of Ephesians chapter 1, as described earlier, set the framework for what matters to Paul: God is bringing "all things together in Christ" (1:10). So what has been hidden is now revealed—and that revelation is not just a single previously disclosed reality, made known in the life, ministry, words, death, and resurrection of Jesus Christ, but an ongoing revelation as God continues to engage people and powers. The Ephesians, along with Paul and his band, are called to be "an honor to God's glory" (1:12, 14) as they perceive and engage God's initiatives. Paul then connects this with what it means to be a church—what we call "doing local ecclesiology."[17]

Even though this letter is sometimes considered a circular letter, it does not foster an esoteric, aspirational church that is disconnected from concrete geographies, specific times, and the lives of actual people. Paul's prayer pushes into this on-the-ground life with God: "I pray that the God of our Lord Jesus Christ, the Father of glory, will give you a spirit of wisdom and revelation that makes God known to you" (1:17). There is specific language in this prayer that goes directly to the specificity of place and context.

Wisdom. While wisdom is sometimes misunderstood as the possession of a few armchair philosophers, its most important meaning is at the intersection of real-life experience, attentiveness, discernment, and judgment. Wisdom is about hour-by-hour life in particular situations, with certain people, in specific contexts. As that verse makes specific, this kind of wisdom connects us to what God is currently doing—God is present and active, and Paul prays that the Ephesians can see and engage this inheritance.

17. We are riffing on Sedmak, *Doing Local Theology.*

Inheritance. This metaphor of inheritance is not to be seen as some amount of money that is deposited in an individual's investment account—it is more like a group of persons receiving the gift of a city in which the Spirit is prompting love and justice and beauty and salvation. So Paul continues, "I pray that the eyes of your heart (desire and volition) will have enough light to see what is the hope of God's call (vocation), what is the richness of God's glorious inheritance among believers (daily life in the midst of God's initiatives), and what is the overwhelming greatness of God's power that is working among us believers" (1:18–19). This is church participating in real time with God, and Paul's subsequent sentences about power indicate his awareness of the challenges this church faces.

Power. Paul is fully aware that the gospel is about changing personal and social habits, but such change is not primarily about functional tactics—it's about power. In a city that is shaped by Artemis and Rome—which together form an environment that places Ephesian citizens as the objects of their powers—Paul knows that the vocation of discerning and engaging the Holy Spirit requires countervailing forces. As Nicholas Perrin writes, "It is difficult to do proper justice to the New Testament without realizing that what is 'good news' for the Christians is religious and political deviancy for the Romans."[18] Paul uses four different words for power, and English can only approximate some distinctions: *dynamis* (instantiation of power), *kratos* (might, strength), *ischus* (ability, might), *energeo* (operationalize, activate), plus other related matters such as *arche* (ruler, authority), *exousia* (right, authority), and *kyriotēs* (dominion, lordship). The church is comprised of those who have begun a new journey that disrupts the formative powers of empire and Artemis, and the human activities that are schooled and participative with those powers. Those cultural, societal forces are daily shaping the imagination, desires, belonging, aspiration, and assumptions of those who participate in this city. Their habits (of thinking, feeling, acting, relating) come from this *habitus*—a dwelling that makes claims on who they are and how they live. We will expand on this challenge below (regarding how critical theory helps us see and reshape our assumptions). Basically, Paul is not naive about this situation—being the church is not just a matter of theological assent, religious ceremonies, and new organizational systems.

In order to ground his exposition about power and ecclesiology, Paul bases the discussion on Jesus. Rather than power in the Roman form of military and governance, or Artemisian authority regarding fate and transactional sacrifices, Paul focuses on Jesus' resurrection and ascension. That event demonstrated the limits of Roman power and the weakness of the

18. Perrin, "The Imperial Cult," 133.

fearful reactions of some temple authorities. The resurrection, in defeating death, and the ascension, in placing Jesus over all earthly dominions, demonstrated God's lordship and might. The accounts about Ephesus Acts 19 (Paul's first visit) show how God's power countered earthly and demonic forces. They have seen that "God put everything under Christ's feet" (1:22)—including all other formative claims on the desires, vocations, loyalties, and social arrangements of Ephesus. It is no small matter to alter a person's (or a group's) imagination and commitments—even when there is an awareness that current practices are not life-giving. So that is why a church is needed; as a group that has covenanted together to engage the practices of discerning and welcoming God's initiatives, the church is a social embodiment of the words and actions that give new life. Participating in God's presence and actions is not an individualistic affair; the reshaping of desires and vocation requires a new community. It is a further demonstration of God's power when a church is so receptive to the missional vocation of God that they are transformed from the beliefs and practices of empire and Artemis and into the imagination and arrangements that are only possible when God is honored as the primary agent of life and love. This is just as true today, regarding the challenge of shaping our own local ecclesiologies in a way that moves our desires and vocations and perceptions, collaboratively, away from the empires and spiritualities of our own day and toward walking with God.

Whatever the church of Ephesus has experienced, however they are partaking of the Spirit's provisions, Paul is writing to both commend and persuade. As the letter unfolds, he addresses cultural divisions, how they experience both earthly and non-earthly powers, and what they assume to be their vocation. He makes connections concerning how they shape their social arrangements, the needed shifts concerning families and labor, and how they evaluate their circumstances. He proposes modes of theological praxis that help them embody both an awareness of forces that seek to defeat them (including appropriate defenses) and an embrace of the holy surprises that may have been seen as threats but are actually the disruptions that God brings in service of salvation. All through this letter Paul is focally attentive to assisting these people discern and join God's agency in the midst of their daily lives. This involved the question of how this gospel was in the process of transforming cultural narratives (of Rome and Artemis) as well the fundamental practices around their social, economic, and political lives as God's people. All of this would have had a huge bearing on how the leaders of these small communities would have understood their roles. They would not have been full-time, ordained clergy running congregations; rather, Paul is helping them pay attention to the Spirit's formation of their social embodiment in contrast to inherited arrangements. Before we explore these themes through other chapters of Ephesians we want to give further attention to conceptual frameworks in modern leadership studies in order to note how our fronting of God's agency might make them more generative for reading Ephesians.

THEORETICAL FRAMES: CRITICAL THEORY AND CHANGING ORGANIZATIONAL CULTURE

How we understand these circumstances in Ephesus, and Paul's observations and proposals, can benefit from the two leadership frameworks that we highlight in this chapter. Critical theory, as it has been developed over the last half century, provides resources for seeing how power is at work in our circumstances and how our own assumptions need to be surfaced and placed into communal discernment processes. Organizational theory gives us some access to how organizations are formed in modern technocratic societies and how the praxis of leadership that comes out of these theories can engage groups of people toward new forms of life that foster the kind of discernment that centers on God's agency. As previously, we will show how these theoretical frameworks need to shift when we prioritize God's agency.

Critical Theory

Critical theory is the term to use for a variety of frameworks, developed in the West, that can help us see how many structures of modern societies, such as economics and politics, when practiced, lead to oppression. The term *critical theory*, in a restricted sense, refers to the developments in the late twentieth century among some German social scholars, and in that form it features the critiques rooted in Marxism regarding wealth and labor.[19] Beyond those basics, the term has become a helpful way to describe other social theories that unmask ideologies in order to reveal how power, and the structures that convey power, harm humans. An obvious way this happens concerns how capitalism allows persons with wealth (capital) to use the bodies of others (usually low-cost laborers) to increase their own wealth, and the capacities for shaping more fairness or equity does not lie in the options of those laborers. So critical theory challenges traditional

---

19. Stephen Brookfield provides an accessible historical and conceptual summary in his *Power of Critical Theory*, chapter 1.

theories, and it has broadened to include matters of race, gender, and post-colonial studies.[20]

Stephen Brookfield, a leading US professor regarding education and learning, emphasizes the need for adults to understand the dominant ideology at play in our societies: "Dominant ideology comprises the set of broadly accepted beliefs and practices that frame how people make sense of their experiences and live their lives. When it works effectively, it ensures that an unequal, racist, and sexist society is able to reproduce itself with minimal opposition."[21] Just as the alignment of Rome and Artemis worked to create compliance and productivity among the Ephesian citizenry (because participants could not imagine alternatives), Western liberal economies align the systems of societies in order "to convince people that the world is organized the way it is for the best of all reasons and that society works in the best interest of all."[22] The term *hegemony* is sometimes used to describe basic oppression that is systemic and pervasive, but Antonio Grimsci uses it in a more narrow sense—that those who are oppressed give consent to the power arrangements in which they are proscribed.[23] They have bought into the oppressor's lie concerning what is life-giving, and they participate willingly. This is why critical theorists make much of freedom—that humans need to learn of the oppressive systems so they can become more free, liberated to be agents (subjects rather than objects) and to have the resources for alternative social arrangements. We believe this was going on with the gospel in the Roman world, and that it offers insights regarding how our own social and church imaginations need to be converted.

But definitions of freedom are not uncontested. As we noted in chapter 2, the Enlightenment fronted individual rational autonomy, but that illusion is challenged by basic Christian anthropology (which we engaged more in chapter 3). Roman Catholic theorist Terry Eagleton emphasizes that only in God is there human freedom, where we can claim subjectivity in relationship to God, creation, and others.[24] In this way, the benefits of critical theory (to gain competencies to look behind experiences and systems) need a theological correction (that God's agency is present, and God's invitation is for

20. With numerous authors and related theories, there are many features of critical theories with which we disagree, just as we disagree with matters proposed in the other theoretical materials we are engaging. One advantage of critical theory is that it assumes this critique—that it is an ideology that critiques ideologies, including critical theory.

21. Brookfield, *Power of Critical Theory*, viii.

22. Brookfield, *Power of Critical Theory*, viii–xi.

23. Brookfield, *Power of Critical Theory*, chapter 4.

24. Eagleton, *Culture and the Death of God*, 49.

humans to be agents in collaboration with the Spirit regarding relationships and creation).

So in the West, the myths around individual agency and claims about social equity are revealed; the complicity of economic systems and political power can be seen. If God's agency is introduced as an alternative to these systems, this provides a frame for us to name the imposters in God's world and to become a people who participate in God's rearrangement of powers. This is visible, above, concerning Paul's declarations about the provisions, peace, and future that come from God. Further, critical theory holds up a mirror to the individual critic/actor, revealing motivations and misjudgments. How can individuals and social arrangements change? The initial steps need to "be found in the sense of being 'different' and 'apart,'" which we believe parallels how Paul encourages the Ephesian church to embrace gospel distinctives while also being fully engaged in the local.[25] If we gain competencies and commitments to be critically reflective leaders, then we can begin to see through the socially-constructed frameworks around us and in us. Empire and Artemis (or Western societies, economic arrangements, and malformed spirituality) are unmasked and contested. The social arrangements of Ephesus are challenged, as they can be in our societies and in our church systems.

Organizational Theories and Change

One expectation of leaders is that they have competencies for moving an organization through change. The need for change can come from inside the organization (whether the development of a promising new product or service or the threat of poor performance or volatility among employees) or from outside (new opportunities for success or an environment that undercuts the organization's plans). Some of the organization's capacities for change are embedded in the culture of that organization. Only in recent decades has the topic of culture become recognized as a key element. Edgar Schein is among the primary authors who has engaged this theme of culture and change. He writes,

> The culture of a group can be defined as the accumulated shared learning of that group as it solves its problems of external adaptation and internal integration, which has worked well enough to be considered valid and, therefore, to be taught to new members as the correct way to perceive, think, feel, and behave in relation to those problems. This accumulated learning is a pattern

25. Brookfield on Gramsci, *Power of Critical Theory*, 105.

or system of beliefs, values, and behavioral norms that come to be taken for granted as basic assumptions and eventually drop out of awareness.[26]

This understanding parallels the preceding comments about a social imaginary. In addition to whatever is taught, culture is primarily caught—it is composed of everything that is assumed to be true, valuable, normal, expected, and (therefore) frequently hidden. Such habitual behaviors are usually not considered (reflected upon) but rather are preconscious.

The literature on organizational change has featured various ways that leaders can shape consciousness about underlying assumptions, promote alternative thinking and behavior, and alter the narratives that give participants their identity and roles.[27] Rooted in Kurt Lewin's theories, Schein explains his unfreezing-change-refreezing approach in this way: "Unfreezing is composed of three very different processes . . . : (1) enough *disconfirming data* to cause serious discomfort and disequilibrium; (2) the connection of the disconfirming data to important goals and ideals, causing *anxiety and/or guilt*; and (3) enough *psychological safety*, in the sense of being able to see a possibility of solving the problem and learning something new without loss of identity or integrity."[28] While our approach to leadership and improvisation is not committed to refreezing, we do believe that leaders are important for the transition that Shein describes, and there are new important patterns that a group begins to embody (even if not fully refrozen!).

In addition to recent studies that advance seeing the cultural elements in organizations, other theories have served to create an awareness of how complex and dynamic they are. Rather than a mechanical view, which was especially apparent in the early years of "scientific management," more recent theories propose that we use an overlay of several frames, each frame giving different information while also requiring that leaders see the interaction of the diverse frames. Among the most influential books is *Reframing Organizations: Artistry, Choice, and Leadership,* by Lee Bolman and Terrence Deal.[29] They propose four frames: structural, human resource, political, and symbolic. The work of leaders, in each frame, includes both seeing and acting—become aware of organizational culture, behavior, and

---

26. Schein and Schein, *Organizational Culture and Leadership,* 6.

27. See Alan Roxburgh's discussion on structures and narratives in *Structured for Mission.* We also engaged the role of narratives and change in chapter 5 concerning social construction.

28. Schein and Schein, *Organizational Culture and Leadership,* 320; italics in original.

29. Bolman and Deal, *Reframing Organizations.*

outcomes, and then intervening appropriately toward desired changes. Organizational *structure* includes formal roles, responsibilities, plans, regulations, coordination, and governance, and this frame assumes rationality, specialization, and efficiency.[30] The *human resource* frame concerns the interface of the organization and the people; the literature acknowledges that this relationship may be one of exploitation or it may have features that enhance the well-being, talents, and prospects of participants.[31] The *political* frame brings awareness to power arrangements that are present because of "interdependence, divergent interests, (and) scarcity."[32] This frame concerns conflicts, negotiating, diverse sources, and types of power.[33] Finally, the *symbolic* frame engages how humans make sense of experiences, and includes numerous ways of meaning-making like myths, visions, rituals, metaphors, and ceremonies. Symbols connect minds and hearts and get expressed in the organization's culture and behaviors.[34]

How do these theories morph when we assume that God is acting in the midst of people and systems? Regarding the ways that organizations have their own cultural traditions and dynamics, God may be disrupting habits through internal or external experiences, or God may take advantage of some disruption that has other causes. The disruption may appear as a threat or as a surprisingly positive occurrence. If leaders assume that God is active, then the priority shifts from managing and controlling the people, resources, and goals to the shaping of a discerning people who invite clarity from the Holy Spirit and improvise concerning what they are learning. When we add the perspectives provided by Bolman and Deal's frames, which can help us understand the impact and options that arise in the midst of disruptions, we need to add the frame of God's agency, and that frame overlaps the other four. Leaders have the work of shaping environments in which participants engage threats and opportunities, gain awareness of how their organizational culture sets up the situation, and discern next steps through critical analysis (the four frames) and the practices we outlined in intermezzo 1 so as to see God's initiatives and invitation.

---

30. Bolman and Deal, *Reframing Organizations*, 47–60.

31. Bolman and Deal, *Reframing Organizations*, 121–25.

32. Bolman and Deal, *Reframing Organizations*, 194.

33. Bolman and Deal, *Reframing Organizations*, 190–205

34. Bolman and Deal, *Reframing Organizations*, 247–72.

READING EPHESIANS AS ALTERNATIVE CULTURE

Paul wants the recipients of his letter to see how God's initiatives—in the life, death, and resurrection of Jesus and now in the Spirit's on-the-ground engagement with Ephesus—are related to the everyday life of their neighbors (formed by empire and Artimus). Their society already embodies concrete forms of social life through habits and regulations and rituals. Households and marketplace, civic events and ethnic associations, are structures. Only critical analysis through a probing, conversational, reflective awareness can help the church see the forces arrayed against them as well as the new vocation of walking with God.

Ephesians 2 and 3: New Social Arrangements Impact the Powers

Embedded alongside Roman and religious webs is a prejudice among Jewish believers from their own Jewish heritage—a bias against Gentiles. So even though the particularity of God's call on Israel was intended as a light to the nations, centuries of animosity made association a fraught imaginary. In chapter 1 we explored an early experience in the life of the church (Acts 10), in which the Spirit was making this new social arrangement obvious and powerful. But prejudices are deep and forceful. Paul gives considerable attention toward eliminating the barriers that must have been a challenge among Ephesian believers. This matter of alterity, as we noted in chapter 6, is not just a footnote of the gospel; rather it is central to the "mystery" that Paul conveys from God: if all things are coming together in Jesus Christ, then the vocation of Ephesian believers includes Jews and Gentiles being near to each other.

Paul wants his readers to reflect on their past; they—Jews and Gentiles—have something in common:[35] "You (Gentiles) were dead" and "we (Jews) were dead" (2:1, 4 NRSV). And among his recipients, there is another commonness: "And God raised us (Jews and Gentiles) up and seated us in the heavens with Christ Jesus" (2:6). This grace of God, an outworking of the announced mystery "to bring all things together in Christ" (1:10), includes a gift—a new social arrangement. The Gentiles' status of being "aliens" and "strangers" (2:12) has been drastically altered. By coming into the peace of Christ, they come into peace with each other (2:17–18). As Stephen Fowl writes, "The two, Jew and Gentile, are not simply left standing next to each other with the dividing wall removed. They are transformed into something

---

35. Fowl notes the importance of memory in the work Paul is asking of them. *Ephesians*, 85.

new, 'a new person.'"[36] This new person is created "in him." The Ephesians, previously shaped in an environment where identity, inheritance, and honor are defined by the Artemis-empire imaginary, have become "fellow citizens with God's people, and . . . God's household" (2:19). As we noted in Acts, regarding Peter and Paul, their encounter with God's Spirit in the midst of alterity, included claims about the very foundations of society—in this case, both citizenship and households.

Each of Bolman and Deal's frames is at play. The Jew-Gentile relationship infringes on politics (the exercise of power in the church and in the overflow of these relationships into Ephesus) and the symbolic (that the meaning of the gospel requires changed cross-ethnic social arrangements). So (per Schein and Schein), the culture of the church will be something that had not previously existed; associations are not ruled by convenience or histories or Rome or Artemis—but by the cross (2:16). The church as a new social construction (Gentiles drawn in) is now in the new space ("heavens") where God's agency is readily visible. Paul describes this new space-between by noting they are currently *in the heavens*, living in this space that redefines agency, powers, and relationships. Meanings and relationships and politics and symbols are all being changed; they are "God's household. . .. The whole building is joined together in him" (2:20–21).

This transformation is not just a matter internal to the church. Opportunities are created as God initiates in the context so that the practices of believers are not just about life hidden behind walls—this new social arrangement will be seen by others. According to Paul in Ephesians 3, the powers are to learn from the church about God's presence in this new space: "God's purpose is now to show the rulers and powers in the heavens the many different varieties of his wisdom through the church" (3:10). As we noted earlier, wisdom is about embodied, daily life. When the church embodies a new imagination—when we attend to what God is doing and then live into that initiative—the powers of earth and non-earth will notice. Andrew Lincoln writes that the church, "by her very existence as a new humanity, in which the major division of the first-century world has been overcome . . . reveals God's secret in action and heralds to the hostile heavenly powers the overcoming of cosmic divisions."[37] As the church embodies the telos of God ("all things come together in Jesus Christ") in the stark and unmistakable social creation that reconciles Gentiles and Jews, heavenly powers and those earthly rulers who are enmeshed with them will take note.[38] In other

36. Fowl, *Ephesians*, 95.

37. Lincoln, *Ephesians*, 187; see also Fowl, *Ephesians*, 112.

38. See Barth, *Ephesians 1–3*, 365.

words, because God is active and powerful (doing something that would not otherwise be imaginable), there is an on-the-ground embodiment and witness as believers participate in what happened in the cross and resurrection and continuing mission of God. There is no public-private split; there is no individualistic rationality; there is no ecclesiology behind the walls; there is no subject-object arrangement between ethnic groups. God's initiatives, embodied in the church as it lives in the streets, disorient the powers.

This ecclesial life with God can be fostered by the kind of space-between leadership that we describe. As leaders foster critical awareness of cultural norms, and as they shape learning communities that can disrupt the trapped layers of organizational life, then rather than command-and-control management, such leaders provide generative practices of discernment and improvisation. The discernment starts with attention to the Spirit's activities, then as the barriers embedded in culture and organizations are named, the group also gains competencies regarding the Spirit's promptings.

Ephesians 4: Vocation and Equipping

Paul's letter brings several trajectories forward: the church's vocation is from the telos revealed by God; unity is not social niceness but a radical display of the end times; God is initiating in the everyday lives and society of Ephesus; there is a new social reality that would be unimaginable were it not for God's direct intervention; earthly powers and invisible powers learn about God by the way the church lives into God's initiatives. So when Paul exhorts the Ephesian believers "live as people worthy of the call you received from God" (4:1), we believe that that vocation is the invitation to enter into what God is doing—bringing all things together in Jesus Christ. Fowl writes, "To do this, the Ephesians, and all other believers, will need to develop a set of habits and dispositions. Cultivating such habits and dispositions will enable the Ephesians to perceive themselves, their world, and the standard to which they aspire, thus to walk worthily in a manner that will lead them to recognize some actions as fitting or conforming to the standard and others as not conforming."[39] The church's life (its habits and dispositions) is not one of earthly tactics and organizational command and control—Paul again notes his status as a prisoner (4:1), just as he did previously (3:1). So the extensive pronouncements about power in chapter 1 are about a type of power that is both beyond imagination (resurrection) and humble (prisoner). Paul even uses a conquest Psalm ("That's why scripture says, 'When he climbed up to the heights, he captured prisoners, and he gave gifts to people,'" 4:8; see Ps

39. Fowl, *Ephesians*, 129.

68:18) that gives us a military image (parading up a hill into a conquered city) to show how this type of power reverses the norm. Instead of gathering the spoils, the Lord gives gifts (4:7). Further, Rome may deal in control and death, but God has taken death as a captive—which leaves the church looking for, praying for, and entering into any way that God continues that life-giving initiative. Critical theory helps us develop those capacities by giving us a way of cultivating awareness concerning how politics and economics and violence and indoctrination are forces of death that God is challenging. The Bolman and Deal frames, when used to look at societal entities and the Christian-related organizations and churches around us, help us see our situation and our own complicity in death, as well as our opportunities to live into our God-given vocations.

And this counter-military metaphor (a reversal of conquest norms and the giving of gifts) becomes the basis of how Paul explains leadership. Throughout the epistle, Paul is working with on-the-ground behaviors and how they connect with God. He notes how the Ephesians connect faith in the gospel and their expressions of love "for all God's people" (1:15), which shows that the Jew-Gentile relationships are in some manner an initial expression of participating in God's in-the-streets work. Paul observed, "Christ is building you into a place where God lives through the Spirit" (2:22). Now in chapter 4 he connects God's prevenient mission with what he observes in Ephesus—that some men and women are demonstrating in their behaviors and words that they are aligned with what God is doing, and they do so in a way that augments and fosters faithfulness in those around them. This fits our understanding about leadership. Paul uses words that work at the overlap of common metaphors, Jewish heritage, and everyday activities—apostles, prophets, evangelists, pastors, teachers. These words gained some specialized meanings as time passed, and have become encrusted in functional hierarchies, but that is not how they began. In general, Paul's descriptions got colonized and turned into strategic formulas, which frequently make it more difficult to live into the space-between and the wonder of participating in God's initiatives. Critical theory helps us see through the fog, and Bolman and Deal's lenses can create both awareness and options.

We believe that these named gifts—apostles, prophets, evangelists, pastors, teachers—are not a formula for organizational structures but concrete observations by Paul; they name the improvisations of the church in Ephesus (and elsewhere), and he doesn't want them to miss how this serves their vocation. There is no command here to appoint or hire some experts—rather the passage assumes that the church is (or can be) aware that God has provided some persons, so the focus is on *why*. These five words are clues rather than tactics. In any specific context, as a local ecclesiology is perceived and tested, we have the work of discerning how God's gifts come in different people (in often surprising ways) as they serve the rest of us in wisdom and walking. We believe a key to these words is that they all describe activities in the neighborhood, or beyond the internal life of the church. *Apostles*, in its basic sense, concerns being sent, usually beyond comfort. The work of *prophets*, as Barth emphasizes, is about, "applying the gospel to specific contemporary circumstances."[40] In the Jewish tradition, prophets specifically helped others hear from God, and this frequently concerned connecting worship with how believing related to matters of righteousness (e.g., Amos 5:21–24; Mic 6:6–8; Isa 58). Their observations and exhortations frequently concerned those who were ill-treated by those in power—immigrants, widows, orphans, any who were marginalized. Leaders who nurture discerning God's initiatives need these traits. *Evangelists* are observed as speaking, often in the midst of other activities, so the gospel regarding life transformed by God is announced. The metaphor of *pastor,* while often associated with the internal life of a congregation, is more about a shepherd's life away from the corral—the hillsides (and its challenges) are more akin to marketplaces and streets. And *teachers*, usually now focused inside church buildings, schools, or maybe publishers, frequently practice in the Graeco-Roman culture, and in Acts, in the marketplace or other civic setting. Teaching is for everyone to hear.

So Paul sees in Ephesus that the gift (singular) from Christ becomes apparent at the interface of the local church and their world; in the daily life of markets and families and social encounters and labor, the people of Christ are "made suitable" ("equipped") for participating with God in *diakonia*, or the work of drawing everything into Christ. Paul notes that these leaders, in varied ways, have a generative and transformative impact on others, and this impact is not recognized in titles and structures but in where they are, how they live into God's initiatives, and how they diffuse the vocation through the body of Christ. Leaders—those who increase awareness and faithfulness in the church—influence connections, opportunities, conversations, observations, and reflections. When they are attuned to the Holy Spirit's life around and among participants, the church then lives into its vocation of joining God in bringing all creation into Christ.

The remaining exhortations of Ephesians expand and detail how the church of Ephesus needs to reconsider their own social arrangements and the habits they have acquired from their cultures. Famously, the passage on armor attends to how disruptive it is to participate with God—it draws fire. The collaborative operations of visible and invisible forces that work against

---

40. Barth, *Ephesians 4–6*, 436.

God require the church to acquire new habits of discernment, love, faith, justice, and courage (6:10–20). Paul indicates that they may not yet be up to the task—so these earlier passages on the vocation and gifts, and the on-the-ground life with God, frame how transformative grace and the engagement of faith provide a new and powerful counter to Rome and Artemis.

GETTING REORIENTED IN EPHESUS

Citizens of Ephesus are being shaped by Roman politics and economics, and by the assumptions regarding identity and power furnished by Artemis. Their imaginations, social arrangements, labors, and rituals are shaped by these powerful and comprehensive forces. God is about an alternative. Without critical capacities, which we see being offered today within the frames of critical theory, regarding societal assumptions and obligations, leaders are unable to see, engage, and shape options regarding God's counter-initiatives. That is how loyalty to God gets colonized by nationalism and the church's vocation gets confused with careers and industries. Ephesians moves back and forth between becoming aware of what God is doing and the shape of the church's life as those initiatives are engaged. Organizational change theories can help us see the overlapping and interrelated systems that have formed Christian organizations; they can awaken us to how church habits easily get stuck in symbolic, political, and relational patterns that proscribe discernment and faith.

As assumptions are displaced and new habits are engaged, diffused leadership continually perceives and names God's love as God engages the neighborhood in ways that draw others toward building the body of Christ (4:15). This is God's love in action. These encounters and experiences become diffused throughout the church, so with all the social, ethnic, class, and generational diversity that Paul notes, the church witnesses and displays in specific and concrete ways the continuing actions of Christ.

PART III: IMAGES & PRACTICES

INTERMEZZO 2

Habitus and Practices

INTRODUCTION

PART I INTRODUCED A way of listening to biblical texts, naming contemporary leadership challenges along with an overview of how we got here, and proposed a theological reorientation for our situation. We gave priority to a theological claim—that God is the primary agent. We have offered a metaphor—the space-between—in order to emphasize a theological interpretation of our context and to provide an imagination that moves us off old maps and into alternative practices.

When God engaged Peter regarding the Spirit's work in Cornelius's household, Peter faced significant changes to his previous beliefs and normal activities. God's initiatives could not be captured by new strategies for managing this disruptive moment within established practices. Peter had already heard some unexpected concepts about the gospel in "Judea, Samaria, and the ends of the earth"—but hearing those concepts, and even ruminating on them, were inadequate for the reality that now confronted him. God's initiatives require of us other kinds of responses: attentiveness, a willingness to be converted, an engagement with (often tentative) new steps that always involve risk, and continuing reflection on what we are discovering. Taking these steps toward participating with God's action becomes challenging and bewildering—not because we can't articulate a new belief or plan but because we are already so deeply embedded in sets of habits that get in the way. Those habits of thinking and feeling and acting, and the means available to be converted, are the themes of this intermezzo. Without an understanding of the role of deep habits and the role that practices play in converting us, our work of leadership will remain inadequate.

Like our first intermezzo, this brief exposition is intended to meet the instructions of our grade school math teachers who tell us to "show your work." That requirement pushed students to clarify and articulate our process, our thinking. In both of our intermezzos, we are focusing on theories that have already been displayed in previous chapters. Intermezzo 1 focused on discernment, showing how the various elements of our writing—Scripture, theology, cultural studies, leadership theories, social philosophy, etc.—come together in the discipline of practical theology. These are the ways a leader brings together critical reflection and participative activities for the purpose of discernment and participation in God's initiatives. This intermezzo, in preparation for part III, provides a brief explanation of what Pierre Bourdieu called *habitus*, which, obviously, relates to our habits.[1] We then explore the concept of *practices*—not just as repeated actions but as a formative process that fits the action-reflection cycle introduced in the chapter on Matthew. Before those conceptual explanations, we provide a warrant—a justification for engaging these theoretical resources.

WHY *HABITUS* AND PRACTICES

In contemporary literature, the work of leadership is often framed somewhat like Mark's first year seminarians' frequently (though perhaps not openly) posit: "finally I get to tell others what to do." Whether in sermons or teachings or planning, this approach of the "expert" dominates the leadership field. Even when the language works to ease this blunt framing, the assumptions around experts still prevail: coaches know what play will work best, consultants know what strategies will turn a company around, a shepherd-teacher (in most Christian comments on Ephesians 4) knows what others need to know and do. During the last three decades, as we noted in part II, some leadership theories have provided helpful adjustments through frameworks such as a learning organization,[2] adaptive leadership,[3] and organizational culture.[4] We draw on these frameworks, but we are still aware that they function inside late modernity (as discussed in part I) and what Charles Taylor called the immanent frame of our secular age.[5] We

1. Bourdieu, *Habitus and Field*.
2. Senge, *Fifth Discipline*.
3. Heifetz and Linsky, *Leadership on the Line*.
4. Schein and Schein, *Organizational Culture and Leadership*.
5. Taylor, *Secular Age* and Smith, *How (Not) to Be Secular*.

will continue to show how various frameworks need theological correctives while we also learn from and draw on these conceptual resources. Here we briefly connect with the theories of *habitus* and *practices* by attending to the theological resources we've been exploring.

When observing modern organizations and the attempts by leaders to shift the priorities and behaviors of such systems, Peter Drucker is credited with the saying, "culture eats strategy for breakfast."[6] Drucker, along with many others, saw the repeated failures of modern management and leadership to change their existing cultures. In our own engagements with congregations and denominations, we have worked alongside numerous pastors, executives, and lay leaders as they named the challenges they face. We would often help them list all of their previous efforts at change—and those long lists, spanning decades, were always about new mission and vision statements, programs for education and training, plans to increase participation, shifts in organizational arrangements, different priorities for staffing, and attention to better self-care among clergy. After creating these lists of initiatives and reflecting on their results, such leaders concurred that even when some benefits could be named, "nothing really changed." Alan would then illustrate this by stretching out a rubber band between his two thumbs. He described how the rubber stretched as long as he held the pressure between his thumbs. But the moment he took the pressure off then the rubber band snapped back to its original position and shape. The point being that most leader-led initiatives don't address the underlying habits and practices of a group. These initiatives are normally leader designed and leader led so that the moment the leader steps away then the underlying habits and practices of the group reassert themselves. Leaders have to understand why this happens within their organizational systems if any kind of transformative change is to be experienced. Pierre Bourdieu's concept of *habitus* helps us understand the powerful forces that make change so difficult. Leaders will mislead others if they do not attend to the profound strength of societal constraints, organizational traditions, cultural pressures, and personal captivities. The habits, practices, and customs that are shaping our organizational systems (congregations, denominations, schools, etc.) are not like clothing we can put on and off with ease. These critical forms of life together are sedimented into our collective lives; they become part of the breath, bones, and sinews of our common life together. As such they are not easily cast off with a vision statement, a bit of adaptive change, or a new innovation. Leaders are without significant influence if they employ only persuasion, explanation, political power, programmatic initiatives, and metrics to the

6. Drucker, "Culture Eats Strategy for Breakfast."

realities of their systems. As leaders we need to engage in reflective practices that match our theological convictions about God's agency. This requires us to get our bodies into new activity patterns that can make it more likely that we shape environments in our churches that invite people into new habits and practices. This is about understanding the power of *habitus* in ourselves and our organizations, and how practices give us ways to be transformed.

Habitus

In this exploration of *habitus*, we can benefit from a cluster of English-language words that assist us in getting hold of its meaning: habit, habitat, habitation, habitable. A *habitus* describes taken-for-granted ways a group of people live in relationship to one another and their context. It describes something we live in, how we understand ourselves, why we perform in the world the way we do. The concept of *habitus* helps us to grasp why these kinds of habits are so powerful in our lives. If one has an appreciation, for example, for soccer, then you become aware of not only the footwork of a player but also her instinctive sense of where other teams members are on the field. It seems as if she anticipates where someone else will be and sends the ball ahead before the team member gets there. How does this happen? The player isn't some complex computer making millions of in-the-moment calculations. Rather, her footwork and her intuitive sense of placement come from years of practice that has put into her whole body these habits of playing soccer. Quite literally, her feet (in relationship to the ball) have instinctively taken into themselves ways of relating to the ball. Her eyes, legs, body angles have done the same in terms of ball placement on a moving, dynamic field. This is what *habitus* is about. In a sense, she couldn't behave any differently without a huge effort in overriding all the knowledge and instincts built into her body. So it is with our participation in organizations like churches or families and so forth. This is why, for example, organizations can run so well and, at the same time, why they are so hard to change no matter how smart a leader might be or how good the plan for change might be. Our explanation parallels Bourdieu's *habitus* with Charles Taylor's concept of *social imaginary*.

Several key elements and assumptions regarding *habitus* need emphasis. First, our interpretation of *habitus* is comprehensive. It is intended to encompass the totality of the environment and behavioral patterns of the organizations and systems in which we live. This involves things like heritage and traditions, the normative ways of acting in a group, the feelings and emotional expressions common to a group. It also involves the approaches we take to structuring our built environment and organizational patterns; it even informs how we live within certain kinds of hopes and expectations. *Habitus* is a *"way of being . . . predisposition, tendency, propensity, or inclination"*[7] within which we live, or dwell. So, just as we live in a house, we also "live in" consumer capitalism, expressive individualism, white normativity, and assumptions about progress. Bourdieu uses the term *habitus* as a substitute for the word *culture*, which he believed had become overdetermined and tended to downplay agency.[8]

Second, a group and an individual are not separate or external to each other—they are mutually interpenetrating. The group is in the individual and the individual is in the group. This is important when we are interacting with materials from a vastly different time period and set of cultures. In the context of this book, for example, we have been looking at the Greco-Roman world, the Jewish culture and its faith, individual Jews, early groups of Christians, individual believers as well as our own contemporary social groups and the individual persons who participate.[9] To understand something of what was and is happening in and across these groups, we have to be attuned to the ways *habitus* is continually present in these interactions and our interpretations. Even in modernity, where individualism is a primary interpretive structure and the center of agency, we have to continually recognize that the *habitus* of this social construction is shaped by a social history. We have to understand this connectivity between people and groups if we want to attend to new situations and the leadership actions that might move us toward new kinds of *habitus*.

Third, as will have become clear at this juncture, *habitus* is mainly a socially internalized, unconscious way of our being in the world. This critical part of social and structural formation is not something reflected on. Like the illustration of the soccer player, *habitus* is assumed and out of sight. Our ways of thinking, feeling, and acting are seen, therefore, as just "common sense," needing no explanation or justification or even awareness. Sometimes Bourdieu compares *habitus* with "a feel for the game"[10]—that responsive yet unreflective way of connecting with a situation and making the next move.

Fourth, while a group's *habitus* gets changed and reshaped over centuries, at the same time, in our own milieu, the time and context in which

7. Bourdieu, *Outline of a Theory of Practice*, 214n1; italics in original.

8. Swartz, *Culture & Power*, 114–15; in reference to Bourdieu, "Structuralism and Theory."

9. Per Swartz, *Culture & Power*, 96–97; Swartz is connecting Bourdieu with social construction in reference to Berger and Luckmann, *Social Construction of Reality*.

10. Bourdieu, *Logic of Practice*, 55–56, 80–82.

we live, "habitus is fairly resistant to change."[11] This is why leaders get constantly frustrated by the limits of their efforts. What is happening is that their plans and hoped-for outcomes are being continually "regulated" by the existing *habitus*. The result is that even when supposedly new actions are engaged, those activities "reproduce the regularities" that are cemented into the *habitus*.[12] This does not mean it's hopeless to initiate change; that is clearly not the case. But it means that one of the frameworks a leader must grasp is the power of *habitus* and how it is addressed.

Finally, while at times Bourdieu seems to resist any significant options, he allows for human agency within the *habitus*.[13] But, human agency requires a *knowing* that is not outside or above the concrete situation. Thus, the leader has "to situate oneself *within* 'real activity as such,' that is, in the practical relation to the world, the pre-occupied, active presence in the world through which the world imposes its presence, with its urgencies, its things to be done and said."[14] Then, along with that situatedness, "the element of time (and tempo) is integral because elements such as norms, opportunities, actions, restraints, and intentions are moving through time, which also allows for different relationships and circumstances and outcomes."[15] This combination of place, time, knowing, intentions, and relationships will be explored as we explain the concept of *practices*. As becomes clear, practices are critical in the formation of any kind of new *habitus*. This is why leadership is about attending to existing practices and understanding how one introduces new practices among people that might initiate new habits. Here the action-reflection cycles within the context of small experiments become a critical leadership skill.

Practices

As a community develops and, over time, dwells in a particular kind of *habitus*, what were once improvisations become habits which, in turn, produce practices that reproduce themselves amongst a people. Indeed, we might say that a particular *habitus* consists of the embodied practices of a group. As we have said, these are mainly unreflective ways of being a group that allow it to engage with those outside the group as well as awake to the nature of their own internal relationships.

11. Swartz, *Culture & Power*, 107.
12. Bourdieu, *Outline of a Theory*, 78.
13. Swartz, *Culture & Power*, 98.
14. Bourdieu, *Logic of Practice*, 52.
15. Swartz, *Culture & Power*, 98–99.

In a sense practices are the ways in which a group goes about working out its *habitus*. They come before and are critical to the formation of a *habitus*. It is the repeated practice of working with the ball, the players, and the field that draws the soccer player into a *habitus* in which she instinctively knows where to place that ball on the field because the practice, literally, embodies a way of playing. At the same time, once that *habitus* is established, it then comes to determine the kind of practices she will attend to. All of this takes place within and over time. Over a time period the practice begins to establish new norms (how one places one's foot around the ball to get a certain spin angle, rise, and direction; how one, at times, holds back for the briefest second as the field keeps shifting with other players). The issue here is that the formation of a *habitus* isn't some kind of a positivist planning strategy based around a series of predesigned steps. Practicing is a dialectic between taking what one knows and has tested then pushing beyond that with new actions that have to be continually tested and retested. There is, for a time, a good deal of frustration; the ball doesn't go where one intends it to go, and it would be so much easier and, initially, more effective, to use the method one has always used. So, practicing is an iterative process that is going to be highly personalized. It will require the player to give the time to the work and to be focally present in this work.

This begins to give us important clues about how leaders involve themselves in the shaping of practices among people. What we are seeing is that such practices are not generalized techniques that can be objectively distributed to a group of people through some kind of handbook or weekend training event. Here, practices involve relationality, a focus on the person with whom one is introducing new practices. Leading a group into another kind of *habitus* through practices is a commitment to a large amount of time and the patience of working through the complexities of being with the other through a wide range of relationships, circumstances, and outcomes. The critical work of the leader is to situate herself *within* the real life of the people, not some imagined, idealized goal or outcome that the leader might have in mind. There is, genuinely, a good deal of complexity in this kind of leadership. At times it might be difficult to imagine how some simple practices (for example, praying the Daily Office) could change the *habitus* of a community. But in times of crisis, deeply embodied webs of meaning and long held habits become open to change. Crisis creates a situation in which a *habitus* can be superseded. This is precisely the kind of time in which many congregations find themselves. The various OT and NT narratives and contexts described in this book are dealing with precisely this kind of situation. The writers are speaking into crisis by inviting people to take on new practices of life. These were the ways they formed the kinds of *habitus* that transformed their worlds. Such practices start to arise from below as more and more people recognize that the habits and practices in which they live simply no longer make sense of the world in which they live.

Leadership happens when one is paying attention to the off-the-map ways people are expressing this disconnection between established practices and their current experiences, between what is being practiced (the current *habitus*) and their sense that things are out of sync. But if a leader is anxious about their own roles and their established patterns of leading, they will miss these off-the-map moments that signal a shift in the culture. One sees an example of this in clergy response to the COVID-19 pandemic. It is quite stunning the extent to which many of them are pouring massive amounts of energy setting up some kind of online worship service for their people. In social media the chats amongst clergy are about how to preach online or how to do a eucharistic service. Here the preoccupation is shaped by anxieties for the established *habitus*. Meanwhile, what is being missed in the crisis were all kinds of small, seemingly insignificant alternative practices popping up on the streets where people live. Being unable to socialize in our habitual ways, because social distancing is important, neighbors are improvising. While doing this, people, at least in Alan's neighborhood and during Mark's hikes, were keeping the new rules while experimenting. Guess what happened? People found ways to talk with one another that had not happened before. While keeping social distance, it was no longer the norm to rush past one another. We were talking to each other in new ways. In other words, this crisis was birthing practices of being with that are at the heart of Christian *habitus*. In the meantime, most clergy kept obsessing how to distribute elements in the right way and how to get their regular preaching out to people. And all the while people were trying on new practices that could radically change the *habitus* of congregations. At the heart of practices is improvisation.

Virtues

All of this brings us back to our earlier proposal that improvisation is a helpful framework for leaders. The question is, however, how does one prepare to improvise faithfully? It is not a given that a leader, on the occasion of God's initiative, will receive and engage that initiative rightly because, as our discussion here has shown, we also have to be very aware of the ways our own *habitus* and practices are at play. How does a leader and a leader's community become competent in faithful improvisation? How do we, in collaboration with the Holy Spirit, become the kind of people who see what

God sees, imagine what God imagines, and engage as God is engaged? We believe this is related to the embodiment of virtues. Practices, over time, create character, and virtues are a particular type of character. This means that at its center the work of leadership involves the formation of a community of character—a people who are increasingly self-reflective about the practices shaping their common life in relationship to God's agency and the people with whom they dwell. This is the meaning of *virtue*. Put simply, virtue is the sum of the habits we, like the soccer player, are being formed in through the practices that we take and make central to our lives. In the end, the leadership we are proposing in this book is about the formation of communities that are rooted in this kind of virtue. As this kind of character forms a local community, they, like the soccer player, when faced with challenges or crises, learn to improvise from within and amongst themselves. Here a leadership is present that doesn't need to have the answers because it trusts the work of the Spirit in the midst of a virtuous people. In this final section of the book we look at how the elements of leadership we have discussed become specific kinds of practices for leadership even as we keep in mind how such practices are developed in the midst of existing habits.

CHAPTER 8

Metaphors: Leadership for the Space-Between

INTRODUCTION: WHY METAPHORS MATTER

IT'S BEING HEARD MORE and more often these days. Over the past several years, Alan has received emails and posts from pastors he knows who have been compelled to go part time because their congregations are running out of money. There are thousands of other congregations and clergy living very close to this reality; they can step off the edge of this cliff at any moment. Denominational leaders see it; they feel the issues and don't know what to do.

While some embrace this trend, most live in the midst of an epidemic of anxiety about this reality of our unraveling. But as long as we let ourselves be imprisoned within these fears we will not discern what God is gestating ahead of us. Part of what is holding us captive to these anxieties are the metaphors that deeply colonize our understanding and practices as congregations and leaders. We live in the midst of metaphors that no longer have the power to help us see what is happening (discernment) and, therefore, can no longer guide us in addressing the unraveling of life that confronts not just the church but our entire culture. We need to recognize these longstanding metaphors in order to lay them down and take up a fresh imagination.

This book has argued for a praxis of leadership formed from within the primacy of God's agency in a context where God, congregation, and clergy have been shaped by narratives of expressive individualism. Our leadership functions in the overriding social imaginary of Modernity's Wager—that life can be loved well without God's agency. Resourcing this wager are metaphors of power, management, and control sourced by the autonomous self. In this social imaginary, God does not disappear but is reduced to the role of useful resource and assistant in human endeavors. This description characterizes one of the primary ways the "principalities and powers" manifest across the Euro-tribal churches. We have proposed theological and biblical resources for framing a leadership that prioritizes God's agency and God's invitation to participate in what God is doing in the places where we're located. *This chapter proposes the metaphor of space-between as one that can shape a new imagination for leaders and faith communities seeking to discern the agency of God.* This metaphor will be used to unfold a series of practices that will be proposed in chapter 9. In the investigation of *space-between* as a primary metaphor for leadership we will need to introduce several other metaphors of leadership as well as propose a moving away from metaphors that have been dominant in the Euro-tribal churches. All of this, first, calls for a very brief discussion of why metaphors are so critical to the proposals we are making in this book.

Metaphors are precritical, functioning as assumed, taken-for-granted ways of reading our worlds. Once established in a culture they're generally not questioned. They come to express a culture's tacit values about a people's place in the world, what it means to be human, to be in relationship with one another, and to form structures for political, familial, and religious life. Metaphors express a group's assumptions about how the world works and the kinds of habits, practices, attitudes, and values that are to shape and sustain our relationships and organizations. Metaphors express the nature of the group's commitments; they provide ways for people to behave within a group; they communicate its traditions to one another. They're hardly ever about individuals.

Metaphors are more than simply words used as pictures. In their book *Metaphors We Live By*, George Lakoff and Mark Johnson point out that metaphors reveal how a group or culture comes to see and understand the world. They argue that the metaphors used by a group become so seeped into their collective experience, their taken-for-granted, unconscious assumptions about the world, that they shape how we read and act in the world. This tells us that our metaphors are very powerful shapers of how we read the world and, therefore, how we choose to act in (and react to) our contexts.[1] The French phenomenologist Paul Ricoeur developed a profoundly detailed accounting of metaphors and how they work in our lives as communities and

---

1. Lakoff and Johnson, *Metaphors We Live By*.

cultures.[2] Metaphors order how we use language; they structure our conversations with one another in ways that express and support the ways we read the world. At the same time our established metaphors are continually being confronted by new situations that are challenging them and, potentially, calling them into question. The way we can understand how a metaphor is working in shaping us isn't just the use of a word itself as an image but the way it is being used in a sentence. Thus to grasp what a metaphor is doing we have to be attentive to the ways it is being used in conversation—how the sentences we are using actually give the structure and meaning of a metaphor. Thus, simply looking up the definition of a word does not give us insight into the use and meaning of a metaphor.

A good example of this is the metaphor *pastor*. It has had a long history in the church and, too often, because the actual word has remained the same through the millennia, it is assumed the meaning hasn't changed. But we will only find out what this image is doing as we listen to its usage in our sentences. When we do this it becomes clear that the ways that image is used today bear little correspondence to its usage in various New Testament texts. A similar kind of thing is going on with another familiar metaphor, that of *household* or *family*. Today, if we listen to their usage in sentences, they connote a massive turning inward of people to find a haven in what Christopher Lasch described as a heartless world. But in New Testament times household had a very different connotation pointing toward the generative space of work, care, production, and worship within which people (male and female, generations together) formed a way of life that was turned out toward the other and embraced a far larger community than our notions of the nuclear or single-parent family. Thus to grasp the intent and meaning of a metaphor, we must be acute listeners who are paying attention to our contexts and the ways words are being used in sentences.

Further, argues Ricoeur, metaphors have the capacity to foreshadow or help us point toward a new world. Thus, the tension of our metaphors. They can locate us in a world even to the extent of causing us to miss a great deal of what is happening that cannot be contained in the metaphors we have taken on from our tradition and, at the same time, they can be irruptive, suggestive of and assisting us in producing a new world. Finally, and of great importance, Ricoeur points out that a metaphor doesn't just describe but frames the kinds of *actions* we might take. They give us the possibility of acting in new, world-making ways in the always changing situations in which we find ourselves. Therefore, the importance of metaphors lies in the

---

2. The notions of metaphor and how they shape us runs through much of Ricoeur's writing. See, for example, *Rule of Metaphor*.

tension of identity, meaning, and action they place before us. They can bind us to a world that is critically important for our tradition as a people; at the same time these very same metaphors can blind us to situations that are before us in the unraveling. But, new metaphors can also point us toward new ways of understanding ourselves and, in so doing, the kinds of actions (practices) we might need to take on in order to structure ways of being God's people in a radically shifting time of unraveling.

This is what makes it so important for us to pay attention to the metaphors we take for granted in order to listen for those that are calling us into new forms of life and practice as the people of God. This is why, as we have argued, change doesn't come from well-formed arguments nor even from the latest methods borrowed from other disciplines. It comes out of our paying attention to the ways certain metaphors have constructed a world of leadership into which we too often have uncritically located ourselves—this is what we have described in terms of the need to be learners in the social construction of our contexts. In order to do this, we are proposing metaphors of leadership substantively different from those that have become normative in the Euro-tribal churches—thus, the language of space-between, alterity, unraveling, discernment, ferment, and so forth shape our proposals.

SOME CURRENT METAPHORS OF LEADERSHIP

Inside/Outside

One of these dominant metaphors is that of *inside* and *outside* space. This distinction between inside and outside has a long history in the formation of Christian communities in the West.[3] The spatial language within which religious life tends to operate is about inside spaces. This language is assumed in architecture: churches are buildings inside which congregations gather, as are abbeys and monasteries. These are spaces within which specially trained and designated people, like clergy, perform certain roles on behalf of ordinary people.[4] This spatial metaphor was largely assumed in

3. Following the industrial revolutions and the almost complete objectification of all life in terms of people as commodities and economic units, the image of *inside* has been transformed to express a place of haven in a heartless world, an escape, a place of protection for the wounded and isolated self, and often the center of consumption.

4. This is an oversimplification for the sake of brevity. In the medieval church those in orders, religious and the clergy, were divided by an understanding of *secular* and *religious* that is completely different from our contemporary use of these words. Secular originally referred to what was called ordinary time among people in their everyday lives. This was the domain of the parish clergy and their specific roles in providing

the formation of most Reformation ecclesiologies at the birth of the modern era in the sixteenth and seventeenth centuries. This is seen in some of the taken-for-granted definitions of the church that emerged in that period. Church came to be viewed as a place in which certain things took place. In Reformed definitions, church was a place where, for example, the Word was rightly preached, the sacraments rightly administered, and discipline rightly given. The Protestant churches' understanding and practice of being church has continued, to a large extent, to be shaped by this spatial metaphor which, in turn, then defines its understanding of the location and role of leadership. The corresponding notion of *outside* then comes to refer to all that happens in the public sphere of everyday life that is not directly related to the *inside* space of church and the roles of its leaders. It became less clear to conceive of the church except as a *space (place)* inside which certain things happened. Correspondingly, leadership then has everything to do with the roles required for life *within that space.* European and North American church leadership would, then, manage the elements of a specific *inside space,* and that work was directed toward assisting and resourcing "lay" people in how to live "outside." This is a significant part of what we would designate as the contemporary *clergy industry* wherein denominations, seminaries, and congregations have been formed within an imagination wherein clergy are not just indispensable but are largely set in this *inside* metaphor. But, as has been shown repeatedly in the biblical sections around Jeremiah, Matthew, Acts, and Ephesians, this kind of imagination, as powerful and deeply colonized as it is in the Euro-tribal imagination, is not sustainable as a primary leadership form.

The narrative developed in the previous chapters tells a very different story. In Ephesians 4, for example, Paul is reporting what he is seeing in the churches in Asia Minor—that as believers live into their communities, their lives as people of God are being shaped in unanticipated ways. That is what is going on in the section Paul writes about leadership. We noted that the language of Ephesians regarding vocations is all about life in the world, in everyday rhythms. Apostles walk among the believers in a way that shapes adventurous new connections; prophets continually link matters of God's voice with their lives in their communities among neighbors (discernment), and so on. Jeremiah's letter to the exiles (Jer 29) is doing the same thing—it

---

the liturgies of Christian life to people. Their work took place, to a large extent, within parish churches. The religious referred to those who had gone into religious orders and were separated from the everyday life of the ordinary. At the same time there were various orders that stood outside this dyadic understanding. They were religious in that they set themselves aside for God's work but rather than locating within cloisters they were present in the ordinary.

calls the exiles to a vocation of being with and among the inhabitants of Babylon. Indeed, the letter suggests strongly that only in this dwelling with and among will the traumatized exiles have any chance at all of hearing God's directions for them. Again, Luke points to this movement when, in Acts 16, the band of fellow travelers around Paul come to Philippi. In the context of what they had practiced in previous travels, they would have sought the familiarity of a synagogue or opportunities in the marketplace in order to present the reality of Jesus. But in Philippi those options did not appear even though they spent some time investigating the city. While they persisted in their search for some form of synagogue ("a place of prayer") outside the gate, they encountered by the river the obverse of what Paul had seen in his vision. It is a group of Gentile women (some "God-fearers") who are the ones to whom the Spirit is leading Paul's band. One can tell from the conversation between Paul and Lydia that Paul found himself in a space-between. It was a space he didn't turn away from, so this northernmost church was birthed in a Gentile woman's home. Rather than leadership metaphors of inside/outside we need to ask how we see our vocation as leaders when we embrace the metaphor of space-between.

Public/Private

Another dominant metaphor in our culture that has also colonized the Euro-tribal churches is that of *public/private*. Lesslie Newbigin, writing about the public/private split,[5] pointed out that the sources of this metaphor were not in the social imaginary of Christendom. For Newbigin, the public/private describes the contours of a modern imaginary. Prior to the emergence of the modern era in the West, God, as Creator, was understood to be the One who established the basis for and ruled over society in its ordered hierarchies. This ruling was carried out through two orders: king and church. Each was given authority to rule by God. The church, therefore, had a huge role in what we have come to call the public realm (in the development, for example, of jurisprudence, in the codes that determined the ways in which goods and services could be used in commerce, in the development of hospitals and educational institutions). Almost all areas of social, civic, economic, and political life were also seen as the realm of the church in the world because they were elements of God's creation. Both church and king functioned together under the rule of God. It was taken as a fact of creation that God, who was understood to be outside the created world, ruled this world from above through the powers of church and state.

5. Newbigin, *Foolishness to the Greeks*, 18–19, 34–39.

In certain periods there was no distinction between the actual ruler and the church leader. At the same time, kings were usually careful to acknowledge that their power to rule was derivative and placed upon them by God through the church. The point here is that there existed no differentiation between private/public or inner/outer in the sense that these metaphors are used today.

As Christendom waned following the Peace of Westphalia (1648),[6] a new relationship had to be worked out between the churches and the new proto nations-states. The Protestant churches, while often given the designation of official "state" churches, were increasingly assigned to the new *private* world of citizens. They came to assume a more and more ceremonial role in the *public* spheres of politics, commerce, social policy, and the ordering of everyday life. It is easy to miss the profound shift in social imaginary this represented for the churches as this modern frame of *private and public* became normative discourse wherein the metaphor *private* became a dynamic equivalent for *church*. This modern metaphor of *public-private* now shapes the self-understanding of church leadership and, as such, it has become the "traditional" way leaders understand the practice of congregational life and leadership.

The metaphor expressed a new understanding of *public* which, in turn, redefined the meaning of *private*. Public now had to do with the secular state and its primacy in determining policy and legislation on behalf of a whole society. It had to do with commerce, economies, the development of expert and professional classes outside the purview and operations of the church. In the case of public life, the churches in modern societies have a voice but that voice is a *private* voice, along with many other private voices, that have no legal or legislative power over anyone or anything within the public sphere. After Westphalia, this emerging definition of *public* resulted in what was effectively a détente between the churches, the state, and the public square. The power of the former was removed from this new *public* (political, legal, educational, social) sphere and relocated in a new *private* sphere (should the individual citizen choose to avail him/herself of these services). This tacit agreement has characterized the modern West up to the present wherein it has come apart at a massive rate that has sent the Euro-tribal churches into a tailspin of handwringing. It is seen in the US in how its Constitution established what became the separation of church and state. The goal was to limit the power of the state over the church but the result was the separation of the two around the public-private imagination.

6. Westphalia ended the Thirty Years War with a treaty that effectively placed control of religious life with a state under the control of its ruler.

Some European countries have state churches, but their roles are limited to ceremonial activities with little to no public influence. In North America the churches continued to see themselves as having a moral responsibility (the so called conscience of society or, less elegantly, a bourgeois morality that came to be seen as Christian) to speak to power or address critical public social issues (the new language developed for those who did this is *public theologian*). But this speaking to power and addressing the moral conscience of citizens operates inside this *public-private* division. The primary space the churches occupy is that of the inner, the personal, and the private, which gets worked out in different ways depending on the theological orientation of the group. So, for mainline churches, this gets worked out in the direction of social action and spirituality; for evangelicals, in the direction of evange-lism and a discipleship of the individual.

These background spatial metaphors (inside/outside and private/public) define the relationship between the churches and the cultures of the West. These metaphors are now embedded in the understanding and imagination of modern societies through their organizational systems (government, business, civic, educational structures, and hierarchies) that structure their values and convictions. Organizations and institutions are how a culture embeds and passes on its deepest values. In turn, these systems then create leadership roles to carry out the task of concretizing the cultural commitments. Social systems are, thus, expressions of fundamental *cultural* commitments that have been given expression in their *organizational* forms. In this way the churches in modernity (but especially the Euro-tribal churches) are structured and organized to be religious centers providing for the private, inner needs of individuals with some limited overflow (helping people and meeting needs) into the outer world. To a large extent the primary task of the *clergy industry* is to form leadership shaped around this social imaginary, though some schools on the right see their role as shaping clergy for political battles.

THE CLERGY INDUSTRY

This strange phrase—the clergy industry—is one of the most powerful metaphors resourcing leaders today.[7] It requires some explanation. An industry is a large, complex organizational system comprising many parts, each designed to interact with the other in such a way that a product is created, regulated, and disseminated across a society. The oil, auto, soft

---

7. While most likely to be heard in informal conversations, it is also common in career literature; for example, see "The Job Market for Clergies in the United States."

drink, entertainment, healthcare, and pharmaceutical systems are examples of industries. In their beginnings, they struggled to establish themselves in a society. To do that they had to provide a rationale for their legitimacy, but once that happens they become pervasive, taken-for-granted elements of a society. These industrial systems, to become successfully embedded in a society, cultivate a whole culture (internally and externally) designed not only to manufacture and sell their products but to enhance their value in the culture. They then need to create narratives that will protect and insulate themselves from alternatives (as in the oil, automobile, and pharmaceutical industries). Thus, these industries develop their own certification methods, their own "industrial standards," along with mission and value statements. Many of them develop their own internal training systems within which they, particularly the management class, learn a set of habits and practices that distinguish their industry and create gateways for people to enter or not (degrees, rings, exams, certification, training upgrades, etc.). Inside an industry people know what the degrees and certificates mean and where they place people in its pecking order or folklore. All of this is achieved from within the particular language world specific and unique to the industry, a language world that not only creates a mystique around its culture but readily identifies who is in and who is outside. Test it out—if you're an amatuer construction builder, or if you plant fruit trees for a small production (these are our own activities), or if you produce your own beer, you have encountered this phenomenon. As you engage these labors you are going to need to learn something of the internal language of the industry. Once established, an industry assumes its role and place within a society without any sense of being challenged (this was IBM's Achilles heel—they assumed the industry they had created was permanent and all their internal systems and narratives supported this conviction).

Part of our argument is that over a considerable period of time the Euro-tribal churches produced a pastor/minister/clergy industry. Today, it is a complex system of denominations, church networks, seminary training schools, conferences, money-sourcing foundations (underwriting the clergy profession), and congregations—all of whom assume there is a central "product" needed to serve the church, which is generally understood to be the "pastor" or "clergy" whose role is to "minister" to people in a variety of ways. This is one of the overarching metaphors determining the ways the Euro-tribal churches see and respond to the unraveling. It was inculcated into the cultural imagination of the churches by using the same methods as any other industry—certification for ordination, degree granting institutions that are the ordaining systems for becoming a pastor, an initiation rite identifying the person as a member of the group, and periodic gatherings of those so identified. All of this is covered over with an internal language world that can only be properly understood by the initiated. This is why a non-clergyperson sitting in a meeting of clergy often confesses to having little sense of what the clergy are talking about. It also goes a long way to explaining why the language of *missional* fails to take hold in most congregations. It is seen as a newspeak of the clergy that can't be understood and, many feel, that is why clergy choose to use such words. Once such an industry is established, people up and down the line (local congregation, denomination, and schools) become dependent, economically and emotionally, on its continuation. Participants see it as the tradition and resist attempts to change its basic structures, forms, and metaphors.

What this means is that clergy/pastors are formed inside a story about their identity that not only presumes a role, but, far more importantly, prevents each of these groups from seeing or imagining that it is this very industry in all its complex forms that prevents the Euro-tribal churches from conceiving of a different imagination or metaphors that might point to a different world.[8] What we confront in making this journey into the space-between, onto a road we cannot name in an unnamable present, is an industry whose systems default to established roles and methods.[9]

The missiological vocation of leadership is forming communities of God's people that are continually discerning God's agency so that they may join with the Spirit's ferment in their neighborhoods. God is the creative agent in the midst of confusing, disruptive change across the modern West.[10] In response to this disruption many institutions are doubling

8. The groups mentioned above—clergy, denominations, seminaries, and congregations—are so embedded in the economics of this industry that they can't afford (their livelihood, literally, depends on the industry) to imagine an alternative narrative. They are continually reinforcing the industry's basic narrative and metaphors. It's hard from within an industry to see its need to end. This is a movement of loss. Within the industry it is more likely leaders will propose means of reforming.

9. Part of the pushback is that the so-called "five-fold ministry" is "biblical" and, somehow, given by God as normative for the church for all time. As we've argued in chapter 7, these so-called "ministries" are examples of how these communities were constructing descriptive accounts of how they were, to be clear, making it up as they went with no intention of establishing for all time some universal identity or role. As with people like Paul, these early Christians were reflecting on what was happening as they sought to make sense of the expanding mission of God. We too are called by the Spirit in this unraveling to work out the mission of God by discerning the practices we need for joining God, rather than trying to rehabilitate an industry that keeps us inside narratives that proscribe us from entering unknown roads.

10. Notions of change can often be presented in a naive, simplified schema that obscure its complexity. See Bude, *Mood of the World,* for a nuanced, thick description of the complexities of change in a culture. An important part of our confession as Christians is that we know, first, because God reveals to us (in creation and in Jesus Christ).

down on their traditional metaphors and existing leadership strategies at great cost both to the people they serve and their ability to discern alternatives. Their metaphors of fixing, managing, and controlling, and even those of pastor and clergy, still powerfully shape the culture of the Euro-tribal churches. These very metaphors have become obstacles in responding to the unraveling. This unraveling can't be addressed through these still dominant metaphors. For example, even though we're in a period when the boomer cohort of leaders are leaving the stage, those leading denominational and church systems were educated, trained, and learned their craft within the metaphors of this cohort. Metaphors formed in an era of optimistic pragmatism and resourced by an unparalleled period of technological and economic expansion built a self-confident conviction that we always have a method to solve any challenge or fix any crisis. These metaphors remain part of the central convictions of clergy identity, denominational planning, and seminary training.

The unassailable narrative has been: we have the capacities to get data through which we can understand what is happening, the creativity to shape new options through innovation, the agility to adapt, the communication skills to explain the vision, and the administrative abilities to manage the needed solutions. When seminaries, denominations, funders, and boards look for answers to the unraveling, their default metaphors go to corporate modes of organizational change, improved products, creative services, and a scramble for better marketing. Alongside such dominant metaphors are also those of a romanticism that believes that simple fidelity to one's denominational heritage or just being "faithful" in a massively transforming context will make the difference. But this romanticism also goes in the other direction with calls to some kind of new, radical risks (which a majority of congregations simply can't imagine) that are off the map of most people's thinking. All these ways of engaging the unraveling remain embedded in the default metaphors of technocratic rationality. This posture, as chapters 2 and 3 proposed, is underwritten by metaphors of human rather than God's agency. Our biblical work (chapters 1 plus 4 through 7) narrated how God's agency is engaged by God's people in diverse times and contexts. Because of the power of these metaphors, and the structures embedded in them, as the unraveling shakes confidence in the technocratic power of human agency, the core biblical and theological convictions of leadership we have proposed fail to get traction.

One of the most important ways of discerning God's revealing work of remaking the world is as we learn, relationally, to listen to the ferment of the Spirit ahead of us in our communities.

In the midst of this turmoil God's Spirit is fermenting a future that can't be managed, predicted, or controlled. This moment invites Euro-tribal leaders into a radically different kind of space. The metaphor of *space-between* invites us into a space of dispossession rather than power, management, and control. In the space-between, the unraveling of our institutions is not something to be fixed but the place where we discern different metaphors (and hence practices) for leadership. It is a disorienting notion to grasp and appreciate. It cuts across and challenges the imagination and practices of current metaphors of leadership (such as CEO, pastor, manager, clergy person, or entrepreneur). It challenges the primacy of human agency in the leadership practices of these churches. The posture of dispossession, as proposed in chapter 3, is at the heart of God's agency in the incarnation. Dispossessing ourselves of the need to control the unraveling and determine all its outcomes is the liminal, in-between space where the Spirit is to be found and God is working. In-between space is where postures of management and control make no sense. It's a space that requires different leadership. Here is the missiological space of leadership in forming communities discerning the Spirit out ahead of them.

FERMENT OF THE SPIRIT

A Metaphor for the Context of Leadership

The metaphors we need for the shaping of leadership are those that assist us to frame an imagination for seeing and joining the Spirit's ferment out ahead in our communities. Such metaphors struggle to emerge because of deeply embedded metaphors of human agency in terms of management, power, and control. While the unraveling is the canvas onto which we propose a theology of leadership, it is not a space we are to manage or control. It is the space where we practice discerning the Spirit's ferment. This alternative imagination challenges metaphors of power and control. The need to fix and to provide solutions is propelled by unacknowledged anxieties about loss of power and a deeply embedded imagination for being in control. It is shaped by confusion about why traditional methods of control and management aren't stopping the unraveling. An imagination informed by the primacy of human agency and power (reforming, helping people, meeting needs, analyzing communities to match church skills with the community, etc.) prevents us from discerning what the Spirit is doing. Leaders struggle because they are locked into narratives: pastor as primarily care-giver, counselor, liturgist, professional, expert who provides solutions, local social justice agent, the champion of the latest identity politics movement. These narratives foreclose on their primary vocation: forming communities of God's people continually discerning and joining the ferment of the Spirit in their neighborhoods.

While becoming expert social analysts (which is helpful and important) leaders seem unable to place such analysis within the frame of God as agent.[11] We're not saying that learning techniques and methods from a broad variety of sources is wrong. There are important methods of leadership available from other disciplines, as we have demonstrated in earlier chapters. We argue that Christian leaders have taken on these methods in ways that make secondary attention to the question of God's agency. Technique and method have overtaken the practice of discerning the Spirit.[12]

The place from which leaders can enter the space-between to reengage God's agency and the Spirit's ferment is in their local communities. The unraveling is precisely the space where the Spirit is gestating God's new world. Therefore, the Spirit-shaped disruptions confronting congregations aren't burdens to be borne, or obstacles preventing "ministry," or problems to be fixed. They're gifts—the liminal space-between where God is already transforming the world and making all things new. Using the metaphor of a recent TV sitcom *The Good Place*,[13] the unraveling of the churches is the real "Good Place" because it is a space we cannot manage or control; it's a space not amenable to our technocratic management. It is where God is working ahead of us. This is why leadership is about forming communities that are discerning God's agency in the places where they live. This absence of the practice of discerning God's agency in the local explains why congregations and their leaders are increasingly anxious and discouraged. As the techniques they use to make their churches relevant or healthy or lively become increasingly ineffective, they have no other posture for engaging with the unraveling other than more technocratic schemes for managing. They are stuck in the default metaphors of fixing.

---

11. One of the most helpful pieces that demonstrates a theological approach to this work of social analysis is Scharen's *Fieldwork in Theology.*

12. There have been many such critiques made over the past half century or more. One of the more striking examples is Jacque Ellul's *Technological Society.*

13. For a brief review of this contemporary sitcom, see Anderson, "The Ultimate Sitcom." The sitcom is built around a simple plot in which a group of young adults die and go to a "good place." But, in actuality, they've been misallocated and are in some kind of in-between place. In this mixup they have to work out their communal and individual lives and purposes.

Early in this new millennium an anxious sense of displacement shapes the Protestant churches.[14] The desire to find ways out of the malaise is understandable. There are now appearing many kinds of experiments in addressing the unraveling that are intimations of the Spirit's ferment. The primary response we get when making proposals around experimenting is no longer disagreement but the question "how?" How do you discern so as to be shaped by God's agency?[15] Increasingly, church leaders no longer have the emotional energy for one more method, process, or book on how to mobilize their congregation or claim that Christians are to be freaky or different or radical or progressive. While some leaders continue to live in an illusion that they can control church life and growth, others leaders are done with aspirational promises. Hard-working judicatory leaders sense the Spirit is disrupting the churches but don't know what it means to engage that. They see these things happening and want to discover how to bring this ferment into the systems they serve. How do you form congregations and shape clergy who can go on this journey of discerning the Spirit and joining God in their neighborhoods?

We are in a very different space from even a decade ago. Leaders face challenges of unraveling on an unprecedented scale. They also sense the Spirit pressing them into this space-between. Once dominant Protestant churches feel like strangers in their own land.[16] Words such as *postmodern, secular, pluralist,* and *globalization,* are expressions of this disorientation but they are metaphors that offer little substantive help or clarification. They are explanations from *within* the once regnant categories of white, majority Euro-tribals who, confronted with loss of hegemony, are creating a new language world (metaphors) that might assist them to continue the control.[17] But what is needed is a *theology* of leadership formed from within the space-between. How might we embody a way of leading shaped by our dwelling in the space-between?[18]

14. See, for example, Bottum, *An Anxious Age*; Jones, *The End of White Christian America*; and Leithart, *The End of Protestantism*.

15. See, Roxburgh, *Joining God*.

16. For an insightful reading of this as a more general malaise across North America see Hochschild, *Strangers in Their Own Land*.

17 Jennings, "Can 'White' People be Saved?"

18. As we have seen, Pierre Bourdieu uses the term *habitus* to describe the precritical assumptions already in us. See, for example, *The Logic of Practice* and *Habitus and Field*. *Habitus* is the system of embodied dispositions through which we engage our worlds. The term *habitus* redirects us from focusing primarily on intellectual ideas as our primary way of knowing. When, for example, we read a book on leadership, the ideas and models given in the book are already based on preexistent habits that are, quite literally, built into the sinews, bodily engagements, and ligaments of the author.

Metaphors for a Theology of Leadership: The Space-Between

Chapter 3 framed a theology of leadership in which the primary image (metaphor) was of leadership informed by God's agency. The primary metaphor we propose to describe theological praxis is that of space-between. Leaders must reflect on the sources of the leadership metaphors shaping their praxis. Thus, our praxis is to intentionally be shaped by such questions as, "What is God up to in the world?," because our primary metaphorical narrative is that this is God's world and God is the primary agent among us in the unraveling. We want to ask: "What is God up to in the neighborhood and communities where we dwell as a community of God's people?" rather than ask generalized, abstract questions of God's nature. We are seeking to discern God's agency in the concrete materiality of our everyday life in the local communities where we live. God's agency isn't, therefore, an ivory tower occupation for those with the leisure time to pursue obtuse questions that real leaders in the trenches don't have the luxury to play with. We have dug deeply into the ways God's agency is central in Jeremiah, Matthew, Acts, and Ephesians. For these biblical writers there is nothing abstract or theoretical about God's agency—God is in everyday life and in the specificities of people's real situations. To take these texts seriously is to be confronted by the fact that God is on the ground.[19] Faithful leadership forms communities that are continually asking: What is God up to where we dwell as congregations? To offer this leadership is to find oneself in the space-between.

We have proposed that in Jesus, God's way of being with us in the world is expressed in the metaphor space-between. As seen in chapter 3, the nature of God's agency is revealed in Jesus, in his incarnation, life, death, and resurrection. That agency is continued as the Spirit of Jesus engages the people and powers of neighborhoods. In the incarnation, God reveals to us in Jesus the true nature of being human, of being-in-the-world. What is revealed in Jesus's Incarnation is that to be human is to live in the space-between.

Christian Scharen, in his little book *Fieldwork in Theology*, offers a helpful window into understanding what's at stake in our use of this metaphor as a central framing of leadership. In terms of God's primary revelation in Jesus as self-giving, Scharen references Rowan Williams:

> Let me start in a bit of a roundabout way by turning to Rowan Williams's little-known but powerful book of sermons. . . .

We have to be sensitive to this reality in order to appreciate the sources and assumptions driving the author's leadership proposals.

19. See this presented in chapter 7, working with Ephesians.

Williams quotes the fifth-century mystic Dionysius, who used the phrase "ray of darkness" to describe the way the light of Christ appears to us in the midst of our blind fantasy of ourselves as the center of the universe. Rather than a comfort, Jesus as the "word made flesh" dwelling among us brings on a "kind of vertigo" in which "the first thing I know is that I don't know, and never did." . . . In the midst of our sin, this coming is disruptive, very strange indeed. So strange, in fact, that the world "loved darkness rather than the light" (John 3:19) and killed Jesus rather than undergoing the radical transformation his incarnation invited . . . God's creative act is fundamentally the act of self-giving . . . the *kenosis* of Jesus . . . [Thus] "we learn to see God's creative act as itself a giving away, a letting go."[20]

In this sense, what we see in Jesus is the way God (in the words of Colossians) emptied himself of power and entered fully (as a dependent baby) into the vulnerability of a space where he cannot be in control. The metaphor *space-between* proposes here a way of understanding God's agency in Jesus Christ. God entered a space within which there could not be power over; it was an ambiguous, fragile space, a space-between the One who was Lord of all creation and the creature. This is the space Jesus came to inhabit. It is, to some extent, like the space that human beings are invited to inhabit in the creation stories. As we wrote in chapter 3, as priests of creation, to be human is to both embody the divine and earthly, to stand in the space-between as the primary space for being human and knowing God. This is the space God enters in Jesus. It is the space-between but, unlike the Genesis stories, Jesus steps into this space-between as one who has laid down all pretensions to power; there is no possibility of controlling outcomes in this space (this is seen most evocatively in Jesus' pleading with the Father in Gethsemane).

In this metaphor, leadership means joining with God by locating ourselves in the space where God has been most clearly revealed in Jesus Christ, the space-between. It continues, after the resurrection and before the eschaton,[21] as the space of the Spirit's fermenting of God's agency. It is a space-between because we both see and do not see where and how the Spirit is fermenting the eschaton. It is space-between because we are too

20. Scharen, *Fieldwork in Theology*, 58–59; citing Rowan Williams, *A Ray of Darkness*.

21. Described by Augustine as the time between the ascension and the coming of Christ again but it does not mean *secular* in the modern sense of that word See R. A. Markus's classic work on this subject in *Saeculum*. The *saeculum* is the space of God's presence and activity. The word carries the meaning of a created order sustained by God's agency without which it could neither be sustained nor could it move toward its renewal and consummation. The *saeculum* is filled with God's agency.

often enclosed within the defaults of Modernity's Wager. It is the space into which God invites us, a space where we can never predict, manage, control, programatize, or turn this movement of God into a strategic technique. In this space of hope and ambiguity, leaders form communities of God's people who are asking what God is doing in their specific context at this particular time in order to join with what God is doing ahead of them in their communities.

METAPHORS AMIDST THE UNRAVELING

Reweaving the imagination of Euro-tribal congregations will be difficult to achieve without something more than techniques of, for example, going out into neighborhoods. There has to be a prior engagement with the question of how to discern where God is at work in their communities. The challenge of joining God in the neighborhood is not that of techniques (how to be adaptive or innovative) but shaping of a liturgical desire to discern God that transcends this inner/outer and public/private imagination. It requires leaders formed in radically different ways than the present clergy industry. It calls for a theologically-oriented desire for the God who can only be known in the space-between. We want to ask about the practices that form leaders who are capable of engaging this question: *If God is the primary active agent in the world and one of the central metaphors for the way God is present as agent is the "space-between," what does this mean for the practice of leadership?*

The Christian communities being formed in the New Testament were constructing a way of life as they, literally, found themselves in a new space (the *ecclesia* of God)—a space-between. They were in spaces they'd never been in before (for example, see Acts 16 where Paul and his companions are confronted with Lydia); they found themselves needing to construct from the raw materials of their contexts ways for structuring and leading that the Spirit was unfolding before them. Questions of organization, structure, and role were resolved by assuming that God was present and active where they were, then, on that basis, asking about the kind of leadership roles that would be required in these contexts. One senses that most of the time the question of leadership roles was being addressed in retrospect—as Paul, for example, engaged the space-between realities of Philippi and the unexpected engagements with people like Lydia, he could look back and then name what the Spirit had been doing.[22] Roles emerged from this kind of engagement with God in the space-between. One wonders, in our own disruptive unraveling,

22. See Weston, "Leslie Newbigin."

why it should not be the same for us. As our examination of biblical texts in previous chapters has argued, so much of what was happening involved men and women taking the risk of following God into these spaces and, in so doing, discovering radically new ways of being both leaders and God's people. The structured, sacred language world of leadership shaping Jerusalem did not become the language world of the early church. These were people who had to reimagine what God was doing in the space-between.

In our own unraveling, the question of leadership cannot be just about the adjustment of given roles (like Jerusalem) that are assumed as normative. We need a willingness to dwell in the space-between where we must practice, risk, and experiment to discover the roles we need in this unpredictable and unmanageable space. The metaphors of this space are going to be very different from those in use today. Our disorienting space invites practices such as being present with, listening with, discerning, asking, evoking, testing; they will be about laying down imaginations of the CEO, team leader, entrepreneur, innovator, strategist, and manager. This is a space of tension, confusion, anxiety, experimentation, and creativity that won't be managed or manipulated to anyone's ends or vision. There, between the mystery of God's working among people of a local church and God's activities in the neighborhoods, leaders discern ways of leading that lie beyond established roles and definitions. The Spirit of Jesus is calling us, like Abram before us, to dwell in a space we cannot manage or control (Luke 10). All of this calls for practices of discernment.

The practices of leadership in this space can only be discerned from within the conviction that God is the primary agent in our communities. As the Spanish theologian Daniel Izuzquiza states, "Any group that wishes to make a significant contribution in a pluralistic world will need to articulate its difference in ordinary practices; if not, it will become meaningless."[23] Given this basis we turn, therefore, to the question of leadership practices in the space-between.

---

23. Izuzquiza, *Rooted in Jesus Christ*, 32.

CHAPTER 9

Practicing Amidst God's Agency

INTRODUCTION

THIS BOOK HAS PROPOSED that the vocation of leaders in the great unraveling is forming local communities of God's people who are discerning and participating in God's agency in their neighborhoods and communities.[1] It argues that the emergence of the modern was characterized by the revolutionary power of technology that, in turn, formed a new class of leader

---

1. As with the incarnation, the bias of this book is the local and everyday. We would argue that if the denominations (which are part of what we call the "clergy industry") are to have any kind of contributive future through their various regional and national structures, they, too, must continuously be asking about their purpose in terms of this basic orientation. Stated in an oversimplified form, this work is about a leadership that is attending to the voices of people at the margins both within the congregations and the neighborhoods where it is located. The temptation within too many denominational systems is to be overly focused on those elements of their organizational systems that are non-local. There is a nodding of the corporate head to the local but little energy is given to actually paying attention to what is happening on the ground except in efforts to boost the larger system. Denominational systems, in parallel with what happened in the broader culture, become bureaucratized and in so doing were directed by whatever the agendas of national and regional staff happen to be in any particular period. An unintended consequence of denominational systems championing the professionalized, technocratic elites that came to dominate organizational systems in the West is how they became increasingly disconnected from what was happening in the local, among ordinary people in everyday, in a refocus on clergy and their roles, the manufacturing of national programs devised and run by experts in national staff, and advocating that their constituencies embrace specific social issues of the time. This has contributed to the massive loss in these systems of any ability to discern the ways in which the local and everyday are, in fact, the primary locations of God's agency.

whose dominant *habitus* is that of the technocratic elite, which is now the pervasive form of leadership in our time. This form of leadership privileges human agency within Modernity's Wager. This *habitus* has produced a social imaginary where any sense of God's agency has no practical meaning for our life together. God as agent has become a vague metaphysical idea with little practical meaning. The notion of God among us as agent has been turned us into a useful resource for blessing our own agency or supporting personal development.

In this overarching context we have asked what was happening in scriptural texts as leaders sought to make sense of their contexts. We have been asking where and how God as agent was present in these situations and what all of that meant for leadership practices. In asking these questions we proposed a primary metaphor for approaching both the texts and our own unraveling. This metaphor is the space-between. This final chapter seeks to outline what we see as the praxis for being God's people in this space.

As the final chapter of part I describes, the theological imagination of the Christian tradition confesses that in the incarnation, God is revealed as agent. God is known to us in all the vulnerability of the ordinary and everyday. In Christian theology, the God who is creator, sustainer, and redeemer, is fully and deeply engaged in this world. What confronts those who are leading communities of God's people across the West is that, practically, this sense of God's agency has been evacuated from our everyday life and replaced by the overarching *habitus* of technocratic rationality. This form of leadership is trained in an imagination that reads the local and everyday as little more than a background canvas over which it paints its own, more generalized, pictures of what needs to happen. Place has become, to a large extent, an interchangeable blank page on which to practice another rationality than that of the incarnation. What is striking about our biblical texts is the extent to which the disruptive actions of God happened in the stubborn particularity of place and among specific, ordinary people.

In the light of this framing, part II invited us into biblical texts that we had introduced in chapter 1, and this underlined God's agency as the basis for the experience of God's people. In the New Testament studies, we saw that local communities of Jesus, as human agents, were invited to be shaped by God's agency in their concrete political, social, and economic realities. What was stunningly clear in these texts was how God continually came to diverse communities to challenge regnant metaphors and call forth alternative ways of being God's people.

Within our questions about leadership and the fate of the Euro-tribal churches, we proposed the metaphor space-between, as the essential location within which leaders and the people discern and engage with God.

This final chapter addresses the question of what, practically, is involved in forming local communities who are discerning and participating in the ways the Spirit is acting ahead of them in their neighborhoods. As leaders and communities we are in an unnamable space where we've not been before.[2] This space-between is not for prognosticators nor for those looking to find five-, eight-, or ten-step methods. This chapter proposes concretely ways of leading in this space-between.

ATTENDING TO GOD IN EVERYDAY LIFE

One of the unintended consequences of the Euro-tribal churches colonization by Modernity's Wager is the extent to which we have lost the habit of attending to God's agency in our everyday lives.[3] When we raise the question of God's agency among leaders there are typically two responses. First, we tend to get agreement that a critical leadership practice in the unraveling is discerning what God is doing to join with God in their communities. Second, leaders confess to having little sense of how to go about this. Part of what is to be recovered are everyday practices that redirect the conscience of our eyes (what we see about us in the concreteness of the everyday). Such practices come from deep within the Christian tradition. There already exists in most traditions habits, such as the keeping of the Daily Office—the *habitus* of reading Scripture, and praying for others, that can form us again

2. This phrase is one introduced by Roberto Calasso in his book, *The Unnamable Present*. He states what this means in this way: "*For we who are living at this moment, the most exact and most acute sensation is one of not knowing where we are treading from day to day. The ground is brittle, lines blur, materials fray, prospects waver. Then we realize more clearly than before that we are living in the 'unnamable present'*" (3, italics in original). This book is written for leaders who can sense that Calasso's words come close to describing their experience. This should not be a troubling thing for a Christian in leadership, as if admitting to being in such a place is to somehow communicate a lack of faith in God. Surely, in so many of the biblical narratives we have engaged in this book, this was precisely the experience of faithful people. But this sense of being in an unnamable present, in a space-between, is the essential element for us to discern the ways of the Spirit in our time. In this context it is important and legitimate to ask the question of how we take this journey. That is what we seek to address in this chapter.

3. In a recent book, the evangelical writer Jake Meador commented on this fact in terms of his own tribe: "At bottom, the recent evangelical movement has been designed to do two things: first, grow churches through innovative worship practices and uncritically adopting the cultural garb of suburban Middle America. Second, to secure political power through an alliance with the Republican Party. . . . In the years since World War II the American church has consistently chosen to chase power, prestige, and mainstream status" (*In Search of the Common Good*, 19). For an excellent historical overview of the development and role of denominations in the American context, see Van Gelder and Zscheile, *Participating in God's Mission*.

as people who are attending to God's agency.[4] The challenge in taking up these practices again is twofold. The first is that so many of us have accepted the lie that in our busy, demanding lives, we no longer have time to come aside, be still, and enter the Office. The other is that even when a practice such as the Office is taken up, it tends to get processed as personal time, inner quiet of the self with God. But, in point of fact, the Daily Office directs our attention away from ourselves to God's reality in the everyday. Recovering these elements of the Office are crucial acts in our capacity to see where God is agent in and around our everyday lives. Leaders can do nothing better than to practice the work of an abbot in forming a people around the practice of the Daily Office. By gradually inviting some in a congregation to walk with you on this road, a circle of practitioners gains the practices that lead to ways of seeing where God's Spirit is present. With the regular practice of some simple questions, a leader can shape the Daily Office in ways that direct people's attention to where God might be at work.

An excellent way to approach questions would be to meet with those who are practicing Daily Office and use something like the Jesuit *Examen* to ask reflective questions.[5] What we have found helpful in this work of reflection are: Where have you seen God present among your neighbors and in your neighborhood this week? What has given you encouragement this week as you have been with others? What have you seen this week that troubles and stirs your spirit? These are not definitive questions but they can guide the beginning of our common discerning of where God might be at work. They are also the kinds of questions that can be introduced into Bible study or Dwelling in the Word exercise. In these prayer practices, the Spirit engages the text, our experiences in our contexts, and the reflective conversations going on around us. Here are simple places where leaders can introduce practices that direct our attention back toward God's agency among us.

4. The Daily Office is a long established Christian tradition of Scripture readings and prayers that begin and end each day. The Office has a regular form built around initiating prayers, readings from the Psalms, selected texts from the Old Testament, the Gospel, and a reading from other parts of the New Testament. The Office orients us toward God at the beginning of each day. Many Offices also direct us in their liturgies into the world where God is ahead of us. Offices are also read at the end of each day in order to reflect on that day and present our life in it to God.

5. The Examen is a prayer of review—a short reflection back over the day, recalling events and taking note of your responses and engagements. It is closely related to Ignatian spiritual practices (Loyola Press, "Daily Examen"). Its purpose is to reflectively deepen one's awareness of the ways God is present to you as part of the critical work of discerning the Spirit's work and calling in your life. The power of the Examen as it was developed is that its focus is not primarily one's personal, inner development but how one is hearing and responding to God at work in the everyday.

Something of this work and practice characterized those who received Jeremiah's letter in Babylon or those in Matthew's community in Antioch. It seemed they were in the midst of disruptive changes, including recent events in Jerusalem. We can imagine that some had lost a sense of how God might be at work in their moment of unraveling. Where to begin to reconnect our leadership with God's agency? Henry Mintzberg in *Rebalancing Society*[6] shares a story based on a character in James Clavell's novel *Shogun*. A "Japanese woman tells her British lover, confused by the strange world into which he'd been shipwrecked, *It's all so simple, Anjin-san. Just change your concept of the world*." But when you're shipwrecked or in a place you don't recognize, what is easy to another person is a terrible loss of identity and role to someone else. This was the world of Jeremiah's exiles, of Matthew's beloved community in Antioch, of Paul and his companions by a river outside Philippi. Each case describes what we call a space-between, where God's people were confronted with the choice of changing their concept of the world. That is precisely the situation in which we find ourselves. In this space, a critical leadership practice is assisting our people to re-focus their eyes to see where God is at work before them. The simple, but extraordinarily powerful practices of the Daily Office, asking simple questions, and reflecting prayerfully together, are important ways of entering into this disruptive space.[7]

Lesslie Newbigin describes how everything in the training and imagination of the Jewish Christians meant that when they were confronted with the unimaginable coming of Gentiles to be followers of Jesus they were convinced that they, first, had to become Jews. In other words, the Gentiles needed to fit into the *habitus* of Israel. Newbigin writes:

> It seems clear . . . that the first disciples also saw the matter in this way . . . What could be more obvious? The law was a hedge protecting an oasis of godliness in a world full of uncleanness. Israel was a garden which Yahweh had planted, watered, pruned, and nourished. . . . The mission of Jesus had been in the first instance to Israel. He had himself been circumcised and had never called in question the fundamental mark of identity of God's chosen nation . . . What more natural, then, that Peter should resist the suggestion that he should compromise himself as a loyal

---

6. Mintzberg, *Rebalancing Society*, 23.

7. Like the conversational studies that occured around tables in Jerusalem following the Spirit's disruption, we hope that some of our biblical explorations can fund the action-reflection of improvisational teams as they seek increased awareness about God's initiatives. Churches can also benefit from other reflective reading—see Smith, *Reading for the Common Good*.

Israelite by accepting the hospitality of an uncircumcised pagan soldier? . . .What resulted from that event was not that Cornelius and his household were added to a church which remained unchanged in its essential nature . . . It was that a sovereign action of the Holy Spirit changed both Cornelius and Peter . . . [F]rom that moment . . . discipling did not mean turning them into Jewish proselytes; it meant the coming into being of a new kind of humanity for which a new name had to be found . . .It surely needed amazing courage on the part of those devout Jewish disciples of Jesus . . . to create something new, overturning old classifications . . . taking all that belongs to the Father beyond the present experience of the church . . .[8]

What was just as radical as this decentering was that in Cornelius and Lydia, for example, there is also a radical decentering of the state and its powers. In this "something new" that was being created, a whole new center of life was being formed that meant that neither the state nor the economy could any longer be the defining locus. Changing our conception of leadership after the shipwreck is about loss to be sure, but it is also the invitation to step into a space-between that overturns the existing *habitus*.

ATTENTION, LOCATION, AND ALTERITY

The work (energy/focus) of leadership is also attending to the Spirit's ferment in our neighborhoods to form congregations that join with what God is doing there. Along with personal and group reflective practices of biblical texts and prayer, we are proposing a shift in the location of leaders and, therefore, a reimagining of some of their primary practices. The location of attending and listening must also become the neighborhood. This attending is not primarily about pastoral care, "ministry," evangelism, or social action. It is the practice of being with the other, as other; our neighbors are not the objects of these targeted actions. If the practice of listening is so critical to discerning the Spirit in the unraveling, then that practice must be practice in this space. Attending and listening with and among the people of a neighborhood are practices that have tended to be displaced by other activities. Why is this the case? Some years ago, Alan wrote a book about change using, as an illustration, the ways single-cell organisms adapt to their environments. These tiny organisms continually work at the delicate task of keeping in balance with their environment. Our skin, for example, is an amazing, complex organism that continually monitors and manages

8. Newbigin, *Signs Amid the Rubble,* 81–82.

the exchanges between our bodies and the environment. It tells us about temperature so that we maintain a healthy balance with our environment. This balance is called homeostasis, meaning we have mechanisms working all the time to maintain balance with our environment. A primary way single-cell organisms, like the amoeba family, do this is through the use of tiny hairs, generically called cilia, that grow out into its environment to send messages back into the cell so that it can adjust (or escape) when the environment changes.

When there's a lot of environmental change (disruptive change like our current unraveling) the organism puts out more and more of these protrusions, increasing its capacity to monitor and adjust. They crave homeostasis. If they don't, they die. Sometimes the organism experiences a very long period of stability. When this happens these hair-like monitoring protrusions atrophy. Given long enough in this stability a majority of cilia disappear as they're no longer needed. This is fine so long as the stability continues. But when the environment changes, as it inevitably does, the organism experiences this as shock. There were warning signs, but when the systems for sensing the environment have atrophied, the warnings aren't detected. Dramatic change then seems to come suddenly, out of the night; it's unexpected and the organism has few capacities to deal with it; it's existed for too long within a range of homeostasis (like the clergy industry) that became the norm.

Modernity's Wager was a massive environmental change for the Euro-tribal churches. After the initial shock they adjusted to this environment but in doing so they disconnected from their communities (parishes) and, thus, lost any practical sense of God's agency. With that came a clergy industry that takes its primary methods from therapy, marketing, business management, and the technocratic elites of the last century. Further, almost all these practices are directed inward toward the congregation, not the neighborhood. Notions of God among us, on the ground, in our neighborhoods, became strange ideas.

Then came the great unraveling. Leaders are at a loss to make sense of this new environment. How to reintroduce the "cilia"? A primary practice urgently needed is that of giving significant time to being with and dwelling in the neighborhood. This is the location of discerning and joining God.[9]

---

9. See, for example, *Joining God*. Also see the important work of Fitch, *Faithful Presence;* and Sparks, Soerens, and Friesen, *New Parish.*

MAKING THE ROAD AS WE WALK

Part of the answer to the question of where we start lies in the story behind a poem written by Antonio Machado (1875–1939). The poem starts with these words: *"caminante no hay camino. Se hace camino al andar"*—"traveler, there is no path. You create the path as you walk." Machado was born in the late nineteenth century, a period pivotal in the imagination of the Spanish people. It marked the ending of the Spanish Empire after a long period of unraveling. Spain entered a time of despondency. The empire which had formed people's identity was extinguished. Machado's poem expresses the feelings of a generation coming to terms with the crisis of identity this produced. Machado's contemporaries were born into a colonial Spain that produced a culture rich in traditions of music, literature, and the arts. It was all ripped away seemingly overnight, but actually the unraveling had been long and slow. Machado knew there was no bringing back this world. He and his fellow Spaniards were confronted with an existential crisis of identity. Their cultural assumptions had been torn away. They were in the space-between —their power gone and with little sense of what to do.

For Machado the established roads that had given place and identity were gone. For some, the option was to pretend, to carve out an enclave of those trying to recreate what was lost, to fix the old roads as if they were still there. Machado, realizing the old roads weren't repairable, expressed in this poem that the task was to make a road as you walked.

> Traveler, your footprints
> are the only road, nothing else.
> Traveler, there is no road;
> you make your own path as you walk.
> As you walk, you make your own road,
> and when you look back
> you see the path
> you will never travel again.
> Traveler, there is no road;
> only a ship's wake on the sea.
>
> from *"Proverbios y cantares"* in *Campos de Castilla, 1912*

Saying the "road is made by walking" doesn't mean a strategy for making a road (it's not about new road construction) to take us to a new goal. Rather, the road is discovered (discerned) as we start walking with the recognition we are in an "unnamable present," a place where we don't know where we're treading.[10] The intent of this walking is to discover how

---

10. Calasso, *Unnamable Present.*

to listen for and discern the way God is ahead of us in the local. The road is not the object (like some blueprint) nor is it to bring us to a destination, an end. This road won't answer questions like: Where are we going? What's the destination? Where on the map do we need to be? Rather, we walk to lay down a road that provides ways of hearing God on the ground.

These are jarring notions for those convinced that God has already laid down a map for us all to follow. It will be jarring for some to read that a destination isn't the goal. There is a destination toward which God is drawing all creation, which we discussed in chapters 3 and 7. We affirm this. But in Jesus' incarnation into the space-between we see that in so many ways Jesus was making the road as he walked. This walking was about listening to and trusting the Father without knowing the blueprint. Such walking calls for trust and humility because we only see the forms of a road after we've walked forward into the space-between. This is the place to begin.

This walking invites us to embrace a hopeful posture of letting go and putting down. It is a confession of our faith in God as agent. Abram was called to leave his settled place and the identity it had given him. He walked to a place he did not know and, therefore, could not recognize at the beginning. He and Sara traveled in the faith that God was leading and would lead them on. This walking invites us to travel beyond the skills and methods this society insists are critical for success, to travel *beyond* "society" to discern God's agency.[11] C. Kavin Rowe expresses this well in his study of Acts:

> [I]n its attempt to form communities that witness to God's apocalypse, Luke's second volume is a highly charged and theologically sophisticated political document that aims at nothing less than the construction of an alternative total way of life—a comprehensive pattern of being—one that runs counter to the life-patterns of the Graeco-Roman world. His literary work is thus . . . a culture forming narrative.[12]

Such traveling requires little gear ("Don't take a backpack for the road . . ." was one of the simple instructions Jesus gave to the Twelve in Matthew 10[13]) and, as anyone who has taken on a simple task (such as choosing to be present in one's community) knows, this requires conversion. Becoming a novice involves embracing postures of simplicity and a conversion to the ordinary, everyday directions of Matthew 10. A novice starts this walking for herself—she is not doing it to get certified or become an expert who

11. Calasso, *Unnamable Present,* 16.

12. Rowe, *World Upside Down,* 4.

13. These instructions are parallel to Jesus' instructions in Luke 10:4: "Carry no wallet, no bag, and no sandals."

guides others. But it genuinely calls for a conversion. We continually hear leaders tell us they have no time for this kind of being with people, and they don't understand what the return on investment will be. A novice is humbly learning how to become an interpretive leader among her people and community. She is learning how to discern God's agency. This means choosing to dwell in one's community and be with the people of one's neighborhood. Interpretive leadership doesn't come in any other way. It is a call to conversion for most busy, goal-directed leaders. It is a radically different *habitus*. What are its practices?

JEREMIAH: DWELL WHERE YOU ARE

The answer to the question of practices, of what does one do when a world unravels, is counterintuitive, as was the case with Jeremiah. Leaders start on this path-making walk as they choose to dwell in and with their neighbors. Interpretive leaders are formed as they place themselves in their neighborhood. As chapter 4 proposed, to lead in the unraveling is to be an interpreter of what is happening in the midst of the community. One doesn't become such an interpreter primarily through books or championing strategies on a set of issues. One becomes an interpretive leader as one dwells in the community. The church is good for little if all it does is champion perceived issues prevalent in the culture and social media. Leaders and churches should embrace social issues (migration, housing, health care, climate change, economic justice—these are issues every citizen must engage), but interpretive leaders have a different purpose and pay attention to different signals. Interpretive leaders focus on the question of how and where, in the midst of multiple crises, God is already ahead of us in our neighborhood. An interpretive leader engages this question by stepping into and dwelling in the neighborhood (Jer 29).

The exiles in Babylon were in shock! The unthinkable happened. They could have raised a myriad of issues about justice, the broken state, the destroyed walls of Jerusalem, and so forth. In this state of shock they knew what was needed—get back to Judea and Jerusalem at all cost. But they were given a vocation they could never have imagined—dwell in the place to which they had been brought. Such dwelling didn't mean forming an identity ghetto; rather they were to enter the life of the city and become engaged with its people. Jeremiah's instructions were a radically different interpretation of the exiles' purpose and how they were to live. Jeremiah interprets the exile in a radically disorienting way: don't strategize a way back to Jerusalem; dwell where you've been brought. Jerusalem for them was the location of God's presence. Jeremiah offered another interpretive framework. God was in Babylon and only by dwelling there could they participate in God's shalom and discern why God had allowed this crisis. The meaning of the exile would not be found in Jerusalem.

The Path Begins in the Local

How does leadership interpret what is happening and where God is in the midst of disorientation and loss? For the exiles the question was, "How do you sing the LORD's song in a strange land?" (Ps 137). The implied answer is that one can't! Jeremiah's interpretive leadership pointed to a different response—we re-root ourselves in the place where we are. In our own unraveling, this is how we make a road as we walk. The dominant identity of many church leaders has been that of overseeing *inside* church (buildings, programs, and roles presumed by such designations as minister, pastor, priest, clergy). They are to care, nurture, and form the faithful in some strange understanding that these *inside* leadership roles equip the people for their work *outside*.[14] For other clergy, the focus is on tactics for changing society, trying to manage changes in social systems. The *habitus* of leaders is a return to "Jerusalem." Jeremiah's alternative narrative to leaders in the unraveling is that the location of our vocation is in the neighborhood.

What are we saying? Making a road means a primary part of a leader's focus and time are directed toward dwelling in their neighborhood, being with the people in that community. This is not about an avocation alongside a busy life of "ministry" but a deliberate choice to be present in our neighborhood and with the people around us. This presence is not about being a chaplain or pastor to the community—that is still about being in control, about being able to name who I am and what I can do for you. The dwelling we are describing involves leaving our "backpack" behind; we are not to be self-sufficient with our own resources, supplies, and strategies. Rather, initially, we lay aside our methods of reading a community (our ethnographies, our asset-based assessments, our metrics for the needs of the neighborhood, and our profiles of who lives there). Instead, we are to be present as ordinary, regular human beings. It is impossible to dwell with and enter into the lives of people, to sit at their tables and eat what is set before us

14. We fully understand that this represents a very reductionistic and innapropriate understanding of what some might describe a "biblical" understanding of the church or being God's people. That is not the point being addressed here. We are not addressing questions about the identity of the church but describing what is, in fact, the actual functioning of the church and its leadership.

if we enter with all these methods of assessment. This entering is hard, disorienting work that takes us outside established roles into a space-between where we can't know what "success" or "results" or "outcomes" look like.

Discernment Only Comes on the Path

Jeremiah 29 proposes a way of answering the discernment question: "What is God doing?" His response is: build houses and plant gardens in Babylon, not Jerusalem. This counter-intuitive imagination was hard to take in as a word from God. Jeremiah's point was that the kind of discernment that gets at the question of what God is doing in our own unraveling doesn't flow primarily out of books, socio-cultural studies (though they are helpful resources), or church-derived programs, but from eating with and dwelling with the people in the neighborhood. The interpretation of our unraveling comes as we make this path.

It would be easy to read all of this as another tactic or strategy: take a bit of time to hang out in the neighborhood. But that would be doing a terrible disservice to Jeremiah's radical reading of what had to change. For the exiles this was not to be a tactic, a "holding environment" to manage activities toward a new accomplishment. It was asking the exiles to do the unthinkable—step outside their social, cultural, and theological expectations—their *habitus*. The interpretive leadership required for our own unraveling is of the same kind. As with the exiles who heard Jeremiah's strange, disorienting words, the roles now required will only be discovered on the road, along the way, in the local and among the everyday. An interpretive leader must dwell deeply in the local, not as an expert, researcher, or analyst, but in the way of the incarnation, without power or control, role or authority. This is the way of comprehending how the Spirit is calling God's people to participate in the making of all things new, of seeking the shalom of the city. You can't be engaged in the shalom of a neighborhood unless you learn, unless you come alongside residents and listen. This is not a capitulation that requires assimilation—shalom is still defined on God's terms—but as they learn that God is in Babylon, they have much to seek/inquire if they are to participate with God. As we noted earlier, prayer practices ("pray to the LORD on its behalf") are in the context of seeking the shalom—learning, partnering, imagining, experimenting. That is why they need an action-reflection learning community. This moves toward our work with Matthew, who proposes, in the midst of the disruptive unraveling of existing narratives, that the work of the leader is to form what we described in chapter 5 as learning communities.

MATTHEW: ACTION-REFLECTION AND LEARNING COMMUNITIES

To walk in this space-between, interpretive leaders need to form learning communities. Such communities are formed, in Jeremiah's language, as a leader's locus shifts from "Jerusalem" to "Babylon."[15] This shift upends assumed roles. It challenges the ways leaders are trained. It invites a deconstruction of established pastoral roles. A common critique is that people will not tolerate their clergy taking on the role we are proposing. The social contract and cultural expectations of a congregation revolve around a taken-for-granted assumption that the pastor's job is managing and taking care of the inner life of the people of the congregation and the habitual organizational activities.[16] We're not advocating a sudden upending of established cultural expectations but an approach whereby leaders focus on creating learning communities that engender an alternative imagination.[17]

Interpretive leaders form co-learners on the walk. Matthew wrestled with how the community in Antioch would come to terms with the upheavals assaulting its self-understanding following the destruction of Jerusalem and the temple.[18] The Antioch community was confronted with massive social disruptions that challenged their identity and interpretation (theology) of what God was doing. These events were undermining their interpretive frameworks. How could they attend to God's agency when their assumptions about how God was working had dissolved? Matthew's interpretive work had to function in such a way that the Christians in Antioch would

15. Again, this is not in order to become a different kind of authority or expert but, on the contrary, to discover how to invite their people onto this path of common dwelling and discerning.

16. It doesn't matter how much one might want to go back, for example, into New Testament texts in order counter people's misinterpretations of roles. The fact of the matter is that there is a deeply embedded *habitus*, a set of socially constructed expectations that go very deep into the ethos of most congregations.

17. While we do not have the space to address this question of leading a congregation through change in this book, we have proposed various ways of going about this in other publications. See Roxburgh and Romanuk, *Missional Leader*; Roxburgh, *Structured for Mission*; Roxburgh, *Missional: Joining God*; and Roxburgh, *Joining God*. See also Branson and Martinez, *Churches, Cultures and Leadership*, chapter 10, and Branson, *Memories, Hopes and Conversations*.

18. It's interesting that in both Jeremiah and Matthew a significant part of each narrative has to do with the loss of what was a primary imaginative and interpretive center (in each of these cases—Jerusalem). The significance of our argument is that something parallel is happening to the Euro-tribal churches in this unraveling—a major center of their imaginative and interpretive life is dissolving; there is now a fundamental need to reimagine not just who we are as God's people in this location but the roles of leadership that, for so long, have been assumed.

step into a new imaginative space. He had to get them to become learning communities. Jesus' prayer named the holy longing by asking God "Hallowed be your name"—make yourself visible among us and our neighbors.

Matthew, following Jesus, shapes us in reflective questions that connect experiences with the words of Jesus. In our contexts, this might mean raising questions like:

- Here is what I'm experiencing in the neighborhood . . . are others seeing the same things?

- How do these experiences connect with what Jesus is saying?

- Is our attention drawn to those named in the Beatitudes: marginalized, sorrowful, hungry?

- How might we participate in Jesus' reign?

- As I'm in my neighborhood, here are ways I'm engaging with people, how about you?

Matthew's Gospel, written to Christians in the midst of disruptions in Antioch, is full of practical insights around the formation of learning communities that can name issues and frame questions they have to address. The influx of refugees and the active power of Rome required them to experiment (action-reflection) to figure out fresh ways of being God's people. Here are some key practices for cultivating learning communities.

Interpreting Contexts in Terms of God's Disruptions

The work of learning communities is that of fostering interpretive competencies through reflective conversations that shape awareness, connections to biblical texts, and continual listening prayers. This is more than cultural analysis. It's not assuaging anxieties (which are real) but offering space-between moments through sharing a different story about the present. The texts explored in this book tell us that the One encountering us is a radically disruptive God. This interpretive frame creates the space for learning communities. Today the Spirit is upending presumptions and calling God's people, in the space-between, to walk a path they couldn't have imagined. Such learning communities require leaders who are interpreting the unraveling as God's disruptive presence. By naming this reality a leader creates spaces for people to start asking: What might it mean to follow this disruptive God?

Setting the space for learning communities requires that leaders assist people to sense that it is God who is bringing us into this disconcerting space. This involves assisting people to see their disruptive unraveling not, primarily, as the result of socio-cultural changes that they're left to deal with in some generic "Christian" way, but that these disruptions involve the working of the Spirit in God's remaking of the world. They are how the Spirit will not leave the churches in their presumptions and patterns. This was what Matthew was doing in how he told the story of Jesus in the face of Rome. Matthew frames a disruptive imagination that undermines people's settled assumptions.

Such practices require skill and patience in cultivating conversations around people's experiences so that they learn to recognize a disruptive God in their own lives. The leader becomes a midwife wrestling to bring to birth what the Spirit is already gestating inside people. Many in our communities never get to this gestating because leaders do not know how to be midwives of the Spirit. Such leading requires preparing a table, setting the places for learning communities that engage the actual questions stirring in people. Leaders who do this work are out on the road, already in the local. Their posture is telling stories and naming experiences, setting tables, inviting questions, forming learning communities.

Antioch and Disruption

In Antioch learning communities were how Matthew encouraged Christians to engage the unraveling. These Christians were in such a disruptive situation that they needed a new place from which to address the disruption. These learning communities were not some new form of small group experience or a task force mandated to come up with programs to make the church more relevant. These interpretive groups provided a means for people to make sense of what God was doing so they could take new actions shaped by the Spirit. Action-reflection and experimenting became critical elements in their process of discernment. Here leaders work with a learning community to reconstruct their imagination as God's people. It is about forming a new language world. For example, when people of a congregation enter their communities they stop asking questions about return on investment, outcomes, or how they minister to people. They ask how to be with the neighbor to listen and, potentially, hear the Spirit. Learning communities assist in this reconstituting the imaginary of a congregation. Here the leader's own experiences and stories on the road are essential. The leader's own traveling the path creates trust in the journey.

Matthew was continually working to create, to remake, a community of learning in Antioch that could discern the ways of God in the radically disorienting space of a Roman-occupied world after the fall of Jerusalem. He was promoting the embodiment and articulation of an alternative social arrangement. This is the work of leaders today—shaping learning communities in the practices of action-reflection that help people be continually attentive to how the Spirit is constructing the new world.

ACTS: ALTERITY AND IMPROVISATION

Acts continues the story of the Spirit's disruptive agency. God is continually pulling the new communities into spaces of alterity (Gentiles becoming Christians in Antioch, Cornelius and his household, Lydia and her household, etc.). In all these situations, leaders were continually needing to improvise. This rhythm called for attentiveness to where God was pulling them. Leading in the unraveling is choosing to be on a path that continually brings us into encounters with unexpected people and requires us to improvise. These people, like Cornelius or Lydia, are the strangers who could never have figured into our calculations. Peter never had a Cornelius in his imagination; Paul never imagined a man of Macedonia much less a seller of high priced cloth named Lydia. These encounters with the other revealed God's ferment. We discern God's agency in our unraveling by making paths that keep connecting us into relationships with people outside our world. The word for this is *alterity*, literally, otherness. But we only encounter the other by laying aside our need to prioritize comfort and to manage outcomes. Managerial power does not see the gift of the other. Without that gift, we won't discern what God is doing.

Locations and Associations

In Acts the Spirit is continually calling the young churches into risky spaces to encounter the other. Two practices are needed for this path. First, listening to the Spirit through the other—listening in alterity. For example, Peter was already in a strange space, a tanner's rooftop in the port city of Joppa. Would this other space, with its swirl of people from many places, have made him more available to God's interruption? So, as a practice, how can we dwell and hang out in places, among persons, who are not our usual ingroup? How can we get beyond the congregation (Jerusalem) into the Joppas around us? Who are those, all about us, living in a world that is different than ours? In the mid-1980s, Mark chose to work in a Black Bible college and to be ordained in a Black church; now he is active in a Latinx church. All this means that he is in different worlds and in these spaces his availability and awareness shifts.

Peter and Paul had, by the Spirit, stepped onto a path that was being made, a path that continually connected them into relationships of alterity. They spent enough time with strangers (Simon, Luke, Cornelius, Lydia, etc.) in ways that made them more susceptible. The leader can prioritize people and places that are harmonious with her type—her *habitus* (which is, generally, the character of a congregation as a homogeneous group)—or she can risk with other conversations and venues—neighborhood groups, social spaces, collaborations.

Imaginations and Improvisations

Second, because alterity is being with those different from us, it is where God takes us outside our expectations. In the neighborhoods of Jerusalem, after the disruption of the Spirit, the homes and alleyways of immigrant Hellenists became venues for meals and conversations that connected Hebrew texts with the stories they are learning about Jesus. In Philippi, Paul's band had no plan for church planting in the house of a Gentile woman; it required on-the-spot rewriting of the play book. Both daily life and on-the-road encounters call for our ability to improvise new kinds of social arrangements and relationships that change us—such as a church in immigrant households, including in a rich woman's household.

What is staggering about these stories of alterity are how, in our modern contexts, we miss what Luke is telling us about alterity as the way the Spirit transforms the world. What was pointed out in the chapter on Acts (chapter 6) is that the households of Cornelius and Lydia became centers of God's remaking the world. These strangers—a Roman centurion of standing and a Gentile business woman—had their whole conception of "household" transformed. In these spaces of alterity God was reordering the systems of empire and power of elites that were part of the Jerusalem and Roman *habitus*. By engaging households, the Spirit was redefining the relationships, production, and sources of meaning and vocation of the first century world. What makes it so hard for us to see what is happening here is that in modern societies our *habitus* is to turn "home" into private space, into "sanctuary" for escape and protection from the world outside. Numerous have been the times when clergy have said to us that they don't have people in their homes because it is their escape, their sanctuary from people. Home has become the locus of the personal and private, where we can be hidden from the larger world in the privacy of our own space. But that was never the case in the New Testament contexts we have discussed. Households were the open windows onto the commons and the everyday. They were turned outward to the world as places that embodied the public narratives of the time (particularly the overarching narrative of the empire). Here in Acts, Luke is continually bringing Paul, Peter, and these young Christians into places and relationships of alterity because these were the places where God's future would be formed.[19]

These accounts help us to see why the practice of dwelling with and embracing the stranger are so critical for Christian imagination and mission. How can life among homes, among apartment dwellers, in civic spaces, be redefined? This becomes a critical question for leaders as they continually practice this way of being with the other. Temple-centered practices and *paterfamilia* are both decentered in Acts. Our lives of consumption, meanings defined in "my career," and building-centered religion are all disrupted as we live among neighbors. The practice of hospitality—in our homes, and as guests of neighbors—opens spaces for conversations, awareness, and discernment, all of which guide us toward the fundamental reconfiguring of life as expression of the kingdom.

Relinquishing Power and Control

To walk this road of listening with the other, encountering alterity, and being called to risk improvisation, is to be confronted by the disorienting issues of power. As a Euro-tribal leader, it is almost unavoidable to live within a presumption of power that is structured into our language and institutions. It is no doubt more so for males than females, but the overarching social narrative of the Euro-tribals has been formed from within this presumption of power. While this question of power ("whiteness")[20] invites a more comprehensive discussion, we want to note several elements of it here relative to the question of engaging with God's agency with the other. Encountering the other within a power relationship is not to encounter the other; without a reorientation we are only getting our own projection onto the other. Someone posted a Facebook question: *How do I make relationships with the unchurched and the unbeliever?* It was a genuine question but it is asked from a position of power. The question already categorizes the other. It is about objectification and power. Often, a congregation looks at their community

19. See Richard Sennett's book, *The Conscience of the Eye*, as an important study of these changed views of home and household in modernity.

20. See Willie Jennings's lecture, "Can 'White' People be Saved?" See also Sechrest, et al., eds., *Can "White" People Be Saved?*.

and starts from the presumption of "needs" they can "minister" to. These are power relationships: I look for something you don't have; I have what you need and can give it to you.

The pathway we're making together can't be made out of the imbalance of power relationships. The posture of alterity is one of *being with* which is other than *doing for*. This is hard work requiring something close to conversion. It's not the way we've been formed to listen in a competitive, exchange-oriented society, but we can be converted by Cornelius and Lydia. Dorothy Day was one of those people who, out of a deep response to her Catholic faith, chose this road of alterity. She embraced the other, especially those whom society had cast aside. But she didn't do that from the middle class perspective of helping and meeting needs from a distance or as a project. All through her life she chose the path of being with the other. In embracing those who were on the margins she wasn't working for or helping or doing for these people. They were her friends with whom she chose to dwell because she knew that within these relationships she had much to learn, receive, and discover about being human from the other. It was in these relationships that Day, and the Catholic Workers, learned how to improvise practices for being God's people. They laid down power and stepped into relationships not focused on outcomes because they had power. Day reminds us what matters—the path we're invited to walk as leaders in the kingdom.[21]

EPHESIANS: CRITICAL REFLECTION AND CHANGE

If we begin to embrace the forms of Christian life in the unraveling we've encountered in the texts we've examined and the practices they invite, it is inevitable that our leadership will require new kinds of social arrangements. That is part of what Paul is telling us in Ephesians. We have already pointed out, for example, that the social arrangements of leadership that were formed over the past century around congregations, denominations, and schools created a self-perpetuating clergy industry that is not sustainable in the unraveling.

Ephesians presents a set of alternative social arrangements for being God's people in relationship to the empire and the religious forms of life shaped around that empire. Paul had become convinced that in Jesus, God had initiated radically new social arrangements that were remaking the world. It is in this sense that he uses the word *spiritual*. It refers to a way of life that is an alternative to the empire; it implies that our lives are deviant when viewed through a society's priorities and narratives. This chapter

21. Day, *Long Loneliness*.

has described some of the practices we believe critical to forming this kind of *spiritual* life in the unraveling of our own empire. These practices also deviate from the clergy industry, which has tended to be formed around an abstracting and universalizing (albeit, modern) of Paul's deeply contextual work of forming communities on the ground in the first century.[22] They are about how leaders address the underlying social arrangements of power, management, and control within the primacy of consumer-oriented individualism. How do such practices become embedded in existing congregations? This section briefly picks up on two responses based in chapter 7, on Ephesians.

The Use of Critical Theory

Critical theory can be a daunting prospect for congregational leaders. While some leaders might want to dive deeply into all the frameworks that lie at its base, there are some basic ways to use this resource. In our observations, conversations, and reflections alongside neighbors, we can attend to the layers of influence in the local—power, resources, goals, structures. It is notable in Ephesians that Paul believes that the new social arrangements of the gospel (Gentiles and Jews together) would be observational education for visible and invisible powers. Leaders can influence the prayers and reflections and improvisations among churches regarding the social arrangements that would be in contrast to the powers around us. The gospel is not just about apologizing to God for sins; it's about embodying the gospel right at the points of society's brokenness.

Also, in chapter 8, we introduced a conversation about the metaphors that shape our imagination and practices as communities. So another way

22. This refers to the much-quoted Ephesians 4:11–13 sometimes described as the "fourfold" ministry." There is much that needs to be discussed about the contemporary usages of this passage. For example, is Paul laying down a firm pattern for the church across all the ages (which one doubts given his own expectations of Christ's return) or is he being descriptive of what is emerging on the ground within the language world of his time? But beyond this critical question and no matter how it gets addressed, it would be difficult to imagine that Paul was viewing these as operating as "full time" roles within the developing young house churches across Asia Minor. It is far more likely that within any or several of these house churches in a regional area, there were numerous persons who manifested these roles as part of their common and broader engagements with the communities within which they lived. What we are proposing is that this more contemporary notion of a special people trained for the inner life of congregations is not something that can be supported from a text like Ephesians 4 and, in the unraveling, can only continue to misdirect a community of God's people in terms of discern the missionary God who, by the Spirit, is out ahead of us. Interpretive leadership must move in this direction.

to begin using critical theory in a congregation is with the leader's own practice of paying attention to the dominant metaphors that people are using with one another to talk about what they see going on around them or what they value the most. As the leader develops his/her own capacities in this kind of listening (keeping notebooks of conversations, reading more broadly on how we are using language together, reflecting with others what we are hearing and what that might involve—here we're applying an iterative action-learning to our own work) then the question is one of how to introduce conversations with your people around the metaphors we use. This is the capacity to form a reflective community that, in the best sense of the word, is developing critical skills at looking at itself in the mirror.

A third way of practicing critical reflection within the congregation is through the stories that begin to emerge as people practice listening as they dwell with people in their communities. This listening inevitably results in people bringing questions and issues back with them. These encounters of alterity create surprises and confusion; they disorient us in terms of the questions or awareness of people about the Christian life. Alan was working with a very large, 25,000-member church in another country. That church had gradually become a place where practically all relationships occurred within the context of the congregation. Al's work was to assist small numbers of people to begin relationships of being with others in the communities where they lived. As church members started to do this they began to report back their surprise at the questions people were asking, at people's responses to church and the ways they were living in a large city. It was these grounded experiences that created new questions in the church members. The critical practice of leadership is in assisting church members to dig beneath the surface of their experiences and conclusions in a way that leads to fresh and, often, disorienting realizations of what God is going.

A leader's work parallels that of Jesus when he spoke about mustard seeds (Matt 13:31–32). When others aspired to be huge trees (a common metaphor for nations), he offered the vocation of being a sprawling, invasive weed. That shift is akin to what we imagine. We doubt that all of his hearers were willing to trade images of being a powerful nation with an imagination for a ground-hugging plant, but Jesus' metaphor was an invitation away from governing power and toward comprehensive embodiment theory that could join with God everywhere, with no concern for barriers and boundaries. In so doing we encounter the other (alterity) in ways that call for improvisation. The move from the disorientation produced in alterity to improvisation will always be through the process of engaging our people in some form of reflective critical engagement with what we are discovering.

Organizational Change

There is so much written in the subject of organizational change.[23] In brief, organizational change is that which happens as a sufficient number of people across a group can name and embody new practices that require a change in the organization. There is no question that congregations need to go through massive organizational change to address the themes raised in this book. These changes will fundamentally undermine the clergy industry. That said, organizational change begins as small numbers of people, out of critical reflection, develop small, simple experiments to test what they are beginning to name, then those experiences are relayed into the buzz of the church. This is critical reflection turned into action learning. The kind of action and learning called for is that which takes this path of being in relationship with the other, which invites improvisation in joining God. Organizational change is a reflective response to these kinds of relationships and how the Spirit is disruptively informing our imaginations as a community. Before these kinds of encounters most organizational change deflects from the work of becoming learning communities shaped by critical reflection on what we are actually experiencing of God on the ground and in the local.

As a leader introduces people to this movement into the neighborhood through the numerous practices outlined above, there will be a continual need to ensure that the organizational systems that express the current *habitus* of the congregation are respected and continued. Leaders always find this a difficult task in that they wish numerous elements of the existing system could just be removed in order to give them time to focus on these other practices. But it is important, as noted below, to start where people are, not where the leader wants them to be. An important way of doing this is by beginning small and slow from within the organizational system that exists rather than creating new programs of organizational systems.

TAKING THE JOURNEY

Learning Together

Making the path as we walk is taking on a Jeremiah 29 or Matthew 10 posture within our neighborhood and community. But it can't be something you decide to do by yourself as a leader, gaining expertise so you can manage others; that is the way of remaining inside the clergy industry. That road can't provide hope in the unraveling. This journey calls you to invite a

---

23. Alongside books mentioned in chapter 7, see footnote 17, above.

community of people who will join with you as co-learners. It is as a community that you figure out the places and people (the Lydias and Corneliuses) among whom you will lay down your backpack (power and resources) to receive the hospitality of the other, sitting at their table and receiving from them, and growing in awareness of the Spirit's activities.

We also believe that, like Paul, it is important that leaders find journey partners in other churches. We noted that Paul may have been more adept at options in Philippi because Luke, a Gentile, had likely joined the team in Troas. Such reflection groups are more generative when the participants are diverse—something also noted in the diffusion theory we engaged in chapter 6. These groups, in addition to having their own meditative practices (like dwelling in the Word), can have three questions: What have you been doing? What have you noticed, especially about God's initiatives? And, what are you going to do next? Stories and imaginations and risk and encouragement are all promoted in such learning communities.

Some leaders will insist that this is an impossible journey—in many ways they are right, but that is usually how the Spirit disrupts and makes things new. A lot of leaders don't believe their boards would allow them to try out any of the actions and practices named here. In our work as consultants and professors, we have learned that church boards can be overwhelmed with a sudden, full-on proposal for their clergyperson to suddenly change the contract of their employment. But what about a small experiment in the spirit of a learning community? What about an initial risk of asking the board for one day per week (or one day every other week) for you to be present in your neighborhood in the ways described here? You will report back to the board. You might propose forming a group of people in the congregation to join with you and that you'd all report back to the board or leadership team (whatever the leadership group of the congregation might be) on a regular basis. It would mean you becoming an interpretive leader who would figure out what information a board would need, what kind of language would help them, and how you could give them a clear "why" for wanting to try out this journey.

Starting from Where People Are

We are writing this to leaders of congregations, to those who are training people for congregations, to those who are preparing to be leaders of some kind in congregations. You are our audience. Congregations are the flawed spaces where God's eruptive life ferments and bursts out. Our theological starting point is that God calls us to lead where God's people are located—flawed, ordinary congregations anyone can critique without breaking a sweat. If, as we stated in chapter 3, God turns up in the most god-forsaken places, then our bet in this unraveling is that these over-studied, over-critiqued places called congregations are where the Spirit's ferment breaks out. Congregations are unraveling. But they're the places where God's people dwell and the Spirit prompts. Here is where the journey starts. We start from where we are.

Making a path as we walk means we don't need to tell people where they need to be. Rather than vision-casting, the walk begins with the stories of the people with whom we dwell. Start by seeking out those in a congregation who sense the old roads aren't repairable and, in the spirit of an interpretive leader, accompany them as fellow travelers (learning communities). An obvious question is: How does one get people in the average congregation to go on such a journey? Why would someone buy a weird story like this:

> Folks, here are some hard things. First, everything we've done to this point won't work anymore. Second, I, your leader, who has spent years at seminary and been ordained by the denomination, don't know what the new road looks like. I've no map. When I started getting really anxious about this a few years back, I signed on to a DMin program thinking if I became a doctor I'd know what to do or, even crazier, that the professors would have answers. It was a bust. Third, as far as I can tell, no one else knows what the road is either. (There are those who claim they know, but, if I'm honest, it's BS.) Fourth, we have to do something I don't know much about—head out on a journey without a road or a map. As crazy as it sounds, we have to make the road as we walk on it. I think that's what the Spirit is saying to us all, not just us here, but to all the churches.

There's a lot of honesty in such a story. It needs to be told. But it's not how people sign on. Start by listening for a few people who might be asking unsettling questions. The clues to how one goes about this are there in the texts we've worked with in this book. You identify such people by asking yourself: How am I present with people? How am I listening to their stories? Where am I creating spaces where people feel safe to share stories about what they experience going on about them? Do I ask questions that open conversations?[24] Alan was recently sitting on the porch with several people talking about a podcast they'd each heard. It wasn't a planned event and there was no leader or curriculum. The podcast was about

---

24. See Branson, *Memories, Hopes and Conversations.*

neoliberalism's[25] effects on emerging generations. It caught their attention because it connected dots inside their anxieties. All Alan had to do was raise some simple appreciative inquiry questions and let people talk. In that conversation, some expressed their sense of just not understanding, but they knew it was all having huge effects on people they loved. These people were ready to step on the road that isn't yet built. We don't need to get everyone convinced about the journey and we don't need to disrupt people who are not ready to be disrupted. The Spirit is already among people in our congregations fermenting a desire for this journey. Begin with them. It doesn't take special skills, some new program, or learning a new language. Rather, it's choosing to patiently start from where people are, not where you think they should be. And it engages the locations and energies of God's Spirit in your own context.

25. See Roxburgh, "A Christian Counter-Movement to Neoliberalism?"

Bibliography

Adams, Samuel L., et al. *Social and Economic Life in Second Temple Judea.* Louisville, KY: Westminster John Knox, 2014.

Allen, Leslie C. *Jeremiah: A Commentary.* The Old Testament Library. Louisville, KY: Westminster John Knox, 2008.

Anderson, Ray Sherman. *The Shape of Practical Theology: Empowering Ministry with Theological Praxis.* Downers Grove, IL: InterVarsity, 2001.

Anderson, Sam. "The Ultimate Sitcom." *The New York Times Magazine,* October 7, 2018, 70–74, 76, 93.

Argyris, Chris. "Teaching Smart People How to Learn." *Harvard Business Review* 69, no. 3 (1991) 99–109.

Arnold, C. E. "Ephesians, Letter to." In *Dictionary of Paul and his Letters,* edited by Gerald Hawthorne, et al., 238–49. Downers Grove, IL: InterVarsity, 1993.

Barth, Markus. *Ephesians 1–3.* The Anchor Bible. Garden City, NY: Doubleday, 1974.

———. *Ephesians 4–6.* The Anchor Bible. Garden City, NY: Doubleday, 1974.

Baudrillard, Jean, and Marc Guillaume. *Radical Alterity.* Semiotext(e) Foreign Agents Series. Los Angeles: Semiotext(e), 2008.

Bellah, Robert N., et al. *Habits of the Heart: Individualism and Commitment in American Life: With a New Preface.* Berkeley, CA: University of California Press, 2008.

Berger, Peter L., and Thomas Luckmann. *The Social Construction of Reality: A Treatise in the Sociology of Knowledge.* Garden City, NY: Doubleday, 1967.

Berryman, Jerome. *Godly Play: A Way of Religious Education.* San Francisco: HarperSanFrancisco, 1991.

Bevans, Stephen, and Roger Schroeder. *Prophetic Dialogue: Reflections on Christian Mission Today.* Maryknoll, NY: Orbis, 2011.

Bolman, Lee G., and Terrence E. Deal. *Reframing Organizations: Artistry, Choice, and Leadership.* 4th ed. San Francisco: Jossey-Bass, 2008.

Bottum, Joseph. *An Anxious Age: The Post-Protestant Ethic and Spirit of America.* New York: Image, 2014.

Bourdieu, Pierre. *Habitus and Field: General Sociology.* Vol. 2. London: Polity, 2020.

———. *The Logic of Practice.* Translated by Richard Nice. Stanford, CA: Stanford University Press, 1990.

———. *Outline of a Theory of Practice.* Translated by Richard Nice. Cambridge Studies in Social Anthropology, 16. Cambridge, UK: Cambridge University Press, 1977.

———. "Structuralism and Theory of Sociological Knowledge." *Social Research* 35 no. 4 (1968) 681–706.

Brague, Rémi. *The Kingdom of Man: Genesis and Failure of the Modern Project.* Translated by Paul Seaton. Notre Dame, IN: University of Notre Dame Press, 2018.

Branson, Mark Lau. "Disruptions Meet Practical Theology." *Fuller Magazine* (2018). https://fullerstudio.fuller.edu/disruptions-meet-practical-theology/.

———. "Ecclesiology and Leadership for the Missional Church." In *The Missional Church in Context*, edited by Craig Van Gelder, 94–125. Grand Rapids: Eerdmans, 2007.

———. "Forming God's People." In *Leadership in Congregations*, edited by Richard Bass, 97–108. Herndon, VA: Alban Institute, 2007.

———. "Interpretive Leadership During Social Dislocation: Jeremiah and Social Imaginary." *Journal of Religious Leadership* 8, no. 1 (2009) 27–48.

———. "Matthew and Learning Communities." *Journal of Religious Leadership* 15, no. 2 (2016) 37–68.

———. *Memories, Hopes, and Conversations: Appreciative Inquiry, Missional Engagement, and Congregational Change.* 2d ed. Lanham, MD: Rowman & Littlefield, 2016.

Branson, Mark Lau, and Juan Martínez. "A Practical Theology of Leadership with International Voices." *Journal of Religious Leadership* 10, no. 2 (2011) 27–57.

———. *Churches, Cultures and Leadership: A Practical Theology of Ethnicities and Congregations.* Downers Grove, IL: IVP Academic, 2011.

Bright, John. *A History of Israel.* 4th ed. Louisville, KY: Westminster John Knox, 2000.

Brookfield, Stephen. *The Power of Critical Theory: Liberating Adult Learning and Teaching.* San Francisco: Jossey-Bass, 2005.

Brown, Raymond E., and John Meier. *Antioch and Rome: New Testament Cradles of Catholic Christianity.* New York: Paulist, 1983.

Brueggemann, Walter. *Cadences of Home: Preaching among Exiles.* Louisville, KY: Westminster John Knox, 1997.

———. *Genesis.* Interpretation, a Bible Commentary for Teaching and Preaching. Atlanta: John Knox, 1982.

———. *Texts That Linger, Words That Explode.* Minneapolis: Fortress, 2000.

———. *To Build, to Plant: A Commentary on Jeremiah 26–52.* International Theological Commentary. Grand Rapids: Eerdmans, 1991.

Brueggemann, Walter, and Richard Floyd. *A Gospel of Hope.* Louisville, KY: Westminster John Knox Press, 2018.

Buber, Martin. *I And Thou.* Translated by Ronald Smith. New York: Scribner, 1958.

Bude, Heinz. *The Mood of the World.* Translated by Simon Garnett. Cambridge: Polity, 2018.

Calasso, Roberto. *The Unnamable Present.* Translated by Richard Dixon. New York: Farrar, Straus and Giroux, 2019.

Carter, Warren. *Matthew and Empire: Initial Explorations.* Harrisburg, PA: Trinity Press International, 2001.

———. *Matthew and the Margins: A Sociopolitical and Religious Reading.* Maryknoll, NY: Orbis, 2000.

———. *Matthew: Storyteller, Interpreter, Evangelist.* Grand Rapids: Baker Academic, 2004.

Chilton, Bruce. "Festivals and Holy Days: Jewish." In *Dictionary of New Testament Background*, edited by Craig Evans and Stanley Porter, 371–78. Downers Grove, IL: InterVarsity, 2000.

Cormode, Scott. *Making Spiritual Sense: Christian Leaders As Spiritual Interpreters.* Nashville: Abingdon, 2006.

Cunha, João Vieira da, et al. "Organizational Improvisation: What, When, How and Why." *International Journal of Management Reviews* 1, no. 3 (1999) 299–341.

Cunha, João Vieira da, et al., eds. *Organizational Improvisation.* London: Routledge, 2002.

Davies, Oliver, et al., *Transformation Theology: Church in the World.* London: T&T Clark, 2007.

Davies, W. D., and Dale C. Allison. *A Critical and Exegetical Commentary on the Gospel According to Saint Matthew: Vol. 2: 8–18.* International Critical Commentary on the Holy Scriptures of the Old and New Testaments. Edinburgh: T&T Clark, 1991.

Day, Dorothy. *The Long Loneliness.* Introduction by Robert Coles. San Francisco: HarperSanFrancisco, 1997.

DeYoung, Curtiss Paul. *Coming Together in the 21st Century: The Bible's Message in an Age of Diversity.* Rev. ed. Valley Forge, PA: Judson, 2009.

Drucker, Peter. "Culture Eats Strategy for Breakfast." https://quoteinvestigator. com/2017/05/23/culture-eats/.

Dumont, Louis. *Essays on Individualism: Modern Ideology in Anthropological Perspective.* Chicago: University of Chicago Press, 1986.

Eagleton, Terry. *Culture and the Death of God.* New Haven, CT: Yale University Press, 2015.

Ellul, Jacques. *The Technological Society.* New York: Vintage, 1967.

Emerson, Michael O., George Yancey, and Curtiss Paul DeYoung. *United by Faith: The Multiracial Congregation as an Answer to the Problem of Race.* Oxford: Oxford University Press, 2004.

Ferguson, Everett. "The Herodian Dynasty." In *The World of the New Testament: Cultural, Social, and Historical Contexts,* edited by Joel B. Green and Lee Martin McDonald, 54–76. Grand Rapids: Baker Academic, 2013.

Fisher, Colin, and Teresa Amabile. "Creativity, Improvisation and Organizations." *Rotman Magazine,* Winter 2009. https://colinmfisher.files.wordpress.com/2012/11 /fisheramabile2009_improvcreativity_rotman.pdf.

Fitch, David E. *Faithful Presence: Seven Disciplines That Shape the Church for Mission.* Downers Grove, IL: InterVarsity, 2016.

Fletcher-Louis, C. "Priest, Priesthood." In *Dictionary of Jesus and the Gospels,* 2d ed., edited by J. Green, J. K. Brown, and N. Perrin, 696–705. Downers Grove, IL: IVP Academic, 2013.

Fowl, Stephen E. *Ephesians: A Commentary.* Louisville, KY: Westminster John Knox, 2012.

Freire, Paulo. *Education for Critical Consciousness.* London: Continuum, 2007.

———. *Pedagogy of the Oppressed.* New York: Seabury, 1970.

Friis, Preben. "Presence and Spontaneity in Improvisation." In *Experiencing Risk, Spontaneity and Improvisation in Organizational Change: Working Live,* edited by Patricia Shaw and Ralph Stacey, 75–94. London: Routledge, 2006.

Friis, Preben, and Henry Larsen, "Theatre, Improvisation and Social Change." In *Experiencing Risk, Spontaneity and Improvisation in Organizational Change: Working Live,* edited by Patricia Shaw and Ralph Stacey, 19–43. London: Routledge, 2006.

Garnsey, Peter, and Richard P. Saller. *The Roman Empire: Economy, Society, and Culture.* Berkeley, CA: University of California Press, 1987.

Gergen, Kenneth J. *An Invitation to Social Construction.* 2d ed. Los Angeles: SAGE, 2009.

Goheen, Michael. *Church and Its Vocation.* Grand Rapids: Baker Academic, 2018.

Green, Joel. *The Gospel of Luke.* The New International Commentary on the New Testament. Grand Rapids: Eerdmans, 1997.

———. *Luke as Narrative Theologian.* Tübingen: Mohr Siebeck, 2020.

———. *The Theology of the Gospel of Luke.* Cambridge: Cambridge University Press, 1995.

Green, Joel, and Lee Martin McDonald, eds. *The World of the New Testament: Cultural, Social, and Historical Contexts.* Grand Rapids: Baker Academic, 2013.

Greenleaf, Robert K. *Servant Leadership: A Journey into the Nature of Legitimate Power and Greatness.* New York: Paulist, 1979.

Groome, Thomas H. *Sharing Faith: A Comprehensive Approach to Religious Education and Pastoral Ministry: The Way of Shared Praxis.* Eugene, OR: Wipf and Stock, 1999.

Gunton, Colin E. *The One, the Three, and the Many: God, Creation, and the Culture of Modernity.* Bampton Lectures, 1992. Cambridge: Cambridge University Press, 1993.

———. *The Promise of Trinitarian Theology.* Edinburgh: T&T Clark, 1995.

Habermas, Jürgen. *Autonomy and Solidarity: Interviews.* Edited by Peter Dews. London: Verso, 1992.

———. *Reason and the Rationalization of Society.* Volume 1 of The Theory of Communicative Action. Translated by Thomas McCarthy. Boston: Beacon, 1984.

Hanciles, Jehu. *Beyond Christendom: Globalization, African Migration, and the Transformation of the West.* Maryknoll, NY: Orbis, 2008.

Hatina, Thomas, R. "Rome and Its Provinces." In *The World of the New Testament: Cultural, Social, and Historical Contexts,* edited by Joel B. Green and Lee Martin McDonald, 557–70. Grand Rapids: Baker Academic, 2013.

Hays, Richard B. *The Moral Vision of the New Testament: Community, Cross, New Creation: A Contemporary Introduction to New Testament Ethics.* San Francisco: HarperSanFrancisco, 1996.

Heifetz, Ronald A. *Leadership Without Easy Answers.* Cambridge, MA: Harvard University Press, 1994.

Heifetz, Ronald A., and Martin Linsky. *Leadership on the Line: Staying Alive through the Dangers of Leading.* Boston: Harvard Business School Press, 2002.

Heifetz, Ronald A., Alexander Grashow, and Martin Linsky. *The Practice of Adaptive Leadership: Tools and Tactics for Changing Your Organization and the World.* Boston: Harvard Business Press, 2009.

Hochschild, Arlie Russell. *Strangers in Their Own Land: Anger and Mourning on the American Right.* New York: New, 2018.

Holladay, William L. "Indications of Jeremiah's Psalter." *Journal of Biblical Literature* 121, no. 2 (2002) 245–61.

Izuzquiza, Daniel. *Rooted in Jesus Christ: Toward a Radical Ecclesiology.* Grand Rapids: Eerdmans, 2009.

Jacobs, Alan. *The Year of Our Lord 1943: Christian Humanism in an Age of Crisis.* New York: Oxford University Press, 2018.

Jeffers, James. *The Greco-Roman World of the New Testament Era*. Downers Grove, IL: InterVarsity, 1999.

Jennings, Willie James. *Acts*. Belief: A Theological Commentary on the Bible. Louisville, KY: Westminster John Knox, 2017.

———. "Can 'White' People be Saved: Reflections on Missions and Whiteness." Lecture presented at The Fuller Missiology Lectures, Pasadena, CA, November 1, 2017. https://www.youtube.com/watch?v=SRLjWZxL1lE.

———. *The Christian Imagination: Theology and the Origins of Race*. New Haven, CT: Yale University Press, 2006.

Jenson, Robert W. *The Triune Identity: God According to the Gospel*. Minneapolis: Fortress, 1982.

"The Job Market for Clergies in the United States." https://www.careerexplorer.com/careers/clergy/job-market/.

Johnson, Luke Timothy. *The Acts of the Apostles*. Sacra Pagina 5. Collegeville, MN: Liturgical, 1992.

Johnson, T. J. "Roman Emperors." In *Dictionary of New Testament Background*, edited by Craig Evans and Stanley Porter, 968–74. Downers Grove, IL: InterVarsity, 2000.

"Joining God." https://joininggod.org/.

Jones, L. Gregory. *Christian Social Innovation: Renewing Wesleyan Witness*. Nashville: Abingdon, 2016.

Jones, Robert P. *The End of White Christian America*. New York: Simon & Schuster, 2016.

Knox, John S. "Christianity." *Ancient History Encyclopedia*, September 2016. https://www.ancient.eu/christianity/.

Kreider, Alan. *The Patient Ferment of the Early Church: The Improbable Rise of Christianity in the Roman Empire*. Grand Rapids: Baker Academic, 2016.

Lakoff, George, and Mark Johnson. *Metaphors We Live By*. Chicago: University of Chicago Press, 2003.

Leithart, Peter J. *The End of Protestantism: Pursuing Unity in a Fragmented Church*. Grand Rapids: Brazos, 2016.

Lincoln, Andrew T. *Ephesians*. Dallas: Word, 1990.

Loyola Press, "The Daily Examen." https://www.ignatianspirituality.com/ignatian-prayer/the-examen/.

Lundbom, Jack. *Jeremiah 37–52: A New Translation with Introduction and Commentary*. New York: Doubleday, 2004.

Luz, Ulrich. *Matthew 1–7: A Commentary*. Minneapolis: Augsburg, 1989.

———. *Studies in Matthew*. Translated by Rosemary Selle. Grand Rapids: Eerdmans, 2005.

Malina, Bruce J., and Richard L. Rohrbaugh. *Social-Science Commentary on the Synoptic Gospels*. 2d ed. Minneapolis: Augsburg Fortress, 2003.

Markus, Robert Austin. *Saeculum: History and Society in the Theology of St Augustine*. Cambridge: Cambridge University Press, 1989.

McConnell, Douglas. *Cultural Insights for Christian Leaders*. Grand Rapids: Baker, 2019.

McGavran, Donald A., and C. Peter Wagner. *Understanding Church Growth*. Grand Rapids: Eerdmans, 1990.

Meador, Jake. *In Search of the Common Good: Christian Fidelity in a Fractured World*. Downers Grove, IL: InterVarsity, 2019.

Mintzberg, Henry. *Rebalancing Society: Radical Renewal Beyond Left, Right, and Center*. Oakland, CA: Berrett-Koehler, 2015.

Murphy-O'Connor, J. *St. Paul's Ephesus: Texts and Archaeology*. Collegeville, MN: Liturgical, 2008.

Newbigin, Lesslie. *Foolishness to the Greeks: The Gospel and Western Culture*. Grand Rapids: Eerdmans, 1986.

———. *The Light Has Come: An Exposition of the Fourth Gospel*. Grand Rapids: Eerdmans, 1982.

———. *Proper Confidence: Faith, Doubt, and Certainty in Christian Discipleship*. Grand Rapids: Eerdmans, 1995.

———. *Signs Amid the Rubble: The Purposes of God in Human History*. Edited and introduced by Geoffrey Wainwright. Grand Rapids: Eerdmans, 2003.

Nietzsche, Friedrich Wilhelm. *The Anti-Christ, Ecce Homo, Twilight of the Idols, and Other Writings*. Cambridge Texts in the History of Philosophy. Cambridge: Cambridge University Press, 2005.

Oded, Bustenay. "Judah and the Exile." In *Israelite and Judean History*, edited by John Haralson Hayes and James Maxwell Miller, 435–88. Philadelphia: Westminster, 1977.

Pascal, Blaise, Thomas Stearns Eliot, and Wiliam Finlayson Trotter. *Pascal's Penseìes*. New York: E. P. Dutton, 1958.

Pazmiño, Robert W. *Latin American Journey: Insights for Christian Education in North America*. Eugene, OR: Wipf and Stock, 2002.

Pennington, Jonathan T. *Heaven and Earth in the Gospel of Matthew*. Grand Rapids: Baker Academic, 2009.

Perrin, Nicholas. "Exile." In *The World of the New Testament: Cultural, Social, and Historical Contexts*, edited by Joel B. Green and Lee Martin McDonald, 25–37. Grand Rapids: Baker Academic, 2013.

———. "The Imperial Cult." In *The World of the New Testament: Cultural, Social, and Historical Contexts*, edited by Joel B. Green and Lee Martin McDonald, 124–34. Grand Rapids: Baker Academic, 2013.

Pew Research Center: Religion & Public Life. "'Nones' on the Rise." http://www.pewforum.org/2012/10/09/nones-on-the-rise/.

Placher, William C. *Narratives of a Vulnerable God: Christ, Theology, and Scripture*. Louisville, KY: Westminster John Knox, 1994.

Polanyi, Michael. *Personal Knowledge: Towards a Post-Critical Philosophy*. New York: Harper & Row, 1964.

Presbyterian Church in the U.S. General Assembly. *The Book of Church Order of the Presbyterian Church in the United States*. Atlanta, GA: Office of the Stated Clerk of the Presbyterian Church in the United States, 1975.

Purcell, Nicholas. "Pater Patriae." In *The Oxford Classical Dictionary*, 4th ed., edited by Simon Hornblower, et al. Oxford: Oxford University Press, 2012. https://www-oxfordreference-com.fuller.idm.oclc.org/view/10.1093/acref/9780199545568.001.0001/acref-9780199545568-e-4775.

Rah, Soong-Chan. *Many Colors: Cultural Intelligence for a Changing Church*. Chicago: Moody, 2010.

Rich, Tracey R. "Jewish Holidays." Judaism 101. http://www.jewfaq.org/holidayo.htm#Extra%20re%20oday.

Ricoeur, Paul. *The Rule of Metaphor: Multi-Disciplinary Studies of the Creation of Meaning in Language.* London: Routledge, 2003.

Rieff, Philip. *My Life Among the Deathworks.* Volume 1: Sacred Order/Social Order. Charlottesville, NC: University of North Carolina Press, 2006.

Rogers, Everett M. *Diffusion of Innovations.* 5th ed. New York: Free, 2003.

Rowe, Christopher Kavin. *World Upside Down: Reading Acts in the Graeco-Roman Age.* Oxford: Oxford University Press, 2009.

Roxburgh, Alan J. "A Christian Counter-Movement to Neoliberalism?" https://journalofmissionalpractice.com/counter-neo-liberalism/.

———. *Joining God, Remaking Church, Changing the World: The New Shape of the Church in Our Time.* New York: Morehouse, 2015.

———. *Missional: Joining God in the Neighborhood.* Grand Rapids: Baker, 2011.

———. *Missional Map-Making: Skills for Leading in Times of Transition.* San Francisco: Jossey-Bass, 2010.

———. *Structured for Mission : Renewing the Culture of the Church.* Downers Grove, IL: InterVarsity, 2015.

Roxburgh, Alan J., and Fred Romanuk, *The Missional Leader: Equipping Your Church to Reach a Changing World.* Minneapolis: Fortress, 2020.

Roxburgh, Alan J., and Martin Robinson. *Practices for the Refounding of God's People: The Missional Challenge of the West.* New York: Church Publishing, 2018.

Royce, Josiah. *The Problem of Christianity.* Chicago: University of Chicago Press, 1968. First published 1913 by Macmillan (New York).

Sax, David. "End the Innovation Obsession." *New York Times,* December 7, 2018. https://www.nytimes.com/2018/12/07/opinion/sunday/end-the-innovation-obsession.html.

———. *The Revenge of Analog: Real Things and Why They Matter.* New York: PublicAffairs, 2017.

Scharen, Christian. *Fieldwork in Theology: Exploring the Social Context of God's Work in the World.* Grand Rapids: Baker Academic, 2015.

Schein, Edgar H., and Peter Schein. *Organizational Culture and Leadership.* 5th ed. Hoboken, NJ: Wiley, 2017.

Schreiber, Rabbi Mordecai. "Rethinking Jeremiah." *Tikkun,* August, 2011. https://www.tikkun.org/was-jeremiah-a-failure.

Schreiter, Robert J. *Constructing Local Theologies.* Maryknoll, NY: Orbis, 2015.

Sechrest, Love L., et al., eds. *Can "White" People Be Saved?: Triangulating Race, Theology, and Mission.* Downers Grove, IL: InterVarsity, 2018.

Sedmak, Clemens. *Doing Local Theology: A Guide for Artisans of a New Humanity.* Maryknoll, NY: Orbis , 2002.

Seel, John. *The New Copernicans: Millennials and the Survival of the Church.* Nashville: Thomas Nelson, 2018.

Seligman, Adam B. *Modernity's Wager: Authority, the Self, and Transcendence.* Princeton, NJ: Princeton University Press, 2000.

Senge, Peter M. *The Fifth Discipline: The Art and Practice of the Learning Organization.* New York: Doubleday, 1990.

———. *The Fifth Discipline Fieldbook: Strategies and Tools for Building a Learning Organization. Series.* New York: Doubleday, 1994.

———. "The Leader's New Work: Building Learning Organizations." *Sloan Management Review* 32, no.1 (1990) 7.

Sennett, Richard. *The Conscience of the Eye: The Design and Social Life of Cities*. New York: W. W. Norton, 1990.

Shaw, Patricia, and Ralph D. Stacey, eds. *Experiencing Risk, Spontaneity and Improvisation in Organizational Change: Working Live*. London: Routledge, 2006.

Shaw, Patricia. "Introduction: Working Live." In *Experiencing Risk, Spontaneity and Improvisation in Organizational Change: Working Live*, edited by Patricia Shaw and Ralph Stacey, 1–16. London: Routledge, 2006.

Simpson, Leanne Betasamosake. *As We Have Always Done: Indigenous Freedom through Radical Resistance*. Minneapolis: University of Minnesota Press, 2017.

Sloterdijk, Peter. *What Happened in the 20th Century?* Translated by Christopher Turner. Cambridge: Polity, 2018.

Smith, C. Christopher. *Reading for the Common Good*. Downers Grove, IL: InterVarsity, 2016.

Smith, Daniel L. "Jeremiah as Prophet of Nonviolent Resistance." *Journal for the Study of the Old Testament* 13, no. 43 (1989) 95–107.

Smith, James K. A. *How (Not) to Be Secular: Reading Charles Taylor*. Grand Rapids: Eerdmans, 2014.

Smith-Christopher, Daniel L. *A Biblical Theology of Exile*. Overtures to Biblical Theology. Minneapolis: Fortress, 2002.

Sparks, Paul, Dwight J. Friesen, and Tim Soerens. *The New Parish: How Neighborhood Churches Are Transforming Mission, Discipleship, and Community*. Downers Grove, IL: InterVarsity, 2014.

Stacey, Ralph. "Complex Responsive Processes as a Theory of Organizational Improvisation." In *Experiencing Risk, Spontaneity and Improvisation in Organizational Change: Working Live,* edited by Patricia Shaw and Ralph Stacey, 124–39. London: Routledge, 2006.

Steinberg, Michael. *The Fiction of a Thinkable World: Body, Meaning, and the Culture of Capitalism*. New York: Monthly Review, 2005.

Strabo. *The Geography of Strabo*. Edited by Horace Leonard Jones. Translated by J. R. Sitlington Sterrett. London: W. Heinemann, 1917.

Swartz, David. *Culture & Power: The Sociology of Pierre Bourdieu*. Sociology, Political Science. Chicago: University of Chicago Press, 2009.

Taylor, Charles. "Foreword." In David Cayley, *The Rivers North of the Future: The Testament of Ivan Illich*, ix–xiv. Toronto: Anansi, 2005.

———. *Modern Social Imaginaries*. Durham, NC: Duke University Press, 2004.

———. *A Secular Age*. Gifford Lectures, 1999. Cambridge, MA: Harvard University Press, 2007.

Trebilco, Paul. "The Province and Cities of Asia." In *The World of the New Testament: Cultural, Social, and Historical Contexts,* edited by Joel Green and Lee Martin McDonald, 501–21. Grand Rapids: Baker Academic, 2013.

Van Gelder, Craig. *The Ministry of the Missional Church: A Community Led by the Spirit*. Grand Rapids: Baker, 2007.

Van Gelder, Craig, and Dwight J. Zscheile. *Participating in God's Mission: A Theological Missiology for the Church in America*. Grand Rapids: Eerdmans, 2018.

Ward, Graham. *The Politics of Discipleship: Becoming Postmaterial Citizens*. Grand Rapids: Baker Academic, 2009.

Weil, Simone. *The Iliad: Or, the Poem of Force*. London: Politics, 1946.

Wells, Samuel. *Improvisation: The Drama of Christian Ethics.* Grand Rapids: Brazos, 2004.

Weston, Paul. "Lesslie Newbigin: Looking Forward in Retrospect." *Journal of Missional Practice* (Winter, 2015). https://journalofmissionalpractice.com/lesslie-newbigin-looking-forward-in-retrospect/.

Weston, Paul, ed. *Lesslie Newbigin: Missionary Theologian.* Grand Rapids: Eerdmans, 2006.

Williams, Rowan. *A Ray of Darkness: Sermons and Reflections.* London: Cowley, 1995.

Wimberly, Anne Streaty. "Called to Listen: The Imperative Vocation of Listening in Twenty-First Century Faith Communities." *International Review of Mission* 87, no. 346 (1998) 331–41.

———. *Soul Stories: African American Christian Education.* Rev. ed. Nashville: Abingdon, 2005.

Winnicott, D. W. *The Maturational Processes and the Facilitating Environment: Studies in the Theory of Emotional Development.* New York: International Universities Press, 1965.

Witherington, Ben. *The Acts of the Apostles: A Socio-Rhetorical Commentary.* Grand Rapids: Eerdmans, 1998.

Wright, N. T. *Christian Origins and the Question of God.* Minneapolis: Fortress, 1992.

Yoder, John Howard. *For the Nations: Essays Evangelical and Public.* Grand Rapids: Eerdmans, 1997.

Printed in Great Britain
by Amazon

57907532R00144